UN AMBASSADOR

HUMAN RIGHTS ACTIVIST

HIGH SCHO

PRESIDENT OF LIBERIA

ton

MOVI

COO. FACEBOOK

SECRETARY OF STATE

Nicole Ma

USAF FIGHT

RodhamClinton

SECRETARY OF STATE

MOVIE STUDIO HEAD

SYMPHONY CONDUCTOR

Rishika Dannyanani

HIGH SCHOOL JUNIOR

FASH

UN AMBASSADOR

Wendy Kopp

TEACH FOR AMERICA

EPA ADMINISTRATOR

PRESIDENT OF LIBER

SECRETARY OF STATE

Nicole Malachowski

USAF FIGHTER PILOT

Catty

MOTHER

FASHION DESIGNER

UN AMBASSADOR

HUMAN RIGHTS

Sheryl Sandberg

Mai

SYMPHON

To Deb –

HOW
GREAT
WOMEN
LEAD

Lead with you!

Bonnie

Also by Bonnie St. John

How Strong Women Pray

Live Your Joy

HOW
GREAT
WOMEN
LEAD

A Mother-Daughter Adventure
into the Lives of Women
Shaping the World

———

Bonnie St. John *and* Darcy Deane

**CENTER
STREET**

New York Boston Nashville

Center Street
Hachette Book Group
237 Park Avenue
New York, NY 10017

www.centerstreet.com

Printed in the United States of America

RRD-C

First Edition: April 2012
10 9 8 7 6 5 4 3

Center Street is a division of Hachette Book Group, Inc.
The Center Street name and logo are trademarks of Hachette Book Group, Inc.

The Hachette Speakers Bureau provides a wide range of authors for speaking events. To find out more, go to www.hachettespeakersbureau.com or call (866) 376-6591.

The publisher is not responsible for websites (or their content) that are not owned by the publisher.

Library of Congress Cataloging-in-Publication Data

St. John, Bonnie.
How great women lead : a mother-daughter adventure into the lives of women shaping the world / by Bonnie St. John and Darcy Deane.—1st ed.
    p. cm.
ISBN 978-0-446-57927-8
1. Leadership in women—Case studies. 2. Leadership—Case studies. 3. Women in the professions—Case studies. 4. Women executives—Case studies. 5. Women politicians—Case studies. 6. Women civic leaders—Case studies. I. Deane, Darcy. II. Title.

HQ1123.S74 2012
305.4—dc23

2011048565

This book is dedicated to Dr. Ruby Cremaschi-Schwimmer, Dr. Fay Deane, and all the great women before us who paved the way for our journey, brick by challenging brick.

Contents

HOW
GREAT
WOMEN
LEAD

CHAPTER 1

— • • —

One Small Step for Womankind

D<small>ARCY</small> . . ."

"Yeah, Mom?"

I momentarily held the undivided attention of my teenage daughter. Her thumbs, free of their ubiquitous texting keypad, quietly dangled by her side. Her computer and its omnipresent Facebook page were completely out of sight. She was even devoid of those little earbuds that seemed to constantly deliver the latest bass-thumping popular melodies directly into her brain. I had almost forgotten what she looked like without all these adolescent accoutrements. As we sat down together on the burgundy leather sofa in our living room, I realized this fleeting state of electronic dislocation was my chance to hatch a plan I had been formulating for the past several weeks. Carpe diem.

"How would you like to write a book together?"

> "About what?" I asked my mom. Write a book? This was a real surprise. I felt a bit suspicious, but still curious. I love to write, and Mom kept telling me I was really good at it. I like writing poetry, fantasy, and sci-fi, though. The books Mom wrote were all nonfiction. I wondered what we could possibly do *together*.

"Well . . ." I hesitated. If I wanted her to commit to any extra work outside her busy schedule at school—not to mention work alongside her mother—I had to make this really great. "It would be about women as leaders," I continued, "a mother-daughter investigation into leadership styles and structures."

> "Leadership?" I blurted. It came out as if I had a bad taste in my mouth—which I did. I couldn't imagine a more boring topic to write about. What is there to say about leadership anyway? When you're in charge, you just get things done, right? Who wants to talk about that?

"We could interview CEOs, politicians like Hillary Clinton, military leaders, and other amazing women."

> The more I thought about this whole idea, the more I didn't like it. I could tell my face showed how I felt.

Her furrowed brow told me I was losing her fast. "Um . . . we could find women leaders *all around the world*!" I said impulsively, frantically casting the ultimate bait.

> "Really? Would we get to travel a lot?" I hadn't thought about that. Heck, I'd write about the mating habits of tsetse flies if I got to go to Africa to do it!

Darcy has always been fascinated with countries and cultures outside her own. Since she was a little girl, she would, for her own entertainment, create entire civilizations from scratch. She designed their social structures and even generated fictional languages and alphabets for their communications. I hoped I was offering her a chance to explore her lifelong passions.

But this project wasn't just about the influence it would have on Darcy. I wanted to do something that could have a potent impact on an alarming trend I had witnessed in workplaces across the country: far too many women appeared to be making a choice *not* to apply for top leadership positions when presented with the opportunities to do so.

Had the pendulum swung back from the newly liberated, ambitious, trailblazing women leaders of previous generations toward a more cautious view of leadership for their daughters in generations X, Y, and Z? Had their mothers paid such a high price for their achievements in terms of family life, harassment at work, and lack of recognition that many of their daughters were now ambivalent about aiming for the top and pushing wider the doors their mothers had opened?

At the same time, I still saw plenty of women who *were* willing to scale the heights no matter what the costs. But these "go-getters" faced a whole new set of frustrations and challenges their mothers wouldn't have even imagined. They weren't yet ready to throw in the towel, but they were pretty close to strangling somebody with it.

A number of books on the shelves today have made deep, scholarly investigations into these phenomena and drawn helpful intellectual conclusions. I wanted to do something different, something that would be more fun and more dedicated to showing how women today view themselves as leaders. I wanted to pull readers into the adventure of leadership. I wanted to strike at the heart—at the emotion of the quest. If I could somehow create a book that would help women of all ages and backgrounds to become more energized and, at the same time, better prepared to step up and *take the lead* in their communities, jobs, and homes, I knew our world would be better for it.

Ultimately, my daughter, too, would be entering the world of the workplace. By taking her on a tour to meet women who were successfully navigating their way around the rocks and hard places of leadership, perhaps we could create a call to action for her and for women everywhere to take their places at the highest levels of every sector in society.

This project, then, was a bit of a Trojan horse. On the one hand, the saga of a mother-daughter journey could seduce female readers, who might never bother to read the Harvard Business School dissertations on the subject, into a meaningful conversation about leadership. At the same time, if Darcy met a series of brilliant, accomplished women—people even a cynical teen would be in awe of—perhaps *they* could tell her all the things I'd like her to know—and more.

And she just might listen.

"Okay…" I told Mom. I was slowly gaining enthusiasm, but I was determined to keep this book from being a total snooze. "Do you want my opinion, though?"

"Of course."

"Well, if you just make the book about CEOs and famous politicians, most people won't feel like the book is for them. We should also talk to some people who are less well-known—people anyone can relate to."

Why didn't I think of that? She was right. I was speechless as Darcy continued.

"What's our budget for this project?" I asked my mother. This thing sounded insanely expensive. It's not like we're the kind of people who vacation in the south of France, you know? How could we afford a huge, global fiesta?

Huh? Budget? "Um . . . I don't know yet." I wondered where she was going with this. So, to stall and gather my thoughts, I invoked the universal parental procrastination position: "It depends."

"It depends on what?" I countered. I wasn't going to let her get away with an evasion like that. "How are we going to travel around the country, or the world for that matter, without a budget and a plan?" My mother does, from time to time, come up with wild ideas—like when she decided to become a one-legged international ski racer from San Diego. I've heard all the stories about her running out of money, breaking her legs, and living out in the middle of nowhere to train on a glacier in the summer. That's so *not* me. She can also be a bit disorganized—just look at her desk. I really didn't want to get involved in this enterprise unless I knew how it was going to work.

Who, exactly, was leading whom? Okay, I probably should have considered some more of the practical details of this endeavor prior to this discussion. For example, we were starting this project not long after the beginning of the worst financial crisis since the Great Depression. I certainly wasn't in a position to name a generous sum of money for travel. "Darcy, we'll make a budget and a plan after we get more information. I'm just trying to get an idea of your interest right now."

"Oh, okay," I said, still suspicious, but willing to give her the benefit of the doubt. I figured, what the heck? Against all my organizational instincts, I would give it a chance. If it did somehow manage to work, it could be the greatest opportunity of my teenage life.

Looking back, this interchange should have been my first clue that this project was not going to be *"mother, paragon of leadership and role model, teaches eager, knowledge-thirsty daughter."* No. This was going to be a true learning adventure . . . for both of us.

The best expeditions start with preparation and help from others. I'm fortunate to have a great group of people who've signed on to my website's "stay in touch" list and routinely give me their input on a variety of topics. This gang is a smattering of friends and acquaintances to whom I regularly turn for intelligent discourse and advice, particularly when I'm embarking on a new book project. Darcy and I crafted an e-mail asking them to recommend women leaders to include in our travelogue. We requested they keep in mind that we wanted not just the obvious choices, but their own, personally near and dear heroes.

Within minutes my inbox was flooded with replies! Not just women, but my male friends, too, regaled us with strong opinions and compelling arguments for women leaders we should hold up as role models. Each e-mail had three, four, sometimes as many as ten names. We were off and running!

"Mom, these women are really cool," I said, surprised after I Googled a couple of the names on the list. Wow… An Iraqi woman who suffered under Saddam Hussein and single-handedly created an organization of women to fight back against dictators around the world… That Buddhist nun who helped AIDS patients in Thailand. Since I play cello in the school orchestra, I thought it would be cool to meet the only woman in the United States who conducts a major orchestra. Then there was Facebook! Right next to Mark Zuckerberg, the founder, there is a woman named Sheryl running the whole world my friends and I need to exist. Meeting her would be awesome!

After a few hours, we had over five hundred suggestions. It quickly became apparent that it would take days to weed through this material, so I sent out a brief "thank-you" e-mail letting people know we were poring through their ideas in earnest and would give them more feedback later. To my surprise, that follow-up note provoked yet another round of responses with hundreds more ideas! For weeks, people stopped me on the street, or after a speech, to say, "I meant to e-mail you back about your next book. You just have to include . . ."

We had really hit a nerve.

Over the next several weeks we delved excitedly into this extensive catalog of extraordinary human beings. Darcy organized the proposals into a spreadsheet to track diversity across age, nationality, ethnicity, field of expertise, and more. With so many legitimate nominations, it looked as if we could write several books. I had never before fully appreciated the depth and breadth with which women are shaping the world today—more than any time in recorded history. This exercise further strengthened our resolve to laud these amazing stories as examples of the incredible capabilities of women as leaders.

But where to start? How would we make it work? I suggested we do most of our research by phone, as I did for *How Strong Women Pray*. My telephone interviews with a governor, some CEOs, actors, sports figures, a college president, and others yielded great stories and information. I promised my intrepid co-author, though, that we could punctuate these conversations with a few visits in person to exciting and exotic places—all with reasonably priced airfares.

> "You know, Mom, if we just interview a bunch of women over the phone and add a few side trips it will be a boring book," I told her as I tried to stay calm. I wanted to meet these women in person, see them laugh, and get to know them. I wanted to meet Sheryl Sandberg at Facebook headquarters. I wanted to hear Marin Alsop's orchestra play. "We need to make this into a story that will draw people in and make them want to read it," I said as persuasively as I could. "These women are so great, everyone should get to know them and truly appreciate their lives." I wasn't just looking for a good time. I had become truly inspired by the women. Plus, this was my first chance to write a published book and I wanted to do it right.

Again, I acknowledged that my daughter was not only dead right, but also thinking way ahead of my curve. We discussed this notion off and on for about a week before we came to, what Darcy called, a "simple" solution:

> "Why don't we follow each subject as she goes about her daily life? That way our readers get to come along with us and get a behind-the-scenes look at what happens to them. Instead of just a boring interview, we—and our readers—get to hang around with these women, see them in their natural habitat, and even see how other people treat them."

Although I agreed it was a wonderful approach, this idea of "job-shadowing" each featured subject didn't seem simple to me at all. I just wasn't sure it would work. The risks seemed huge. Would these high-powered, important women deign to allow us that kind of access? Would they be able to impart the kind of wisdom that would resonate with our readers and truly make a difference in their lives? And, I still had no idea where we would find the financial resources to pull it off. We looked at each other, both of us hooked on a crazy idea that we weren't sure we could pull off.

"It sounds impossible, Darcy," I said. "We might as well get started."

And so, we stepped out . . . on faith.

CHAPTER 2

Her Excellency, Ellen Johnson Sirleaf

President of Liberia, Nobel Laureate

From all the requests for interviews we sent out to our massive spread-sheet of extraordinary women, we secured our first agreement to participate from none other than the outspoken, controversial, twice jailed, and almost assassinated president of the West African republic of Liberia, Ellen Johnson Sirleaf. This incredible role model also happens to be the first elected female head of state on the continent of Africa and was awarded the Nobel Peace Prize for her "non-violent struggle for the safety of women and for women's rights to full participation in peace-building work."

The bad news, though, as we took our first wobbly steps forward on our mother-daughter leadership venture, was that a pair of plane tickets to Liberia was never going to fit into the "reasonably priced airfare" disclaimer I made to Darcy. Europe? No problem. South America? Maybe. But even a couple of super-saver coach seats to Africa would have used up the entire book advance. So we settled for a phone interview rather than pass up the opportunity. It would be okay to interview *one* of our featured women via telephone; we just wouldn't make it a habit.

From the moment we booked the appointment, Darcy was a bundle of energy. We both scoured anything published about President Johnson Sirleaf, as well as scads of literature on Liberia and its extraordinary history. We totally immersed ourselves in research about this extraordinary woman. We read her book, *This Child Will Be Great*, cover to cover. As we turned page after fascinating page, we scratched yellow highlights over all the exciting parts—which gave our copy roughly the appearance of a lemon meringue pie that was heavy on the lemon. To discover the rich details of President Johnson Sirleaf's incredible history, from an abusive marriage straight out of high school to facing down firing squads as a politician, left us completely in awe. We even got some great insights into her life from our online gang of friends and colleagues. Finally, one warm summer afternoon, Darcy and I sat down together to make a list of the questions to ask.

"I really want to ask her: *How do you respond to critics?*" Darcy jumped right in. "I know I worry about being criticized when I am heading up a group. But maybe we should say: *When do you believe your critics?* or *Do you ever take criticism to heart?*"

Darcy's hot pink gel pen instantly filled every line of the tablet in front of her as she wrote, crossed out, and rewrote as fast as she could talk. I tried to be patient with her obsessive wordsmithing, but after spending fifteen minutes on each of the first two questions, I had to say, "Don't agonize so much about the exact wording or the order of the questions. The conversation will flow in its own direction. Try to stay attentive and listen to what she is saying. She could bring up an idea that makes you want to ask something we didn't plan at all." I was afraid we were losing focus on the big picture. As a veteran of this sort of interchange, and far more confident about how the call would go, I did my best to instill a sense of calm and confidence in my agitated daughter.

I took the tablet and wrote: *How do we encourage more young women to be leaders despite the challenges?*

"I think it should be *'young women with doubts to take on leadership roles,'*" Darcy insisted, pulling the paper back.

I couldn't believe she felt she had to reword my questions, too! It was making me crazy.

I wanted everything about this first foray to be perfect. I could feel in the pit of my stomach how nervous I was. Maybe it would be easier on the phone than in person, I told myself. But I still wondered how all this was supposed to work. When you call the president of Liberia, does she just pick up the phone? It seemed crazy that we were going to talk to the head of an entire country.

Never having done this before, I focused all my energy on what I *could* understand and control: wording the questions to the best of my ability. I thought we should try to sound like we were polished experts and that wording the questions carefully would help with that. I made up our very first question list, neatly typed it, and organized it into categories. I finally felt prepared when I printed it out. It spanned three single-spaced pages starting with: *How do you define leadership?* and ending with: *What do you find most rewarding about being the President of Liberia?*

When the actual day arrived, I took the morning off from school so that Mom and I could make the call together from home. It felt a little like cheating to be out of school when I wasn't sick, but this was really *important*. I began to feel the scope of what we were about to do—not just today, but with this whole project.

I was still worrying, too—especially about how we would record the interview. We'd purchased a pair of digital recorders (one primary and one for backup) to use at our in-person meetings, but they didn't have a mechanism for jacking in to pick up both sides of a phone conversation.

"Don't worry, honey," Mom had told me with an easy smile. "We can use *Old Reliable*, the cassette tape recorder I used for the interviews in my last three books. It has a special plug that hooks directly into the phone line. It works great." Smiling fondly, she patted the antique black plastic RadioShack box that had been her trusty companion through interviews with people like Edie Falco, Barbara Bush, and Amy Grant.

I stared at this clunky looking gadget. "*Old* Reliable" was ancient technology. Fatter and heavier than an iPad or even a notebook computer, it was at least ten times the size of our sleek, new digital recorders. Those cassette tapes inside it seemed so fragile—easily ruined by water damage or breakage. You can't even upload them to a computer to back up the recordings! But Mom made one of

those parental-authority rulings. She pushed aside "high tech" and
stuck us with "good-bye tech."

Those tiny little digital devices made me uncomfortable. Barely bigger
than a cigarette lighter, they seemed so dainty and insubstantial. You can't
see where the interview is stored. I like to watch the wheels turn inside
the tape player so I know the thing is actually recording. It feels good to
pull the cassette out afterward, and label it to save for later. It's something
you can physically hold in your hand. You know you have the interview.

I got a little misty-eyed as I inserted four fresh D batteries into the
plastic container on the back of my old pal, and connected the phone
jack wire to her side. I peeled the plastic film off a brand-new cassette
tape, labeled it carefully, and heard the satisfying click as I loaded it into
the slot and closed the lid. I tested the recording. Twice. I smiled my
most satisfactory smile. It worked beautifully—just like always.

"See?" I said to Darcy, "Just 'cause it doesn't have any 'apps' or an LED
display doesn't make it a dinosaur. Now, are you ready to dial Liberia?"

> I checked my notes and pens, and gave Mom an enthusiastic
> thumbs-up. I felt a bit shaky inside, but excited. This was our maiden
> voyage together, and I still wasn't sure what to expect.

I winked to my daughter and dialed the impossibly long series of numbers it takes to access a foreign country. We had decided against using the
speakerphone, so instead we sat next to each other, each of us holding
her own handset. Simultaneously, we heard the familiar, yet still unusual,
"blip-blip" ringing signal of an international telephone interchange.

"The number you have dialed is not in service. Please hang up and try
again . . ."

My heart began to beat faster as I frantically double-checked the number. I dialed again, carefully examining each digit on the page.

"The number you have dialed is not in service. Please hang up and try
again . . ."

Oh, *no!*

Whoa! My heart skipped about a dozen beats. What the heck was going on? Mom was moving around way too fast, and I had no idea what was happening. Is this going to work? Is there something weird about the phone system in Liberia we don't know about? Does this kind of stuff always happen?

I raced over to my computer and pulled up an e-mail from the president's assistant. There was another phone number there at the bottom. I added the international access code and the country code to the number on the e-mail signature and slowly punched in the numbers. And prayed.

Blip-blip. Blip-blip. Blip-blip... click!

"Office of the President," finally came the heavily accented answer.

"This is Bonnie St. John and Darcy Deane. We have an appointment to talk with President Johnson Sirleaf...?" My voice trailed up at the end, like it always does when I'm nervous.

"One moment please."

Darcy looked at me in wide-eyed panic, jumped up from the table, and ran into her room! I thought, *Oh, great. She's overcome with stage fright and she's losing it.*

This deafening, reverberating echo was emitting from our phones. My handset was too close to Mom's and the signal was feeding back. Suddenly the already questionable international connection became almost inaudible. I grabbed my notes and sprinted to my bedroom to put as much distance between our two phone units as possible. "I'm still here, Mom," I said quietly so she wouldn't think I had abandoned her.

"This is President Johnson Sirleaf." Her elegant voice filled my ears.

"Hello, Madam President. This is Bonnie St. John, and I'm on the phone with my daughter, Darcy..."

I couldn't believe the President of Liberia was actually on the other end of the line speaking to us! It was really happening. I knew Mom

had done a lot of high-profile interviews, and I was completely relying on her to make this a success.

As I continued to greet the president, I quickly glanced toward Old Reliable. The tape wasn't moving! Those little circles that go around and
around, winding the cassette from spool to spool, were stubbornly still.
How could this happen after all these years? Okay, so "all these years" is
probably the operative phrase. A cold sweat gripped my entire body. My
hands flew to the controls and, in the process, I knocked the recording
relic right off the table!

> I listened to Mom's voice becoming increasingly shaky, distracted,
> and unsure, and I started to wonder what was wrong. Then I heard
> a crashing sound.

As the machine tumbled onto the floor, I mustered all my acting ability
to pretend there was no problem. ". . . Um, thank you so much for taking this time to speak with us . . ."

> I flung the bedroom door open and came pounding out into the
> living room. As I raced toward her, Mom lunged for the recorder
> and all her notes went flying in the air, adding a snowstorm of paper
> on top of the fractured old recorder. I was terrified.

So much for setting an example of professionalism for my daughter. The
Three Stooges, on their worst day, were more composed than I was in
this harmonic conversion of disasters.

> As adrenaline coursed through my veins, I took stock of our situa-
> tion:
>
> 1. The President of Liberia was on the phone.
> 2. Despite all the chaos, my mom was still talking to her.
> 3. Nothing was recording the interview.

If I didn't do something right now, we'd have to write all this from memory. That thought alone was my call to action. I grabbed one of the abandoned digital devices off of the table and turned it on immediately.

I'm still not sure how it happened, but, to my delight and relief, I saw Darcy had managed to get one of the digital recorders going. I quickly pressed the speakerphone button on my handset so that we could record both sides of our conversation. Not the greatest way to preserve the session, but desperate times called for desperate measures. I looked gratefully at my daughter, as if she had performed a miracle. Perhaps she had.

Though the bedlam had felt like an eternity, only about fifteen seconds had actually elapsed. As a bonus, with the digital recorder doing its job via speakerphone, Darcy and I were now able to sit together. The interview—and this entire project—had now officially begun. "The recorder is rolling and we're ready to start," I said triumphantly. "Madam President, how do you define leadership?"

After a long pause to choose just the right phrase, Her Excellency replied, "Someone who unites people to work towards a common goal. A leader is someone who creates collaboration."

Her voice emanated from the tinny little speaker with a surprising softness that melted my stress and anxiety away. The serenity of her tone reminded me of the time I recorded (on Old Reliable) a dialogue with the legendary Maya Angelou. Both of these great women speak as though their throats are coated in a rich, silky cream; the essence of their thoughts slips smoothly and gently into your soul with such a warm resonance you feel as though they've infused your entire being with profound wisdom. I could listen to this lyrical, calm, yet impassioned voice for hours.

"How do you create collaboration with the enemies you have in your midst and their fierce opposition on a day-to-day basis?" I heard Darcy ask.

"In my government I have many of my harshest critics right beside me. I don't have real enemies that remain enemies throughout my lifetime, only temporary political adversaries, perhaps. One has to be able to avoid spending time worrying about your enemies, and do the things that diminish them. Focus on your achievements for the greater good and you leave them less to say. You diminish them with your success."

It is worth noting that when President Johnson Sirleaf came into power in 2006, her government opted to have a truth and reconciliation commission instead of a war crimes tribunal, following Nelson Mandela's example in South Africa. Her commitment to heal past hatreds, extinguish the legacy of violence, and build cooperation for the future permeated her whole approach to governing and legislative decision making.

> Mom pointed to another question, somewhere on the second page, that related to the subject of dealing with opposition. I swallowed my irritation with her for going out of the order we had originally devised because I knew she was my mentor as well as my mother. So I asked: "Many women are afraid to become leaders because they don't know how to handle the criticisms that are so frequently aimed at those in charge. How do you decide which criticisms to take to heart and which to ignore?"
>
> This was one of the questions I had crafted carefully because I worried about criticism as a leadership issue myself.

"It depends on what it is. Constructive criticisms are valuable when they point out my deficiencies and shortcomings. I examine them and decide whether I can improve. Criticisms based on falsehoods and accusations are annoying, but I dismiss them. It's not worth dignifying them with my attention. Truth is the criteria for judging the value of criticism."

> I really agreed with her answer, but she didn't acknowledge how criticism can be deeply impactful emotionally. I guessed her sense of having a cause made it worth the pain. While she didn't actually say that, her life example definitely does. I went on to the next question.
>
> "Do you think men and women lead differently?"

"Oh, yes," she answered quickly, as though it were perfectly obvious.

"Women bring to their responsibility and leadership a sensitivity that most men do not have; a certain passion, a certain commitment, a certain concern about the welfare of human beings. It may be in the genes or from the experience of being mothers."

Madam President's succinct answers were allowing us to get in a lot of questions in this brief allotment of time. Proud that Darcy had changed the direction of thought with surprising flexibility, I asked, "If you had a daughter, would you give her leadership advice that was different from what you would tell your sons?"

"Whether I was talking to sons or daughters, my advice would be the same." Madam President's voice became a bit sharper now. She took a breath and then spoke in her characteristically poetic way, pausing for emphasis:

Reach for your full potential.
Aspire for the biggest thing you can.
Be diligent,
Work hard,
Get as much education as you can, and
Stay focused on your goal!

In each sonorous caesura, I heard the wisdom of a woman speaking across the decades to herself at age eighteen, married out of high school to an abusive husband and having babies as rapidly as humanly possible. By following the same advice she gave now, Madame Johnson Sirleaf changed the entire trajectory of her life when she could have easily lost hope as so many young girls do. These were words packed with meaning and motivation.

"What about women further along in their careers? What advice would you have for them?" I followed up.

As usual, she paused and then gave an eminently quotable answer.

"Have the courage of your convictions—no matter what the challenges are. And by all means," she answered in her deep melodious voice, "choose your battlefields."

In her world, this meant leaving the country—even leaving her children and family behind at times—to avoid being killed for sticking to her beliefs about the right thing to do. At other times, it meant staying put and going to jail to force the world and her fellow countrymen to see the truth.

Again, her words began to flow rhythmically:

Retreat to strengthen your resolve.
Pull back to recharge and address the situation.
Don't destroy your goal by taking undue risks.
You can destroy everything you've worked for by risking too much.

After all the preparation we had done to learn about her Liberian history, the one question that I most wanted to ask was this: "How did you deal with your fears? How did you become so courageous?"

I got chills as she began to respond in a near whisper, her voice growing slowly in sound and intensity…

That first risk…
That first challenge…
That first responsibility.

That first experience in which fear is a factor—
You have to take that first step forward and rise above it.

After that, as you move on,
The fear diminishes.
You reach a place where you have complete freedom from fear.

What is the objective?
I'm willing to take the risk that gets me there.

Now it was time for Darcy and me to pause. So moving was her response, it was a moment or two before we could continue. This was a quote I knew I would share with every group of young women I had a chance to address about great women leaders.

Darcy finally asked, "Where do you find your strength in these grueling and dangerous situations?"

"I would direct you to the words of your President John F. Kennedy: 'For this, each man must look into his own soul,'" she answered, and then continued, again in her own poetry:

After you've taken some risk,
And you've been able to meet the challenge and rise above it,
It strengthens your character,
It strengthens your resolve,
It enables you to be more determined.

One event, one experience,
Leads to another
And strengthens you to take on a bigger battle.

She moved into talking about her faith, "I grew up in a family of prayers. My mother was a Presbyterian teacher and preacher. In difficult times when man cannot help you, we always prayed. That's part of my faith, part of my spiritual upbringing."

Building on that faith idea, I asked another question I had specially prepared because it fascinated me. "In your book you describe how calm you became in some of the most dangerous situations. You never seemed to lose your temper, even when others were hostile and confrontational. I think a lot of women would want to know: *'how do you manage your emotions?'* "

"First of all, I am a very reserved, calm, and private person, even though I am good at campaigning and I can shout and speak at rallies with the best of them. In the most difficult circumstances, I go back to my faith, say a quiet prayer, and see it through."

It surprised me a little to think of Ellen Johnson Sirleaf as more intro-vert than extrovert. Could a reserved and private woman rule a country with enough authority?

I chimed in with my next question: "How do you hold people ac-countable for misconduct? It's a challenge for every leader, but with the political dynamics in your context, quite a tricky task."

"One has to demonstrate very clearly that there are consequences and be strict enough to make people accountable with penalties . . . yet you don't want them to perform only because of fear. It is important to en-courage and motivate people to do the right thing; you have to recognize their progress, congratulate them, and let them know you appreciate them. You have to balance both sides if you want to lead, and not rule."

It was my turn again, and I asked a question for my generation. "There are so many challenges and hardships associated with lead-ership that young women often get discouraged from taking on leading roles, even though there are more opportunities than ever before. How do we encourage them to aim higher?"

"I hope your book will be an inspiration for young women to lead, when you tell the stories of so many women. I am just one. We need more role models, more life stories, so that young people believe you can rise from any level and achieve what you aspire to," she said. "I was en-couraged by Rosa Parks, Winnie Mandela, and many other women who came before me."

I realized our time was running out, so I reluctantly skipped to the end of our very long list. It really hurt to jump over my carefully crafted questions, but I could see Mom's point that the interview had developed a flow of its own. So, I sucked it up and asked what was designed to be our final question.

"You have worked so hard to be where you are today. What is the most rewarding thing about being the President of Liberia?"

"During my campaign I often said that one reason I was running for president was because I wanted to see the children of Liberia smile again. They have gone through such horror: running from guns, facing starvation, seeing their parents mutilated and killed. As I traveled the country during the campaign, I could clearly see signs of despair, the loss of hope. Too many children still did not know where their next meal was coming from. Too many still knew nothing about school.

"So my greatest reward as president is changing that situation for our country's children and fulfilling the promises I made. My commitment is to get them decent food, decent housing, and decent education. To get them back into an environment in which they can feel themselves to be a real and vital part of a real and vital society. To create for the children of Liberia an environment in which they feel the future is bright.

"That's why every sacrifice seems well worth the cost when I see children smiling with hope in their eyes, see them back in school, and know they have a future."

We thanked her profusely and, reluctantly, said our good-byes.

As soon as we hung up, I looked with wide eyes at Darcy, pointed at the tiny technological wonder on the table, and nervously said, "Is the interview really in there?"

She pushed several buttons and replayed the first two questions. We had to strain to hear it, but it was there all right. We hugged each other with relief.

Once breath returned to my body, I asked Darcy, "Doesn't Madam President inspire you to want to be a great leader?"

"Truthfully, Mom, it kind of scares me. Does being a leader mean risking death like she did? Even if not death, it just sounds like a really harsh and difficult life. Is that always the cost of leadership?"

That was definitely not the reaction I wanted or expected. While I internalized and embraced President Sirleaf's profound advice to lead rather than rule, it seemed this brave woman had actually thrown a wet blanket on Darcy's aspirations—rather than kindle them as I'd hoped. It never occurred to me that this experiment might backfire.

"I admire her—no question. She's awesome," Darcy replied, looking at my crestfallen face. "But that's not the kind of life I want for myself."

"Not all leaders risk life and death or struggle to create peace in war zones," I said, hoping to get the train back on the track. "Just take the lessons you can from what she says. You'll find ways to apply it in other contexts. Plus, we have lots of other leaders to meet in many other situations."

It sounded a little lame, even to me, but it was the truth.

I was feeling somewhat deflated as we collected up our notes and began putting things away. Papers were still scattered everywhere, and my useless tape recorder sat accusingly in front of me. To regain my poise as a parent and author, I decided to turn this into a teachable moment.

"Well, Darcy," I said, "the lesson here is that no matter how much practice you get, no matter how long you have been at this author game, you always have to be prepared for Murphy's Inimitable Law to rear its ugly head. You did a great job, by the way, rolling with the punches. Thanks."

"Actually, Mom," I said, "in my opinion, the lesson for today is to embrace change. Like Madame Johnson Sirleaf said, 'we can make the future better than the past.'"

I ceremoniously dropped Old Reliable with a heavy thud into the nearest trash can and wondered to myself, *Why is it so hard for adults to learn how to use cool technology? Why do they hang on to old stuff that doesn't work?*

Don't get me wrong—I admire my mom totally. I mean, she has accomplished all sorts of great things in her life. Besides, I could never have put this project, or even this interview, together myself. But having things go so wrong made me realize she's not perfect, either.

I could see that from now on I really needed to be part of the team—not just along for the ride. And what's best is, I was pretty happy about that.

CHAPTER 3

―――――――

Leslie Lewin

Executive Director, Seeds of Peace

The Egyptians are coming, the Egyptians are coming!"

Far from the late-night ride of that infamous tinsmith heralding the arrival of red-coated oppressors, this New England call to action ripples through a remote enclave deep within the forests of Maine. Right on cue, a throng of teenaged campers and their counselors assemble around the main courtyard of their idyllic campground. Gradually, but deliberately, the peace and quiet of this bucolic setting is interrupted by a cacophony of joyous sounds that reverberate through the trees and seem to infuse the whole scene with energy and purpose. African drums, maracas, bongos—and almost anything else you can bang on to make a sound—blend with saxophones, guitars, horns, and fiddles into a glorious chorus of musical celebration. Even as observers, Darcy and I can't help being swept up in the excitement. We grab some drumsticks from a small bin on the ground and add our own clicking and clacking to the beat of the fray.

A large yellow school bus appears on the horizon and ambles its way over the bumpy dirt road that defines the entrance to the camp. It draws closer to the clearing where we are gathered, and the sense of anticipation swells to the point of explosion. As the coach slowly jerks to a stop, the welcoming party swarms this mammoth vehicle. Arms raise higher, hands clap, bodies swirl in rhythm, and smiles seem to jump right off the faces of everyone involved. Finally, the long vertical doors snap open and fresh, new campers spill out—happily stunned by the magnitude of their reception. Cowbells, triangles, wood blocks, and tambourines are thrust into their hands, immediately enfolding them into the celebration. Nowhere is there any evidence of the weariness they must feel from their seven-thousand-mile journey around the world. To the contrary, they bound into the melee with enthusiastic delight.

Next come the Palestinians. And then the Israelis. And the Jordanians, Bosnians, Iranians, Pakistanis, and Afghans . . . each time the flames of music and dance flicker higher and higher as the burgeoning numbers of previous arrivals pass on the joy to the newbies.

This is Seeds of Peace. A summer camp unlike any other. For the past twenty years, Seeds of Peace has brought together over four thousand future leaders, ages fourteen to sixteen, from conflicting nations, particularly in the Middle East. For three weeks the teens partake in canoeing, campfires, and, most important, crushing barriers to foster peace and understanding between people who have been taught all their lives to hate each other.

In the rustic log cabins that dot the shoreline along the aptly named Pleasant Lake, you'll find Bosnian Muslims bunking with Bosnian Serbs. No guns. No violence. You'll see a teenage girl from India on a rock-climbing wall, suspended in the air while completely trusting a Pakistani boy to hold her safety line. Israelis, who previously knew only one phrase in Arabic, *"Open the trunk and give me your ID,"* sit and converse, side by side, with their Palestinian neighbors. It's absolutely extraordinary to witness.

"This feels like a magical place," one Palestinian camper told us. "People can actually come together as humans. Here, we live day to day along side Jordanians, Egyptians, Israelis, and Americans. We forget about nationalities. We talk. We have fun. We can be friends.

"I am sad though, knowing that it won't last," he continued. "Before, I never believed such a thing could happen. Now I don't want to go back to the real world."

His eyes watered and his voice choked up a little, communicating an inkling of the deep pain we could only imagine. It was as if he had moved into a home in the Garden of Eden, only to find out he was scheduled for eviction.

He smiled, spying a group of his peers sporting a mix of yarmulkes, hijabs, and ball caps walking together, laughing and enjoying each other. "I will always hold in my heart one of the slogans of this camp: *This is how the world should be.*"

As I looked around at these kids my age from countries where bombings and gunfire broke out routinely, I felt a sense of nervous anticipation for the challenges they faced. What was it like to sit at dinner with people who have been blamed for all of your family's problems? I would think that I would be angry all the time. I marveled at their willingness to be open-minded and to try this experiment. Even though Mom and I were not allowed to sit in on the daily, intense, dialogue discussions where tempers did flare and painful layers of history were peeled back like Band-Aids, I was well aware that happy hiking trips were not the only activities. I heard about how hard it is for them to go home afterward. Looking around me, I felt the wonder, but also the weight, of the peacemaking work on the shoulders of my peers.

The chanting now reaches a crescendo...
    Boom... Boom... Boom, "Seeds of Peace!"
    Boom... Boom... Boom, "Seeds of Peace!"
As I gaze over the joyous chaos of the arrival ceremony, I realize this festival isn't chaotic at all. Everything about this place has been brilliantly honed over the years to create a safe, warm, welcoming environment wherein real communication can take place. This opening ritual transcends language differences and cultural barriers with music and movement to immediately put anxious teens at ease and soften their landing in a strange and potentially fearful environment.

I really had a fun time banging on the drums. I was enjoying the evolution of the music as more and more people were added. Everyone had a place, whether they were riffing on a sophisticated instrument like a violin or trumpet that they had played for years

> or just shaking a maraca. I wove in and out of the rhythms as they
> moved from an African-style thumping into a more varied, exotic
> kind of world-music. Then people began dancing; a red-haired girl
> brought out long scarves that traced graceful arcs in the air. It was
> a cool, vibrant energy. You know how people sometimes do an ex-
> ercise to get a group going and it feels faked? This had substance. It
> felt primal. It was very real.

My eyes travel over the sea of bouncing and stomping and fall on the
front porch of one of the more prominent log cabins. Slightly larger than
the others, this is the virtual "Capitol" of the camp. Standing there at the
center of it all, orchestrating the proceedings like a symphony conductor, is Seeds of Peace Executive Director, Leslie Lewin—the woman we
had come this long way to interview.

With her dark brown hair pulled back into a bouncy ponytail, the
ever-present Dunkin' Donuts coffee cup, baggy sweatpants, and freckles
dancing across a makeup-free face, Leslie looks almost as young and optimistic as the counselors and campers she leads. Part camp director,
part mother hen, part world-class diplomat, her dynamic spirit is the
spark that keeps this amazing place going year after year.

We had arrived the night before after a grueling road trip all the way
through the heart of New England. We awoke at the crack of dawn to
begin the eight-hour drive from our home in Princeton, New Jersey,
hoping to arrive before darkness fell at the other end. Due to her penchant for carsickness, Darcy was a bit dubious about making such a
long trip on four wheels. We decided, though, that it made a lot more
sense to drive up to Maine in our own car rather than book flights and
rent a car, since the camp was nowhere near an airport. Plus, as Darcy
never failed to remind me, we still didn't have a budget for this mother-
daughter escapade and there were many more places we needed to go.
Prudence and economy, then, put us on the highway in our blue Ford
Escape—well armed with a GPS on the dash, a goal in mind, a spirit of
adventure in our hearts, and a secret stash of Dramamine (just in case).

I was looking forward to this time in the car with Darcy. If I spend long enough cooped up with my talkative daughter, she will eventually tell me everything that is going on inside her teenage hormone-infused brain—often things she never really means to share with her parents. Boredom, for Darcy, is a form of truth serum.

"People at my old school told me I should lose weight before I start at a new high school in a new town," Darcy shared with me. "They said I will have more friends if I do."

"That's horrible!" I said, taking my eyes off the road briefly to look at her directly. "You're a size six . . . you have a beautiful figure."

"Aw, Mom," Darcy groaned and slumped, "you don't know what it's like. I want to be pretty. I want to have lots of friends. Maybe even a boyfriend someday. Do you think I ever will?"

"Of course you will . . . and you are beautiful," I said. Steering the conversation was a lot harder than steering the car. Did my words counterbalance the peer pressure at all? Was I setting a bad example with my own constantly changing diets? Would I be able to handle seeing my daughter go on a date? As our chat continued, I found some of the topics uncomfortable, but I was certainly glad we had lots of time to talk.

By the end of three hours in the car, Darcy had pretty much downloaded, in excruciating detail, every tidbit of drama with her friends, what she hoped to achieve socially as a sophomore in a new high school next year, struggles with her sense of racial identity, how she felt about moving back and forth between divorced parents, and many other things that loomed gigantic in her life. And we still hadn't even completed half the trip!

When we stopped to refuel—both the car and our stomachs—for the next leg of the journey, I discovered a five-hour-long book on tape in the convenience store to get us through the rest of the drive. The gripping spy story and exquisitely dramatized reading had us on the edge of our electrically adjustable seats all the way to Maine. Laughing together while having our imaginations titillated by the mystery unfolding in literary twists and turns was so much fun we missed that crucial left turn after we got off the freeway . . . a mistake that added yet another hour to the already long trip. All this entertainment provided an extra special bonus, too, since Darcy never once mentioned an upset tummy.

Finally, at dusk, we arrived—tired, groggy, and wanting to never, ever, see the inside of our car again. A staffer working late pointed us to our overnight accommodations. We picked our way over muddy dirt trails (thank goodness for four-wheel drive!) to the row of white clapboard cabins near the housing for the adult chaperones who accompany the Seeds from each country. The lodging was spartan, with charmingly mismatched furniture—probably inherited through donations or acquired at flea markets—and permeated by that unmistakably familiar woodsy/musty aroma such barracks always contain. After unloading our gear, we bravely set off on foot to find our host in what was, by now, a pitch-black night.

> I reluctantly followed Mom out of the comfy, well-lit cabin into the limitless darkness outside. It had been a long time since I had been out in the woods after sunset. A noise to my left made me jump, which made Mom laugh nervously. Was it an animal? Had I heard there were bears out here? I recoiled again, feeling something touch the back of my neck—and slapped hard as I realized it was just a tiny mosquito looking for a late-night snack.

I knew this was the kind of situation that made Darcy really uncomfortable. The peace and stillness of this summer evening was pleasant, but at the same time, a little disconcerting. I could see Darcy's eyes large and alert—her entire body ready to dash screaming away from the nasty critter that was certain to jump out of the desolate void before us any minute. Her vividly imagined fears were making me edgy, too.

Just when we both were sufficiently creeped out, ready to turn tail and run back to the sanctuary of our wooden hut, a pair of bright lights appeared rounding a corner about a hundred yards in front of us. Eerily quiet, the brilliant orbs closed the distance between us at an alarming rate. At first, I thought I might be hallucinating from the numbness of the previous ten-hour car drone. But, no, this apparition seemed quite real, otherworldly, a close encounter with a couple of bouncing-ball ETs way out here in the boondocks! I glanced over at Darcy. Her mouth was open, but nothing came out.

Good. I wasn't crazy. She saw it, too.

I steeled myself, ready to throw us both diving for cover. The beast stopped right in front of us . . .

"Hi guys! Welcome to Maine!" an incongruously sweet voice called out.

And there she was, the object of our odyssey into the wilderness, Leslie Lewin, piloting an electrically powered golf cart with two great big headlights.

I threw off my crepuscular anxiety and burst into a smile at the lovely woman before us. We had first met Leslie, briefly, at her office in New York City. There, atop a sleek high-rise office building with the big-city din providing an edgy, urban soundtrack, Leslie wore a lovely suit, sat behind an elegant yet practical desk, and flawlessly played the role of a successful nonprofit executive. But here, among the crickets and tree frogs, a softer, easier woman appeared. Fashionably tailored hems were replaced by comfortable, unconstructed T-shirts and sweatpants. Even in the dark, I could clearly see this was Leslie's natural habitat. She seemed somehow more alive, more herself than back in town. You could feel the energy crackling around her.

"I'm doing rounds, if you want to join me," she announced with a perkiness that belied the hour. Eager to begin our mission, we jumped aboard.

I think Leslie may have been apprehensive about being shadowed by people planning to write about her (who wouldn't be?), but she was more than gracious about including us in her ride around the campus. Little did she know we were as nervous as she was. While we already had our Liberian phone interview under our belts, this was to be the very first job shadow we would perform for this book. As we climbed onto the backseats and bounced with her around the camp, I was awash in the reality of the moment. We were actually doing this. My daughter was beside me and we were embarking on an epic journey we would remember for the rest of our lives.

Leslie Lewin was the perfect person to begin with. Her easy, unflappable, warm, and welcoming spirit was just what we needed to get our feet wet. I was also glad we were starting with a subject Darcy had fought to put at the top of our list. Seeds of Peace connected deeply with her passion for building bridges across cultures, languages, and religions. In her early thirties, Leslie would be one of the youngest leaders we would interview—not to mention an expert in motivating teenagers—so I felt she would easily engage Darcy's imagination and get us off to a rousing start. I could already tell that our visit would turn into something marvelous.

We scooted back and forth over the rocks and roots of the narrow forest paths. Leslie delivered some sleeping bags and towels to a cabin that was in short supply. She saw a broken screen door and radioed in the repair request. We stopped to talk with staffers who had questions. She gave encouragement and support to others where needed. Basically, she was buzzing around like any other sleep-away-camp administrator—making sure everything was physically ready for the influx of arrivals that would descend upon us the next day.

When a bright, shining summer sun crested the horizon the next morning, day one of this Seeds of Peace session commenced. Everyone hustled about with excitement and anticipation. Camper arrivals began after lunch, so last-minute details were furiously scratched off the many and varied to-do lists all morning. The calm in the eye of the storm, Leslie mainly stayed by her "command post" cabin. The large, wooden porch and broad front steps seemed to be the central point from where all activities and directives rippled across the camp. This benevolent captain stayed constantly available to troubleshoot problems by radio or in person as a constant flow of team members stopped by to seek her advice and input.

And the parade of challenges began . . .

The flight from Jordan was canceled. The delegation is re-routing and
    not sure when they will arrive.

The father of one of the counselors died last night. She's going home.

A leaky sink flooded one of the cabins rendering it uninhabitable.

We watched in awe as Leslie deftly authorized cabin reassignments and kept tabs on the situation in Jordan. She even made time to comfort the bereaved young woman who lost her father and help make arrangements to get her home.

Crises don't follow a schedule. They seem to arrive in clumps.

"This is kind of like bird-watching," Darcy observed as we sat on the porch waiting for the next upheaval. "You wait a while, then you see something exciting. Then you wait again." As she spoke, her prophecy was fulfilled.

"Mommeeeeee!"

The uncharacteristic screech echoed through the thick, humid air. It seemed as though we were about to watch a very interesting bird.

Like a whirling dervish, the adorable little carrot-topped source of the outcry soon appeared in all his glory. No bird at all, Leslie's two-and-a-half-year-old son, Sam, who was also in residence here at camp-central, came whizzing by with his Seeds-alum nanny, Jesse, hot on his heels. They were on their way for a diaper change. The moment he caught sight of his mother, it suddenly became imperative for the little fellow to have her attention *right now*.

"I want *Mommy* to change my diaper!"

When this particular outburst presented itself, Leslie happened to be deep in conversation with a group of local community leaders who were responsible for organizing an alumni outreach program.

"Honey," replied Leslie calmly, "You have to go inside with Jesse right now, but I'll be there in a few minutes to have a snack with you."

Do the terrible twos listen to reason? It was like seeing a baseball pitcher wind up for the toss as Sam's cherubic little cheeks began to glow beet red.

"Nooooo! Mommy! NOW!" he erupted.

My body tensed up in empathy. Would Leslie's work be derailed by the tantrum? Would she give up and go inside for the sake of peace? Would she signal the nanny to drag away the screaming child while she pretends he isn't really hers at all? Who would win this round of work-life balance?

In the true spirit of conflict resolution between diametrically opposing views, Leslie managed to stay respectful of both parties without missing a beat. Before Sam had a chance to completely disintegrate, Leslie smoothly crouched down to his eye-level:

"Sammy, you know you may not talk to me like that," she told him firmly, but kindly. "What do we say about yelling?"

"I don't get what I want if I yell," her toddler replied with an "aw shucks" kind of obedience.

"That's right. Now go with Jesse and I will see you in a few minutes," Leslie told him again. Only then did she give the nod to the nanny to herd him inside willingly . . . or unwillingly.

All of this drama took less than a minute before Leslie was able to bounce back up and resume her discussion of strategic matters that reached worlds away from this forest and her motherly obligations. I wondered how her working-mother lifestyle, with a husband who visits from the city on weekends, was being viewed by the contingents of campers and delegates from countries where women seldom come out in public—and when they do, they cover everything but their eyes and remain completely subservient to men. As the first woman to head up the camp, Leslie seemed to cut a brand-new path through these woods.

We spent the next few days enmeshed with Leslie, the counselors, and all the Seeds. It was great to see Darcy connect with this international gathering of colleagues. She was like a kid in a candy store. She immediately donned the signature green and blue SOP sweatshirt, and fit right in.

> I was hanging out with a group of girls from Egypt who invited me into their bunkhouse. We were aware of the ghosts of previous campers who had carved their names and years with hearts and warm words into the dark, wooden walls. I felt something sacred about the friendships formed here in the past; there was an obvious sense of love. The girls with me popped in a CD, and strains of Arabic music filled the room, along with their laughter and mixed

English-Arabic chatter. Although they had welcomed me in, I still felt like an outsider not being able to participate in the discussion about the latest pop songs from their country. I could see how they were going to become intensely connected together, and I wished that I could be a part of that connection. I wished I could stay to absorb their culture, learn some of their language, and bond with them. But that wasn't going to happen. I only had a few days here. Far too soon, I would bid my new friends farewell.

After dinner on the evening before our final day in camp, we sat down with Leslie for a more formal interview. As we arranged our notes and digital recorders around a folding card table in one of the rustic activity rooms, we could hear just outside the open windows the laughing and screaming of kids enjoying the last few hours of sunlight. Darcy led off with the first item on our sheet of prepared questions: "So, we want to start out by asking, what's your definition of leadership?"

"Hmmm. Leadership or a good leader?" Leslie mused. "Let's go with a good leader because it's easier to explain. A good leader is someone who can remain strong even in difficult and trying circumstances; someone who is empowering those around them; and someone who is as interested in the needs of the people they work with and the larger needs of the project or the organization as they are in their own needs. I think a positive attitude is essential."

"How would you describe your leadership style?" Darcy followed up.

"Well, my leadership style is very positive, but still evolving—I know I am on the young end. I'm very committed to and consistent about bringing out the best in people and reinforcing their strengths, while also providing guidance for areas of weakness. I believe it's important to empower people by providing them with the big picture and also giving them ownership over a project and the results of it. Tim Wilson, my predecessor as camp director and my mentor, has taught me a lot about delegating effectively, but empowering people goes further than that. That's more my style.

"I don't get overwhelmed very easily. I can handle juggling a lot of balls in the air at one time, which is certainly necessary in a unique organization like this. I have to imagine, though, that it's a pretty transferable leadership skill, being able to handle whatever is thrown at you, no matter when or how, or how many other things you're dealing with at the same time."

"What is one of the toughest challenges you've had as a leader?" I asked. "A time when you felt like quitting or when you really had to dig into your reservoir of leadership skills?"

"A lot of times when things start to disintegrate here it has to do with events that happened back home," said Leslie, taking a deep breath. "The most challenging moments at camp happen in the years that there have been major bombings while the kids are actually here in Maine, like during the 2006 Gaza crisis. Events from home can suddenly set back our progress in camp."

"Oh, okay. Wow." I shook my head. I couldn't imagine what that would be like.

"People are being killed. No one knows who is alive or dead. Those are very painful feelings for the campers—and even more painful because they're staring this enemy in the face.

"It's suddenly very real and very intense. They're far away from home and processing all this emotion with these 'others' around them. They're confronting feelings of betrayal like: 'I was just starting to get to trust you and like you, but now look what your people are doing to my people!'"

"What kind of training and skill does it take to get through something like that?" I wondered aloud.

"Recognizing the pain that they're going through. Finding it, legitimizing it, and giving them space to deal with it before putting the pieces back together. Not being too *'Rah-rah,'* or saying, *'We can do this, we're Seeds of Peace!'* That's the sort of artificialness that they expect from someone who doesn't live in what they live in. We're not telling them not to feel what they're feeling. But rather, helping them to see this as an opportunity for processing what they're feeling and to embrace that opportunity.

"There are two models for this situation. One is to bring the whole camp together, refocus, and take a deep breath. The other is to separate them into their delegations, give them some time to talk, be angry and get it out, and then build them back together again." Leslie clasped her hands together consciously or unconsciously acting out her words.

"We've done both, and they're both effective. But the process is rooted in having leadership that people believe in and trust. That's the most important."

It was so interesting to me that there were models for how to bring people back together after a crisis. This was a discipline, a field of expertise, a type of leadership specialty.

"The kids have to believe in me. I have to stand in front of them all, remind them of the importance of our mission, and actually have it mean something to them. In this situation, one of the most challenging parts about being a leader here is that I'm not facing what they're facing on a daily basis. I don't have the fears they have. At the end of the summer, I'm going home to Brooklyn to live my cushy life. But I still have to stand up and ask them to keep talking, keep pushing."

"How do you personally refuel and reenergize yourself in these tense times? What do you do to clear your head or to re-stoke your engine?" I followed, amazed by her stamina.

"Here in Maine, I go in the lake, take a swim, and cool off. It's a quick fix, and I come out refreshed, clean, and woken up. That's a personal outlet I need sometimes. The sheer amount of responsibility that's involved in being a leader can be a little overwhelming in a place like this, where you have the safety and lives of campers in your hands. We have kids swimming, rock climbing, and up on rope courses, as you saw today, so there's danger involved. Knock on wood—we haven't had any major accidents, but that sense of responsibility is very real in a place like this. Your mind is always thinking about safety—emotional and physical—when camp is in session. As much as I love what I'm doing, there's no 'off' switch. It's constant.

"When I am working in New York City I can take more of a real time-out. I would probably spend some time with my family, shut down my phone for a little while, even an hour, and just get my mind off things. That's a recharger. My son helps, too. He's fun. He helps remind me of what's really important so I don't sweat the small stuff."

"How do you work with others who have very, very different values from your own?" Darcy asked.

"This is an easy one for me to answer in some ways, because Seeds of Peace is about establishing communication and respect across major differences. If I can't model that, or my staff can't model that, then we don't really have any business being here and asking everyone else to do it.

"There's certainly room for different values. Earning the participants' trust from the outset is important and helps down the line when difficult moments arrive. The more I can give them information and collect information from them—listen to them and be listened to—the stronger our foundation becomes.

"Proactively building good communication is critical—you never want to be playing catch-up to explain things that could have been disseminated earlier. In a crisis situation, we are engaging people in the process, the solution, and the steps that need to be taken in order to create that solution. Getting their buy-in fast is key.

"It's my job to make the final decision, but getting input from people is very important—even if it's not input that I agree with. Sometimes I have to say, *'Let's take a step back here. What is it that we're really about? I hear what you're saying, that you prefer it a different way, but for now you're going to have to trust me.'* When we don't see eye-to-eye, that foundation of trust is critical."

"That's a good segue to another question we had," I said. "Being a woman and being Jewish must be a little challenging given some of the cultures and people you're working with."

"They're really only minimal challenges," Leslie answered easily. "You heard a little bit about the push back Tim faced when he put my name forward for head counselor. There were some folks who felt that this camp and this situation needed a man. But Tim saw it as sort of a double bonus: I was the most qualified and at the same time we had an opportunity to empower people here even more deeply than we already were.

"As far as the complications of being Jewish, that has been a long-standing concern here since our founder was Jewish. Seeds of Peace, thankfully, has built up a strong enough reputation where having a Jewish leader doesn't mean that we're one sided. It's something I'm definitely sensitive to, but I don't think I've ever faced direct issues over it. We talk with the counselors, too, about how and when to reveal yourself, as far as your ethnicity or your religion. It's a difficult balance here.

"More than being Jewish or being a woman, I think that being a mom can change the way people look at me. When I have a two-year-old on my hip, it's a physical symbol, a reminder, of the kinds of reasons that anyone would question a woman leader. Maybe certain people can more easily put me in a different category.

"This is a camp where issues of gender are very, very real. Having someone like Wil who reports to me as my second in command, and Tim who promoted me, shows other people a model of men and women equally supporting each other. It happens naturally; we don't go out of our way to display our working relationships, but I've been told by many that the way we work together sends a great message about gender and leadership."

"When you first started out as a counselor," asked Darcy, "did you ever see yourself as becoming the leader of the whole organization?"

"No, I didn't. That's a good question. When I graduated from college, everyone was on the hunt for a real job; but I decided to come back and be a counselor again—the head counselor. As much as my parents love Seeds of Peace, they thought I should not be going back to the summer camp of my childhood once I finished college.

"I didn't think it would become my career. At best, I was thinking that I might be able to balance having a real job with camp during the summers. I was thrilled when they offered me a full-time job working on the camp logistics and planning in the New York headquarters at the end of that summer. Who knew it would lead to becoming Camp Director several years later, and now Executive Director? I just stayed here because nothing, to me, could be more exciting."

Darkness settled once again on the shores of Pleasant Lake as we wrapped up our interview with Leslie and headed back to our cabin in the woods. As Darcy and I got ready to bunk down for the last night in our surprisingly comfortable twin cots, a bloodcurdling scream suddenly rang out, piercing the thin walls.

"There's a spider in my towel! And it's *huuuuuuuge!*" Darcy screamed. With eyes as big as saucers, she jumped up on her bed. Her entire body clenched—every cell transfixed on the vicious terry cloth mass on the floor, as if the entire thing might leap up and attack her at any moment.

Bravely, I picked up a corner of the towel with the tips of two fingers and carefully examined every inch. No spider. Under the bed? No spider. The chair? No spider.

For the next twenty minutes we gingerly scoured our hut from top to bottom—searching through our shoes, jackets, pj's, even the other bathroom towels—all with no success. Finally we gave in, exhausted from a hectic day in the great outdoors and longing to snuggle up under the covers and drift into sleep.

Naturally, before getting into bed Darcy had to pull the blankets all the way back to check...and there, as big as your thumb, was the mother of all spiders waiting patiently in her bed.

Darcy nearly fainted. She locked herself in the bathroom and hyperventilated for ten minutes.

I tried to figure out how to remove the annoying arachnid without actually touching it. We were way past a clump of tissue paper here. This was spider*Zilla*. A club or a baseball bat seemed more suited to the task. I spied a small broom, more like a brush actually, lurking in a corner behind one of the beds. Armed now with a perfectly good weapon, I opened the door and quickly swished the little bugger right back to his wilderness home.

"It's gone!" I exclaimed with a triumphant flourish. "Mom saves the day!"

"I don't believe you," came the muffled response from my sequestered daughter.

"Honest, honey. Come see."

Darcy sheepishly emerged from her porcelain sanctuary, still a bit traumatized by the whole experience. I tried to distract her by asking about what she thought the most profound moment with Leslie Lewin had been. I felt certain she would pick the welcoming festival, or the impact she felt from meeting all the diverse personalities from around the world, or maybe even the rousing talent show put on by the counselors featuring their rendition of Michael Jackson's introspective tune "The Man in the Mirror."

Darcy released her phobia and reflected on her time with Leslie. "I think it was that first night, in the golf cart. It stuck in my mind because it surprised me so much. She was rolling up her sleeves and really setting an example. I guess I had these preconceived notions about what leaders are like."

"Like what?" I asked, relieved to see the spider stiffness in her body relax.

"Well, you know . . . the boss, the all-knowing authority, way out in front, issuing orders to her subordinates from on high. But Leslie wasn't like that at all. Everybody really likes her. She got them to do what needed to be done by creating an environment where they took responsibility themselves. She helped them, sure. She supported them, definitely. But in the end, they did things on their own—putting their individual sense of self into the work. They weren't just following orders. It's like, she didn't have to behave like a ringleader in order to be one."

"Interesting," I replied. "And why did that surprise you?"

"It's not that I didn't think anyone would act like that," she explained, "it's just . . . I didn't think it would work so well. I didn't think that stuff would get done without the leader being more dictatorial."

Our last day in Maine was a profoundly moving experience. As one of the major centerpieces of each Seeds of Peace session, an incredible ceremony takes place. We had all been asked to gather immediately outside the main entrance to the camp in a large clearing along the road. Surrounded by everyone—Seeds; counselors; support staff; chaperones; politicians; a phalanx of local, national, and international media; and today, Darcy and me—Leslie stood up and led the assembly. Her impassioned speech set the tone for the entire mission and purpose of the Seeds of Peace experience. Cameras clicked as she welcomed the crowd and, in her own inimitable style, spread a warm and inspirational message:

"This summer, these friends, this extraordinary melding of mind, spirit, and emotion is just the beginning. All one hundred and seventy of you Seeds were selected from among eight thousand applicants and have a responsibility to use this rare opportunity to go back to your homelands and lead. You have a responsibility to become advocates of understanding; to spread messages of patience and tolerance; and to bravely stand up and chip away, however slowly, at the hatreds so deeply embedded in so many hearts, minds, and cultures. Governments negotiate treaties. Peace is made by people."

As Leslie wrapped up her address, I saw that the large metal gate to the camp had been pulled closed, leaving us all curiously stranded outside the grounds. A semi-circle of empty flagpoles surrounded the space where we stood. Darcy and I had heard this was to be the "flag raising," but we could not have imagined what was about to happen.

Rameesh, a delegate from Afghanistan who had attended the camp last year, took the microphone. "This camp is a lot of fun," he happily shared, "a *lot* of fun! But it's also a lot of hard work. To make peace with your enemy, sometimes you have to go to war with yourself."

As he finished his speech, the black, red, and green stripes of his country's flag slowly crept higher and higher up the first pole. His Afghan compatriots joined him there, in the front of the crowd. They lifted their eyes to the sky and passionately began to sing the Afghanistan national anthem.

One by one, each delegation assembled and repeated this ritual in front of their own flag. As the waving fabrics splashed their striking colors against the evergreen background, Darcy and I watched as all around us arms wrapped over shoulders. Seeds of all shapes and sizes linked themselves together in long chains of warm embrace. Soon, the teens were hugging each other so tightly their identical T-shirts seemed to meld into a unified mass—a great green sea swaying in time with the national hymns. Tears streamed down faces as they honored symbols they've been taught all their lives to despise. The poison of hostility seemed to melt away and, in its place, a harmony emerged that transcended the wooded setting.

When the last flag reached its zenith, the singing stopped and all eyes were called to focus on the closed metal gates.

"Outside, the symbols of all the countries represented here fly side by side. But separately. Alone. Each unto itself..."

It was Wil, now, who addressed the crowd from immediately outside the gate. With this pronouncement, he signaled two other counselors to ceremoniously open the barrier, revealing a single, solitary flagpole on the other side.

"But as these gates open, only one flag will fly inside the camp."

Wil pointed to the great, green Seeds of Peace banner flapping in the breeze, proudly proclaiming unity to all who go before it.

"That one."

Once again, that glorious chanting, stomping, and cheering we heard at the arrival celebration seemed to spontaneously engulf us all. An extraordinary league of nations surged across this magical threshold into a place with no borders, no hatred, no war.

Leslie leaned over to me.

"This *is* how the world should be," she said, softly.

CHAPTER 4

Dr. Condoleezza Rice

Former United States Secretary of State
Professor at Stanford University

The noise must have been devastating. *Despite the fact that it came from across town on Sixteenth Street, the little eight-year-old girl heard the thud and felt the concussion from a bomb that shattered the peace of this otherwise quiet Sunday morning in 1963. A group of terrorists, hiding behind the cowardly white sheets of the Ku Klux Klan, had placed a stack of dynamite in the basement of an all black church and set a timer to detonate right in the middle of Sunday school. Twenty-two defenseless people were injured, and four young girls, including one of her playmates, were killed. But for a few blocks of Birmingham geography, young Condoleezza Rice could have been among those taken from us on that day.*

Thankfully, that brave little girl not only survived, but went on to become, among other things, a world-famous Russian scholar, Stanford professor, National Security Advisor, and the first African-American woman to be named U.S. Secretary of State. And Darcy and I were on a plane heading to meet her.

Since we'd interviewed the President of Liberia by phone and driven to Maine to meet Leslie Lewin, our first airline trip of the project felt like a milestone. It had taken literally months of back-and-forth planning with her assistant, Marilyn, to find a slot in Dr. Rice's incredibly busy schedule. Once we locked in a date, I'd booked the flights, hotel, and rental car well ahead of time to get the best rates. Darcy and I spent hours crafting, honing, and arguing about the best questions to ask and how the flow of the meeting should unfold. We were as ready as ready could be. But, staring at each other thirty-five thousand feet over Nebraska, we couldn't help reexamining our preparations one last time.

Darcy, who still struggled with her own sense of racial identity, was taken by Condoleezza's frank discussion about "the complicated history of blacks and whites in America" in her book, *Extraordinary, Ordinary People: A Memoir of Family*.

We took turns reading to each other from the opening chapter:

"We came to this country as founding populations—Europeans and Africans. Our bloodlines have crossed and been intertwined by the ugly, sex exploitation that was very much a part of slavery in America. Even in the depths of segregation blacks and whites lived very close together.

"We still have a lot of trouble with the truth of how tangled our family histories are. These legacies are painful and remind us of American's birth defect: slavery. I remember all the fuss about Thomas Jefferson and Sally Hemings a few years back. Are we kidding? I thought. Of course Jefferson had black children. I can also remember being asked how I felt when I learned that I apparently had two white great-grandfathers, one on each side of the family. I just considered it a fact—no feelings were necessary. We all have white ancestors, and some whites have black ancestors."

Darcy was keenly aware of her own mixed bag of DNA. Despite inheriting facial features from her black mother and grandmother, Darcy's coloring mostly took after her Caucasian father and grandfather, making her look virtually white: blue eyes, pale skin, and sandy-blond hair. Yet, she felt proud of her African-American heritage and sad whenever black or white kids invalidated her mixed-race sense of who she is.

> I feel like people try to tell me what race I am all the time. When I tell them that my mother is mixed and my father is white, they respond one of two ways. *"Oh, you're black! That explains why you dance so well!"* Or, some people—white or black—will say, *"Black? You're not black! C'mon, that doesn't count...you look so white."* But it's not for them to decide. I am what I am. It's more complicated than just being a label.

I admired Condoleezza Rice, this extraordinary woman who, as a child, couldn't eat at lunch counters in the segregated South, yet rose to hold what some say is the second most powerful office in the United States of America. She fought her way to the top of the Good Ol' Boy network in the Republican Party and, at times, weathered more criticism than support from African Americans. She served as Secretary of State in the midst of an extremely unpopular war. And she did it all with a smooth, calm style. There were so many questions I wanted to ask this dynamic world leader, I hardly knew where to start.

> While I admired her achievements, I had also heard a lot of criticisms of Condoleezza Rice from African Americans and Democrats who are plentiful in my New York area peer groups. I wanted to connect on a personal level with this mixed-race international icon and Russian scholar, but I was afraid that I wouldn't really relate to her and would have to let my mom do most of the interview. To be honest, I was very intimidated by her. But I was also intrigued and wanted to see for myself who she really was.

"Please be sure your tray tables are folded, and your seatbacks in their full, upright position..." the familiar instructions interrupted our reading.

As soon as the plane touched down, I turned on my phone, as I always do, to check in with my office at home. While I'm in the air, my trusty assistant loves to fill my inbox with all sorts of valuable information that I can deal with as I trudge through the airport. I scrolled through the subject lines.

Rescheduled appointment for conference call with board members; Received two more firm offers from WSB (my speaking agents); *Have flight itinerary for Wednesday's trip to Louisville; CALL DR. RICE'S OFFICE IMMEDIATELY; Scheduled hair appointment for Tuesday...*

Uh-oh! I was just guessing, but an urgent call from Dr. Rice's office probably wasn't an invitation to dinner.

I almost smashed the little button that controls the curser on my

BlackBerry as I frantically dialed Marilyn's number, which I knew by heart after so much planning and coordinating over the last few months.

"Oh, Bonnie, thank goodness we reached you. The husband of Dr. Rice's closest friend passed away suddenly," Marilyn said with an efficient, yet emotionally concerned, tone. "We are canceling everything on her schedule so that she can be with her friend. They want her to speak at the funeral, too."

Darcy watched all the blood drain out of my face as we talked.

> I only heard one side of the conversation, but I could tell what had happened. It was clear we weren't going to get the interview, even though we had flown all the way here to see her. Frustration gripped my entire body. I was missing several days of school...for nothing. I'd have to catch up on all that work while staying on top of an already difficult course load. At the same time I worried that we wouldn't get another chance to meet this amazing woman. Why was everything so hard?

"I am so sorry!" was all I could muster for Marilyn, as my mind reeled. "Please extend my condolences to Dr. Rice and to her friend."

"We feel just awful that you've come all this way," Marilyn said with genuine remorse. "Maybe we can try to fit you in sometime tomorrow..."

"Oh, no!" I exclaimed. "Of course not. We wouldn't dream of intruding on her grief right now." Not only would it be rude to press for a meeting under the circumstances, I couldn't imagine that we'd really get her at her best. It would have been pointless.

"Thanks so much for understanding," Marilyn said. "We will definitely work to get you back on the schedule soon, okay?" I knew that she could feel my frustration, but there was nothing either of us could do.

As I clicked off my BlackBerry, I felt deflated. Months of planning and preparation, not to mention the time and expense of flying across the country, were all rolling up into a big, fat goose egg. I knew too well how interview dates with busy people go. Despite the best of intentions, the harmonic conversion of time, effort, and resources necessary to pull off a meeting like this might never occur again. We may have just missed our shot.

Darcy looked crestfallen as I confirmed for her that our whole trip was for naught. There is nothing worse than feeling like a failure in your child's eyes.

Even if we turned around and got back on a plane home, we'd still have to pay for the lodging and car rental because, in the spirit of careful budgeting, I'd booked both through Priceline. William Shatner had karate-chopped us into a great deal, but there would be no refund. We might as well stay the night.

As we shuffled through the drab, gray baggage claim area of San Francisco International Airport, I wallowed in the string of disappointments I'd suffered while trying to connect with extraordinary women to feature in the book.

> *Sally Ride, the first woman astronaut? "I'm sorry. She isn't giving out any interviews at all."*
>
> *Mary J. Blige? Inquiry after inquiry with no response whatsoever.*
>
> *Ursula Burns, CEO of Xerox? "Would love to, but there are just too many requests."*

Losing our meeting with Condoleezza Rice felt like a death knell for this whole enterprise; this great adventure, this brilliant opportunity to help my daughter learn about leadership. The interview with the President of Liberia? Well, that was on the *phone*. That rousing adventure with Leslie Lewin at the Seeds of Peace camp? Not exactly the kind of heady, globetrotting experience we'd promised the publisher. I'd thought we were finally reaching escape velocity, so this crash and burn really hurt.

I had dreamed about following an enchanted yellow brick road that would guide us to just the right places, at just the right times. I would glow with pride as my daughter sipped cool drinks from the font of leadership knowledge. But as I stood in front of baggage carousel 3D and watched the endless stream of black, look-alike luggage go round and round at a maddeningly slow pace, I realized life isn't always magical, is it?

I thought about all the leaders on our list. All had faced setbacks. All had faced challenges. If I was going to make this project work, I would have to find a way to borrow some of their strength and fortitude right here, right now. I wanted Darcy to learn that leadership often means finding the faith to mold your own miraculous world from the hard clay of life's bitter and inexplicable realities.

"All right. What do we do now, Mom?" Darcy asked, a little too matter-of-factly for my mood.

Then it hit me. "What do you think about a college tour of Stanford? We're here. We've got a hotel room and a car..."

As a high school sophomore next fall, Darcy was still a bit young to begin the process of college selection, but I was improvising.

> "Sure, why not?" I said easily. I had never done a college tour before; it seemed like fun. Plus, the stress of interviewing a high-profile person was lifted off my shoulders and I could enjoy the time off school without feeling like it was wasted. I was getting excited. "Nice way to spin things, Mom," I said, hoping to brighten her disposition. She smiled at me. It felt great to be in this together.

We checked into our hotel room, and, with renewed vigor and a rehabilitated sense of purpose, we beseeched today's modern equivalent of Oz: the great and powerful Internet. Within minutes, an entirely new plan for our day in Palo Alto took shape. We booked ourselves into the official Stanford admissions office orientation session and campus tour at 2 p.m. We looked up the departments where Darcy's interests lay, Linguistics and Anthropology, and found, to our astonishment, Stanford was one of the top-rated institutions specializing in these fields of study!

A couple more keystrokes provided us the e-mail addresses of some professors whose research spanned both fields—whom we boldly convinced to meet with us.

As Darcy enthusiastically embraced the redirected energy of our excursion, my mind raced forward to the vision of a brilliant, late May afternoon in 2017. A cool, California breeze dances across the grand

Mediterranean archways surrounding the academic quad, ceremoniously decorated for an illustrious occasion. Elgar's brassy "Pomp and
Circumstance" heralds the arrival of the newly minted Stanford graduating class as they flood the commencement courtyard.

As only a mother can, I scan the throng of black robes and immediately spy my child, mortarboard cocked confidently upon her head,
grinning from ear to ear in anticipation and joy. She waves her hand and
I return the gesture, beaming with pride. Randomly, another parent sitting next to me leans over and asks how she ended up at Stanford. A
smile crosses my lips . . .

I was getting a little ahead of myself; although, as I looked down, the
bricks below my feet were beginning to show a slight tinge of yellow . . .

—————·•·—————

CHAPTER 5

Sharon Allen

First Woman Chairman of the Board,
Deloitte LLP

Darcy and I have had a special deal about the way she dresses ever since she was little, homeschooled, and spent a good deal of her time traveling with me. Most often I let her use her own judgment (within reason) for her look when she is with her friends. But when she flies with me for business, I get to decide what she wears. As far as the book was concerned, this agreement hadn't, up to this point, been onerous for her. We didn't have to dress up for the phone call with Ellen Johnson Sirleaf, and the clothing for shadowing Leslie Lewin was all comfy sweatshirts and jeans. Even our abortive visit to the Stanford campus only called for comfortable "business casual" attire.

This time, though, I had to insist that she wrap herself in the most conservative kind of business suit possible. Not only were we going to meet with the head of a Fortune 500 firm in New York City, but as Chairman of Deloitte, Sharon Allen was the number one person at a Big 4 accounting firm—which meant that many of the other top companies looked to her as a member of their winning team as well. If power were a storm, we were heading into the eye of it.

Fortunately, I had kept some of the business clothes I wore twenty pounds ago. Determined to raise her popularity quotient, Darcy had slimmed down from a size six to a size four, which meant one of my chic Tahari suit jackets fit her perfectly. By adding one of her own tops, a simple black skirt, and some nice pearls, my teenager looked like she absolutely belonged in the executive suites.

My mom knows I'm the kind of person who would always choose words over numbers. I don't relate much to the traditional corporate world—the stereotypical images, at least, never attracted me. Having to wear bland, impersonal clothes to blend in with everyone else felt stifling to my sense of identity. Even though I've been interested in having my own business, like my mother does, I didn't think I would fit into the kind of gigantic, conservative organization where we were headed. But for today, I would have to give it a try.

Since the commute time into the city from Princeton can vary, we left plenty early and arrived thirty minutes before our scheduled meeting. After finding Deloitte's headquarters address in the famous Paramount building at 1633 Broadway, we parked ourselves in the small café on the ground floor to enjoy a hot cuppa Joe before heading into the inner sanctum above us. We grabbed a couple of seats right in front of the picture windows, giving us a perfect vantage point to "people-watch" the melee of midtown Manhattan on that busy, summer morning.

Once caffeinated and ready to go, we gathered our things and entered the mammoth gray building. We flashed our IDs at the security desk to obtain the badges that would allow us passage in the express elevators— all the way up to the executive-level C-suite offices. Whoosh!

Whoa! This was probably the fastest elevator I'd ever been in. It wasn't as though I'd never been in tall buildings in New York. After all, we lived on the twentieth floor of a forty-story, Upper East Side apartment building for several years. But this was an ultra-fast, ultra-quiet starship to the nether galaxies of Titans. I started to get a sense that this powerful, elite world would be different from anything I'd ever experienced before.

The elevator doors slid open, revealing a vast open expanse of space with plush carpeting, comfortable sofas, and floor-to-ceiling glass walls framing a panoramic view of the NYC skyline. A well-coiffed receptionist sat behind a large round counter that reminded me of a backlit bar in one of those trendy downtown watering holes.

"Welcome to Deloitte Ms. St. John, Ms. Deane," she greeted us. "Would you like something to drink? Water or coffee?"

"No, thanks," said Darcy, "our tanks are full."

"Have a seat over there," the receptionist continued warmly. "I'll let you know when you can head upstairs."

> Everything here reeked of power, riches, and the capability to shape the world. It was attractive, even beautiful, in a slightly frightening way.

Sitting in the chairs waiting for our meeting, I explained to Darcy why accounting firms were so influential. I knew it was a pretty abstract idea for someone who had not yet worked in the business world at all. My training as an economist began to kick in.

"Big accounting firms like this keep track of the money for all sorts of other big businesses," I imparted. "Public companies are legally required to be audited by these licensed firms and report the numbers to their shareholders."

Her eyes met mine, and I knew that look. She wasn't getting it.

> I didn't want to get it. This was exactly the kind of Econ 101 discussion that put my feet to sleep whenever I heard anything like it. Do I really have to know about this?

"It's about scandals," I said, hoping to wake her up with something salacious. "A large global company cannot easily cheat its investors and employees out of billions unless their auditors fail in their responsibility. The huge, multinational accounting firm that served Enron, for example, Arthur Andersen, went out of business because they lost the trust of the corporate community by being complicit in some of the things the crooked executives were up to. Deloitte prevents corruption and keeps businesses running smoothly around the world. They partner with clients in every industry, to not only provide audits, but also to provide consulting, give tax advice, and show them ways to grow."

> "Really?" I said. "They're kinda like the business police?" Okay. Now you're talking. That's kind of cool.

She understood! I wanted her to grasp how companies like Deloitte represented the centrifugal force holding the fabric of our world together.

"Without what Deloitte does," I continued with my lecture, "investors wouldn't be able to effectively pick where to invest, regulators couldn't monitor illegal activity . . . why, the whole capitalist system would come crashing down. World panic would set in. The global money supply would collapse. There would be no jobs, no growth . . . we'd all live in huts!"

Darcy smiled. She liked the idea of living in huts. It was the budding anthropologist in her.

> My mind drifted outside to the sharp city landscape of elegant, geometric figures: rectangular black windows all up and down the endless rows of skyscrapers that stood against a clear, blue horizon. And behind every one of those windows is at least one person. That person is doing something. And the "something" that person is doing is important—or at least lucrative—because it costs a fortune for the privilege of standing behind that window!
>
> Another glance around the space overlooking this multimillion-dollar vista made me realize that the room we were sitting in actually reflected the view. Everything around us had clean designer lines and simple modern shapes, from the high-style chairs and tables to the line of video screens marching across the walls all around me.

"She's ready for you now," the receptionist told us. "Just go up the stairs and into the conference room on your right."

We walked up a freestanding spiral staircase gracefully suspended between the two floors. In many executive suites like this, you can't reach the inner sanctum from the elevator used by the hoi polloi. This triple line of defense—special elevator, receptionist, and extra staircase—provided super security for this very, very VIP.

We had seen Sharon Allen several weeks before when she participated at a UN conference we attended. She was on a panel with the former Prime Minister of New Zealand, the founder of womenforwomen.org, and other global influencers discussing the private-sector role in empowering women around the world. We spoke with her briefly at that time, so when we saw her rise to greet us there was already an easy familiarity to our discourse.

"Bonnie, Darcy, so nice to see you again," she welcomed as we settled in around the massive glass conference table. And then it was straight to business.

"I looked at the questions you sent, but I didn't have much time," Sharon told us. "I really couldn't print them until late last night, so I didn't get to ponder each one fully."

"Were there any that particularly stood out that you might want to start with?" asked Darcy, taking the lead.

"No, why don't you tell me where you want me to go."

"Okay," Darcy said, nodding. "Well, the first question we've been asking people is—very basically—how would you define the term 'leadership'? What does it mean to you in particular?"

"I define leadership by the admirable qualities in the leaders who inspire me. A good leader is someone who sees beyond themselves and really thinks about how they can move their organization forward by helping others to fulfill their potential. The great thing about leadership is that it can be done in so many different ways. It doesn't have to be predefined; it doesn't have to be packaged. It's important for people, and especially women, to recognize that. Sometimes women try to define their own leadership style by looking too much at those around them—and many times those people are men. Finding your own way to provide leadership is one of the most important discoveries that we find as we evolve in our careers.

"Let me tell you a story about another woman partner here who is a real fireball—an emotive type of person. Early on in her career she decided she should try to emulate another woman who was much more of a control and command kind of person. In the next meeting she led, someone actually said, *'What is wrong with you?'*

"When she explained that she was trying to be more authoritarian, the other person said, *'Forget that. Just be yourself.'* She has done that and she's been very successful.

"I can't tell you about a specific moment in time along my journey where I found my own style. But I will say that I became a lot more successful after I did."

"So what is your style, the style you found for yourself?" asked Darcy.

"The style that has worked for me, because it's natural for me, is a very direct, very inclusive, and welcoming style. That's typical for me. I like to look someone in the eye, be very present, and have a direct conversation. In today's world particularly, not being in the moment really gets in the way. I see far too many leaders who are worried more about the next meeting than the one they're in. They're worried about the next interaction more than the one that they are currently having. Some leaders have their BlackBerry sitting next to them and are constantly checking it while they are talking to you. That isn't my style. If you look at the leaders you admire most, I think you'll see that they are very present with people.

"Being in the moment and being direct helps to establish trust. If people trust you as a person, they will trust you as a leader . . . and that's an important component that some leaders don't ever get to. Now some leaders overcome that if they really have a strong command and control style. Sadly, I don't think that style works very well for most women. Is the world equal? Yes . . . sort of.

"A command and control style may not be right for women—either because it's not the way we tick or because men won't accept it from us—but the future of leadership actually lies in a different direction anyway; a direction that is more compatible with women's strengths. The collaborative nature of the changing workplace will demand a more collaborative leader.

"In the future we'll have flatter organizations, ones that require the ability to have a real impact and influence when it may not be so clear who the leader is in the room. You need to be able to dive into complex group dynamics and create excellence. We will need more leaders who know how to inspire a team and know how to help them come to a group conclusion; leaders who know how to let their team succeed without them making all of the choices and decisions. The old corporate ladder, hierarchies, and organizational charts just don't work so easily anymore.

"Technical competencies, whatever your expertise is, are important, but they are only the groundwork you need. The soft skills are even more crucial for leadership: the ability to communicate, the ability to organize a meeting, even the ability to think through what you want to have as an end point and allow for the discussion and process along the way. Those competencies come from a different kind of learning. In college and business school, you take courses to learn technical skills and information, but the group projects and the extracurricular opportunities for teamwork and leadership are where you learn the soft skills. I believe those are even more important today.

"Speaking is another one of the soft skills that becomes more and more important as your leadership responsibilities increase. Over the years, I took the time to work at it, accepted coaching from others, and got lots and lots of practice. I used to hate public speaking, honestly, and now I really enjoy it.

"But it wasn't easy. At least once a year, I sat down with different coaches and mentors to watch video recordings of me speaking. They pointed out little things I didn't even realize I was doing. They gave me ideas and suggestions that made me better. Some people think it's fake to watch yourself and change your gestures, but I think it's just self-awareness. Not very many people are natural public speakers; you have to spend some time figuring out how to do it. No one would go onstage and try to play the piano without practicing first.

"I'm talking a lot," said Sharon. "Is this what you want to hear about?"

"You've been great! You've been answering a lot of questions on our list before we're asking them . . ." I replied, hoping to keep her going.

"She's a quick study," said Darcy, agreeing with me. "She read the questions once and she's been answering them all the way through. But I'd like to hear more about what is essential for leadership regardless of individual styles or skills. What is the core or spine?"

"I like the way you asked that question," Sharon said. "While styles may vary, all good leaders need to have three basic things: clear vision, tenacity, and empathy.

"When I say vision I mean an ability to stop and look ahead. You have to think beyond what's happening in the moment, and see how actions today will create results in the future. Being clear—being very confident in where you're trying to go—is important.

"Having tenacity, a measured tenacity, also differentiates good leaders. In whatever style you use, you need to be clear and stick to your guns about your expectations: expectations for your own positioning, expectations for other people's performance, and expectations for how a meeting should be conducted. By measured tenacity, I mean that you need to persevere toward your objective but be willing to accept some advice, counsel, and suggestions along the course. It's a balance.

"I was coaching another woman here regarding a project that didn't go as well as it should have or could have. I thought that she had actually been forgiving to a fault with people. When they didn't accomplish what she asked, or they rearranged her priorities, she would say, *'Oh, it's okay.'* Leaders generally, and women in particular, must be willing to be very clear when the result is important, create an expectation, and not back off.

"The third, and perhaps most important basic ingredient for leadership, is having the appropriate amount of empathy; and it can't be insincere or faked. I really think the secret weapon for many leaders is emotional intelligence. So many times I see leaders who may have all the intellectual intelligence, strategic thinking, and tenacity that is needed, but if they are not able to read a room and interact with individuals, they're not going to achieve their objective."

"When you talk about not backing down from your expectations and coaching that woman, you are talking about delegating, trusting, and relying on others," observed Darcy. "Was that hard to learn?"

"It takes experience. Eventually everyone has that 'a-ha' moment when you actually start leading rather than managing. The epiphany happened for me when one of the folks working with me said, '*You know, you're a much better leader in Portland than you are in Boise.*'

"This came as a real surprise to me. I had started my career in Boise and was, over time, promoted to be the managing partner for both the Boise and the Portland offices. This particular person worked with me on business development in both places. We had conducted a meeting on the marketplace with our management team in Boise, and then we held the same meeting in the Portland office. It was afterward, when we were debriefing, that he told me I was a better leader in Portland.

"'*How can that be?*' I asked him. '*I'm still the same person.*'

"'You still think you know everything in Boise,' he explained to me. 'You created a lot of the systems there and so you're still trying to manage everything. When you are in Portland you have to rely on a lot of other people. It's clear you've let loose of the details. In Portland you are truly leading instead of managing.'

"You always hope you will have someone who will be honest with you like that and tell you, not what you want to hear, but what you need to hear.

"Leading versus managing is an important distinction for individuals. If you have an incredibly large group of people to lead, you have to get to the point of trust and confidence and really rely on them to exercise judgment in executing against your expectations. With a smaller group you could find yourself trying to micromanage. But in a larger group you really can't do that or you'll never succeed. Ultimately when I moved to Los Angeles to become the regional managing partner, I led people by knowing the business and understanding what I was looking for, but nevertheless relying on competent people to execute against my expectations."

"Darcy is interested in delegation," I mentioned, "because she has struggled with that in places where she has been a leader."

"Is that right?" asked Sharon.

"Delegating, right," said Darcy. "And letting go of the desire to micromanage."

"Exactly." It seemed that Sharon and Darcy were really connecting on this issue. "I must say, I think sometimes women tend to do that more. Why is that? I don't know. Are we more perfectionist?"

"Actually there is brain research that shows women actually do see more detail than men," I responded. "So we really are more prone to that."

"It's important to know when to get into the details and when not to," Sharon continued. "There will be times when you'll be disappointed in the result if you haven't really focused enough on the details, yet you know you can't really manage them all the time. Being detail-oriented is a strength and weakness you have to balance."

"Knowing when to get into the details seems a lot like knowing when to be tenacious and stand your ground," I said. "You have to pick your battles."

"Exactly," said Sharon. "When I was first elected as Chairman of the Board, I had an opportunity to redefine the role. There were many situations where I had to choose what was most important.

"Before me, the chairman had always had another full-time job in the firm. Once he left the boardroom, he wore a different hat. We decided as an organization that we needed to have more independence in the chairman's role and made it a full-time job reporting to the Board of Directors. We wanted to ensure the strength of our governance processes. But beyond that, I had freedom to define the job to include some work with our biggest clients, leading the partners and directors, and doing some eminence building for our brand.

"I was very clear about positioning my new job at a very high level because it was really being created as we went along. I made sure that we fully utilized the title of chairman in the marketplace and had the opportunity to really leverage that position, as opposed to allowing it, and me, to be suboptimized. There were times I had to stand my ground and say, 'No, this is the way it's going to be. This will happen this way because it's the right thing to do.' I knew it would affect the way people would see the position of chairman."

Darcy, looking professional in her sleekly tailored jacket, leaned forward to ask one of the questions she'd put on the list. "What scares you most about being a leader? What are some of the negative things, and how do you overcome them?"

"One of the things that scares me most about being a leader, particularly in today's world, is having someone else define who you are or what your organization is by something you may say unintentionally or something taken out of context. Trust is so important, especially in our profession, that it bothers me how a totally unintended action or mistake could define the organization in such a significant way that it could actually have a tremendous negative financial impact.

"It scares me that my comments or someone else's comments could have a devastating result. That possibility is increased by the proliferation of social media and bloggers. You can spend years raising the bar on governance, emphasizing integrity with all of our associates, and building the reputation of the firm globally and have it destroyed with a few careless words gone viral. We've done research on appropriate boundaries for our associates online as well. This is big."

"So how do you deal with that fear? What do you do about it?" I asked.

"Well, you know," said Sharon, "you can't control everything. What I can control about this type of risk is myself. I am always very careful about what I say and how I represent the organization. My media team is very selective about whom we talk to. We don't give many interviews."

Sharon looked at us pointedly, reminding us that we had been granted one of very few interviews.

"Thank you," I said immediately.

"Thank you for trusting us," Darcy reiterated.

Changing the subject I asked, "I was thinking about you growing up, when you were in your twenties and thirties. You probably weren't thinking, 'I want to be the Chairman of Deloitte,' were you?"

"It wasn't the case, no," said Sharon with a smile. She was probably remembering how they didn't even let her meet customers face to face back in the early days. A woman chairman was truly unthinkable.

"Now that women can hope and dream of being the Chairman of Deloitte or some other Fortune 500 company," I said, "they often think it sounds like too much work. What would you say to women in their twenties or thirties to make them want your job?"

"I love my job," she said without hesitation. "When you really believe that you have been able to influence the entirety of an organization as big and as important as Deloitte by your actions and by the way you interact, it's very rewarding.

"As chairman, I also find it very fulfilling to be able to give more support to our initiative for the Advancement and Retention of Women, and also on diversity in general. I do believe that defines our culture in so many ways, and it has made us a better place for women . . . and for men.

"Our people have a great appreciation for what has happened to our culture, and I take at least a part of the credit for that. It is a collective effort clearly. But as a leader, the consistency of your approach, attitude, and resolve to do the right things at the right time make a difference. I am proud of that. I love my job every day.

"I remember when I was first elected. Out of the three thousand plus partners, you have to have enough people say, 'Yes, she's the right person to fit the role of chairman.' After I was voted in, one of the members of the nominating committee pulled me aside and handed me a bottle cap. I flipped it over in my hand and saw inside that it had one word on the inside: Trust.

" 'That's why you were elected,' he said.

"I keep the bottle cap on my desk . . . and the idea front and center in my mind. Trust is very important to me."

On that note, it was time to wind up. We'd already gone past our allotted hour.

"What a pleasure to get to know you!" I said, standing up. "We know it's time for you to catch your plane."

"Well, it's my pleasure," said Sharon warmly, reaching out to shake our hands. "It really is. And I must say, it's fun to watch the two of you together. I think this is such a great adventure that you're going on."

We snapped a quick photo. I smiled at seeing each of us in our power jackets—Sharon in an elegant, short-waisted butter cream, Darcy in black and white twill, and me in basic black: the unwritten uniform for successful women. We definitely made the right fashion choice!

The elevator dropped like a stone, and we left behind the shiny, polished world of high finance.

"Wow," Darcy exclaimed as our ears popped, "she lives in a world I never really knew existed."

"How do you mean?" I asked.

"Well, she has responsibility for all these people, and all that money, and all those rules and regulations, and if she makes a mistake it affects thousands of people all over the world. I mean, I knew politicians had that kind of power, but I never knew people in business had that kind of role, too."

"Yes," I agreed, "it's staggering how much influence the handful of folks who occupy the C-suites actually have. It's awe-inspiring to see how far Sharon Allen has come in a generation or so."

As we spilled out onto Times Square and mixed back in with the common folk, I looked up and thought again about those windows. Some people say that New York City is the center of the universe. Well, at that moment, it sure felt like it!

CHAPTER 6

Hillary Rodham Clinton

United States Secretary of State

Foggy Bottom.

Sounds funny, doesn't it? Like, maybe something a baby gets after scarfing down too many Gerber's mashed kidney beans.

Actually, the term refers to a geographic district within the borders of our nation's capitol, slightly south and west of the White House. But inside the beltway, and throughout governments around the world, "Foggy Bottom" is universally known as the nickname for the imposing, concrete, bunker-style Harry S. Truman building—the headquarters of the United States Department of State.

It is here that Darcy and I carried *our* bottoms, foggy or otherwise, to meet the most powerful woman in the United States and therefore, arguably, the most powerful woman in the world: United States Secretary of State, Hillary Rodham Clinton.

We had garnered an invitation to join Secretary Clinton at a special luncheon she was hosting in support of international women leaders who actively engage in mentoring. Titled "Diplomats, Leaders, and the Next Generation: Sharing and Strengthening an International Network of Women," this event promised to be an amazing opportunity not only to see Secretary Clinton in action, but also to participate in a celebration of the very essence of this project—the passing of wisdom and experience along to the next wave of women leaders.

"You are invited to attend with a member of the next generation who you are mentoring to benefit from the advice and insight of our diplomats and leaders," proclaimed the gold-embossed formal invitation from

Capricia Penavic Marshall, United States Chief of Protocol, requesting the pleasure of our company.

> Powerful women from around the world *and their younger mentees!* I wasn't sure how this kind of thing would work, but I thought it sounded really cool. To be honest, though, I found Secretary Clinton pretty intimidating. She is the most famous woman leader in the world as far as I know. Would I be able to hang in this fast crowd? Would I get to meet the legend herself? And if I did, what was I going to say to her?

Darcy and I were only beginning to grasp the enormity of the sandbox we were about to play in. We were going to Washington to have lunch with ambassadors, heads of global nonprofits, business leaders, and more—women who are quite literally shaping the world.

The only thing disappointing about this whole opportunity was that we had been warned we probably wouldn't get any alone time with the secretary. But we didn't care. Just to be in the same room with her and this distinguished group was exciting enough.

It was a warm summer's day when we pulled up to the main gate of the State Department at the intersection of 22nd and C Street in our nation's capitol. I must say, situated as it is among some of the most exquisite architecture on our shores, the Truman Building reminded me of the architecture from one of those deliberately drab depictions of a heartless "Gotham City" you see in the Batman movies. All concrete and bland, the entrance was surrounded by blocky pillars, naked of any sort of adornment, with boring square windows running as far as you can see in either direction.

All of this was neatly tucked away behind a phalanx of armed guards and imposing steel barricades that rose from the ground like a garden of limbless trees—an unpleasant fact of life in post–9-11 Washington.

We had been issued detailed instructions as to exactly where and when to enter the building, which we were following to the letter. Only security-cleared vehicles could enter the complex, so we parked our car down the street and walked up to the intimidating silver guard house bearing the not-so-subtle placard: ALL VISITORS CHECK IN HERE.

I twisted the handle and opened the door into a space that served as the clearinghouse between the outside world and the highly secure interior. The balmy summer atmosphere quickly disappeared. Winter inhabited this little shanty all year round—and I'm not talking about the temperature.

Stern military eyes stared down at us. Why are these guys always so tall?

"We're here for the luncheon?" This place made me nervous. Well, maybe it wasn't just the place. Maybe it was the guy with the loaded submachine gun and the dark, black and green camouflage flak jacket standing there giving us the hairy eyeball.

"May I see some identification?" ordered the guy next to Rambo.

We gingerly handed over our IDs. He scrutinized my driver's license and Darcy's passport as if he were authenticating the Dead Sea Scrolls.

Sheesh! I felt like we were exchanging espionage at Checkpoint Charley in East Berlin during the height of the Cold War. I know these guys are trained to be suspicious, but I find it hard to imagine that this five-foot-two, one-legged black woman and her fashionably conservative teenage daughter looked so threatening as to warrant all this attention.

"All right." Our officious host lightened up a bit after seeing that we were, in fact, supposed to be there. "Head to that blue awning across the courtyard."

He pointed to a long canopy about fifty yards to our right. As soon as we turned in that direction, I knew he was steering us to the right place. Exploding from underneath the faded blue canvas was a veritable sea of color, gleaming in bright contrast to the stark backdrop of the Truman edifice. Bright dresses and jackets trumpeting reds, yellows, and oranges; traditional multicolored turbans; saris; hats with feathers and flowers. The ladies had arrived, wrapped in all their finery.

I was struck by the incongruous nature of what I was seeing. Even as little as fifteen years ago, when I worked in Washington, the doorway we were about to enter would have been almost exclusively populated by standard-issue blue or gray suits, power ties, and wing-tipped shoes. The few women who were given the chance to cross this threshold back then would have done so constricted by extremely conservative formality of dress and demeanor.

I looked over at my daughter and mused that this is the kind of experience my mother could never have given me when I was her age. A gathering of powerful women like this didn't even exist back then, much less waltz its way into a bastion of male dominance like the U.S. State Department. And even if they did, my mother didn't have anywhere near the kind of connections needed to get you into a place like this.

Her alcoholic mother, my grandmother, never went past the fourth grade, and my grandfather left before Mom was born. Though she grew up with Jim Crow laws and segregated schools, my mother found enough optimism in the Civil Rights Movement of the sixties to cross the color lines and marry my father, a WASP through and through. The fact that his family never acknowledged our existence and that my dad left her struggling to support my brother, my sister, and me, didn't stop her from continuing to believe that she could build a better future for herself, for us, and for many others.

Mom grew up poor. She ferociously fought to graduate from college and become a teacher. By the time I was Darcy's age, my mother had earned her master's degree, went on to complete her Ph.D., and become a high school principal. Even though she was an acclaimed turnaround leader who transformed schools, she could hardly conceive of circulating comfortably in the Ivy League, Wall Street, and Washington milieu that she had propelled me into by pushing me to win scholarships for prep schools, Harvard, and Oxford. As I climbed higher and higher, the air got thinner and thinner. Although I had gained beaucoup access, it still felt more like a tourist visa to me than a local passport—compared to my peers who came from generations of politicians, Ph.D.'s, and financiers. By starting earlier, I hoped that Darcy would have even more entrée, see even more opportunities for herself, and be better prepared to step up and carve out her own leadership role.

A sense of awe crept over me even while Mom and I were still in the bustling group of women entering the building. Everywhere I looked there were high-profile, globally influential women. The international diversity was even more than I had expected. Although we take for granted that gatherings of men like this exist, most people, I would think, are unaware that this international women's entourage is so healthy and well established. Just getting the first impression, I already sensed that the normal competitive aura of a powerful men's gathering was replaced here by a collaborative, more interconnected sensibility. I felt drawn to this wonderful energy and wanted more than anything to be part of it.

We merged into the kaleidoscope of costumes and were immediately whisked onto an elevator for the ride up to the third floor where the formal reception rooms are located. I could already feel the air thinning.

A soft *ping* signaled our arrival. The mottled gray, steel doors slid open . . .

. . . and we stepped through the looking glass.

Unfolding before us, in stark contrast to their exterior frame, were the grandest, most elegant series of rooms I have ever seen.

We walked off the elevator into the Entrance Hall. Our shoes were cushioned by the soft, thick weave of an intricately patterned Tabriz rug covering polished mahogany floors. Thirteen feet above our heads, the ornate ceiling supported an exquisite antique crystal chandelier bathing the creamy, paneled walls with soft illumination.

"I don't know what I was expecting these rooms to look like from the outside, but whatever it was I definitely wasn't expecting *this*," Darcy whispered to me. "It looks like the White House."

I smiled. Darcy had been to the White House at age thirteen and gave herself a tour of the China Room, the theater, the Map Room, the Green Room, and the Blue Room, while I was being prepped to receive an award for Black History Month in the East Room. *"It looks like the White House"* was an honest remark from her personal experience. Another stamp in her passport to a better future.

My attention moved past the beauty of our surroundings and began to absorb the meaning, the purpose, and the history of this place. These diplomatic reception rooms are the official spaces where the secretary of state, the vice president, and members of the Cabinet meet, greet, and entertain visiting foreign dignitaries. The rooms are meant to provide an appropriate backdrop for engaging in the art of diplomacy while surrounded by the fine and decorative art of our land. Most of the pieces date back to the early years of our country's heritage, particularly the eighteenth and nineteenth centuries. In its entirety, this display comprises one of the finest collections of this period ever assembled.

Soon we found ourselves clustered around an intricately detailed rococo-style table covered with rows and rows of perfectly aligned little tents made of creased, cream-colored card stock. On the face of each card, in perfect calligraphy, was the name of a guest and, on the back, her specific seating assignment for the banquet—table *and* chair number. That's the Office of Protocol for you. I chuckled to myself thinking both houses of Congress were probably consulted to approve the seating arrangement.

As we cruised over the names in search of "Bonnie St. John" and "Darcy Deane," my little joke about Congressional oversight seemed to cut frighteningly close to the bone. The list went on and on, and became more and more unbelievable with each name and title.

> Kolinda Grabar-Kitarovic, Ambassador of Croatia
>
> Her Excellency Dr. Inonge Mbikusita-Lewanika of the Republic of Zambia
>
> Janet Murguia, President, National Council of La Raza

As I read though the illustrious guest list, my jaw dropped. I looked to my right. Darcy had the same bulging eyes and unhinged mouth that I did. Like mother like daughter.

A young state department staffer approached us. "You are Bonnie St. John, correct?"

"Yes..."

"Excellent. Welcome to the State Department. You'll be meeting with the secretary in the Monroe Room," she said in a quiet, almost conspiratorial tone, to keep from alerting the less fortunate that such a meeting was possible.

"Please come with me. I'm JoAnne."

"Is she kidding?" came a panicky, sotto voce scream from Darcy as we followed JoAnne down a meticulously decorated corridor.

All I could do was stare forward as my eyes slowly widened.

JoAnne guided us into yet another masterpiece of neoclassical décor. Named for James Monroe, our fifth president, who served as Secretary of State for six years prior to his taking the big chair, this room was much more intimate than any of the others we had seen. The soft yellow walls, colonial blue fireplace surround, and private nooks with small groupings of chairs and sofas gave the room a cheery, homey yet still elegant feeling.

"The secretary is on her way," JoAnne informed us as she stood guard by the door. "She should be here in about ten minutes."

Darcy and I huddled in a niche near the center of the chamber. We'd been granted our wish: a quiet, intimate moment with the woman who had personally transformed the way women leaders were treated around the world, and we had no script or plan.

"What the heck are we going to say to her?!!" Darcy would have grabbed my lapels and shook me if she wasn't trying to play it so cool. "Mom?" Darcy implored. She had that panicked *you're-the-one-steering-the-ship-and-if-you're-going-down-then-that-means-I-am-too* look I had seen before when the interview with Madame Johnson Sirleaf was going sideways.

"Well," I said to Darcy, trying to sound more calm and confident than I felt, "she will most likely ask us about the book. Think of three examples of the women we are interviewing to share with her. Practice saying something about each one."

Knowing that Darcy would probably find herself less articulate than usual in this kind of intimidating setting, I had her practice saying a few intelligent things about herself, the book, and her gratitude for being included at this luncheon. Having a few phrases on the tip of your tongue helps a lot when the blood isn't quite circulating to the top floor.

Mom always does this to me! She puts me into a position where I have to perform when I am not prepared. It scares me to death. Now, when the real, actual Secretary Clinton could walk in the door at any minute, I am struggling to find the right words. Even though we were told this wasn't going to happen, we should have thought of this. We should have practiced!

As we lobbed our stock phrases back and forth, a man came into the room with a big camera, a long lens, and a giant flash attachment all hung around his neck.

"Hi, I'm Rob, and I'll be taking your picture with the secretary." His charming smile immediately lowered our personal threat levels from orange to yellow.

"Hi, I'm Bonnie," I said, reaching out to shake his hand.

"Darcy," she offered, following up with her own handshake.

I am always so proud of my daughter's self-assurance in these very adult settings. The years spent on the road with me at business events all over the country have made her extremely comfortable with professional etiquette. Even though, as a teenager, she hates wearing conservative jewelry and business suits in place of her usual torn jeans, hoop earrings, and layered T-shirts, her excellent manners and people skills always come through.

"I can't believe how nervous I am to have my picture taken with the secretary!" I admitted to Rob.

We all laughed a little, which helped ease the tension even further. We weren't the first nervous people he'd met in this room.

Why is it when we meet really famous and powerful people our brains cough and sputter like an engine that won't start on a frosty morning? We all dream of that moment when we are given an audience with one of our idols, right? We think we'll dazzle our hero with a beautifully erudite bit of insight, wrapped in a witty phrase, slightly droll, but still so perfectly impressive that our cleverness elicits a private chuckle between the two of us, leaving everyone else in the room irretrievably jealous of the attention.

But it never happens that way. Ever. And sitting there on a spindly, 250-year-old love seat, all I could do was hope for the best.

Just then, the emotionless, government-trained bodyguard stepped aside slightly, and from the shadow behind him *she* appeared. As I watched her walk forward, I felt a real bond of sisterhood with this stately figure. Like me, Mrs. Clinton had struggled to raise an only daughter while working full-time and more. She'd had her personal life dragged through the tabloids both here and abroad. Yet she still braved unthinkably brutal personal insults and sexism to run for president. To say I admired her just wouldn't be sufficient.

Like a shot, she crossed the distance to us with a grace that seemed to carry her on air. Not regal, that would be too stuffy, but powerfully warm and inviting—the epitome of elegance. Gone now were the plain blue pantsuits of the campaign trail. Instead, she wore a soft-shaped, hip-length red business jacket with understated, but exquisitely tailored, black pants. She looked feminine, stylish, comfortable, and strong all at the same time.

"Thank you so much for coming, Bonnie. It's a pleasure to have you here."

I smiled and took her hand as she immediately moved on to my daughter.

"And, Darcy, what a great joy to meet you."

I knew she had been briefed on who we were just thirty seconds before arriving—because I worked in the White House and I knew how these meetings went. Any political official couldn't possibly hold in their head details about all the people they come in contact with, so there are teams of people whose job it is to make sure the officials they work for have just enough information to greet every guest with a warm, personal connection. But what Secretary Clinton did with that information in the next few minutes showed why she cared enough to make space for us on her calendar. After the first polite few seconds, it was as if I had disappeared. Her entire attention, her being, her powerful presence was aimed squarely and completely at Darcy.

"So, tell me about this project you are working on," she queried my teenager. Hillary Clinton wanted to find out what Darcy thought and what Darcy was learning—not what Darcy's mother had to say about it! The only thing more wonderful than having your idol focus her attention on you is for her to focus her attention on your child. I beamed with the intensity of a supernova as my poised daughter responded.

"We're writing a book called *How Great Women Lead*," Darcy said, looking far more at ease than I knew she felt. "It's a mother-daughter journey to meet amazing women leaders like you, and Ellen Johnson Sirleaf, Leslie Lewin, Sharon Allen..."

> Mom's last-minute practice technique worked like a charm. The words just spilled out! I hoped I was making sense...

"How old are you, Darcy?" Hillary asked.

"Fifteen."

"So, tell me. What are you learning about leadership?"

Even though the questions came in rather rapid-fire form, Darcy seemed to easily fall into a rapport with this dynamic, powerful presence. She was able to hold her own, not fall apart, and engage in an intelligent, interesting dialogue.

"What is your most profound impression of the experience you're having with this book?" I heard the Secretary of State ask Darcy.

"Well, I'm discovering—and today's luncheon is a perfect example of this—there is a great big circle out there of good and powerful people who really want to continue to expand the progress of women as leaders by passing along to others the wisdom and experiences they've accumulated. They make a conscious effort to stay connected—to nurture and support one another's efforts. So, the circle keeps growing and expanding in strength and influence. And, that as a woman, I can be a part of this circle and benefit from it if I just make an effort to reach out and embrace it."

Hillary's entire face smiled as she held Darcy's hands in hers. From writing *It Takes a Village to Raise a Child*, to speaking out at the global women's conference in China, Secretary Clinton has always been a vocal advocate for women and girls. In this moment, I was seeing her passion in the most simple and genuine way. She was truly fascinated with this one young girl's quest to learn about leadership. In her eyes I saw a mother, a leader, a woman, and a spirit overjoyed with hope and confidence in the future. "That's exactly right, Darcy," she said with a look of intensity that I'm sure my teenager will take to her grave. "And don't you ever stop reaching out and participating."

> Meeting the secretary, the world's most recognizable woman leader, wasn't nearly as scary as I thought it would be. I had met other strong women in business and government who talked in short sentences and seemed to be weighing your response, almost challenging you with every syllable. They give you an intense stare that translates into: *"You'd better say something good, and say it quick, or I won't listen again."* But Mrs. Clinton wasn't like that. She didn't approach me with that cold, scrutinizing energy I expected. It felt more like, *"Hey I'm here, it's nice to see you. I want to know a little bit about you."* It was surprising how easy she made it to talk with her.

Staffers I hadn't noticed before began to hover, signaling it was time to move on. Hillary subtly nodded in response and gracefully moved us into place for the pictures—perfectly centered in front of the fireplace directly under the portrait of President Madison. Clearly this was an intricate bit of choreography routinely performed by photographer, staff, and secretary—and the boss knew how to hit her marks.

Pop, pop, pop . . . Rob's camera flashed in our faces, capturing the moment for posterity.

With a big smile, hugs, and more warm sincerity, Hillary bid us farewell. Just as quickly as she arrived, the secretary was swallowed up by her cadre of deputies and whisked out of the room. As the last blur of red fabric disappeared, we could hear a roar of applause on the other side of the door. I felt the honor of that intimate moment, the private audience we just had with the woman who is responsible for the relationship between the United States of America and the rest of the world. In an odd way, any doubt I had about whether we could see this journey through receded in the face of Hillary's vote of confidence in us. If she saw our mother-daughter global adventure as important to expand the ranks of women leaders, then it must be. And we'd better get it done!

JoAnne quickly ushered us down a side hallway, into the back of the ballroom, and directly to our table—just as the sumptuous meal was served. Still reeling from the whirlwind of the past few minutes, Darcy and I took our places among our distinguished lunch mates. The Benjamin Franklin State Dining Room was certainly the most spectacular of all the spaces we'd visited thus far. I counted twenty-four gold-leafed, freestanding Corinthian columns that surrounded the gigantic space, with twelve stunning chandeliers brilliantly lighting the formal place settings in front of us.

I nudged Darcy to make sure she wasn't bewildered by the vast array of flatware, china, and crystal glass before her. Just to be sure she didn't start drinking the Finnish Ambassador's water by mistake, I conjured an old memory peg I'd read in a book somewhere. Under the table where only Darcy could see, I surreptitiously formed the letters "b" and "d" with my thumb and forefinger of each hand (kind of like the "ok" gesture). The "b" on the left means that's where your bread dish is found. The "d" on the right indicates which drinking glass is yours.

Working from the outside in, we moved from fork to fork happily devouring the delicious mixed greens and delicate salmon tartar amuse bouche already set out as appetizers. As we did, Cheryl Mills, the secretary's Chief of Staff, began the program with a welcome message and introductions.

"Not only has she been a great mentor to me in the world of politics," quipped Cheryl in her formal introduction to the secretary, "but she also taught me how to find a really great handbag!"

The audience loved it.

It was fun for me to see Cheryl again after so many years. From the inauguration of the Clinton administration in 1993, she had served as a Deputy White House Counsel while I had come on board a few months later as one of the directors on the National Economic Council. At that time, there were only about four or five young African-American women in their late twenties running through the corridors of the West Wing, so we were routinely mistaken for one another. Through thick and thin, Cheryl always remained fiercely loyal and close to the Clintons.

"And now, please welcome the United States Secretary of State, Hillary Rodham Clinton."

Everyone jumped to their feet clapping and cheering, and they wouldn't stop. Secretary Clinton stood and smiled broadly from behind the podium adorned with the official seal of the U.S. State Department. The applause continued for almost a full minute before the secretary herself had to motion for everyone to sit down.

"Welcome to the State Department," she began. It was a monumental moment; she was the host. This was her place, her time. "I am delighted to see so many of you gathered here to share and strengthen the international network of women leaders. I see so many friends and colleagues from across the government and private sector, ambassadors and diplomats, media representatives, and of course all of the members of the next generation brought here by your mentors."

She took a moment to recognize another hero of mine, Dorothy Height, one of the foremost pioneers of the Civil Rights Movement in this country. In an era where African-American women were often banished to the lowest positions in society, Dorothy Height dedicated her life to one purpose: that equality for women and equality for African Americans are issues that go hand in hand.

I looked up, along with the rest of the crowd, and spotted Dr. Height, resplendent as always in her trademark fancy hat. Well into her nineties, she was confined to a wheelchair but still retained an aura of spunky enthusiasm as she waved to the podium in thanks.

Once again, the crowd was on their feet in honor of this beloved national treasure.

The secretary continued after the ovation for Dr. Height.

"I've experienced mentoring from both sides, having been both mentor and mentee. I look around and see so many here who I have worked with on one side or another of that line."

As a professional speaker, I couldn't help noticing how well the secretary made everyone feel included and connected with her via powerful use of presence, eye contact, and a warm, inviting smile.

"What I like about the mentoring relationship is that it promotes creativity and collaboration. It may seem like it's a one-way street, but believe me it's a two-way street. Mentoring gives each of us a chance not only to be a teacher, but also to be a student...there is so much we learn from each other. But, you know, the best-kept secret is how much this experience means to the mentors. We get such positive feedback.

"It's also about friendship. The friendships that arise over time as two people go through ups and downs, crises, and all kinds of life's challenges.

"I know I don't have to convince this audience why it's important still, today, in 2010 for women to go out of their way to make sure they mentor other women. It's amazing to me that we still need to do it, but I know we do."

Here there was a strong reaction from the audience.

"I see some heads nodding!" Hillary acknowledged.

"Mentoring may be a fairly new practice in the American workplace, but in fact women have been mentoring each other for millennia. There's always something to learn...and always some personal barrier to push your way through.

"I recently read a letter that Amelia Earhart wrote in 1936 to a girl named Beatrice Pugsley who asked the famous pilot how she could break into aviation. So Amelia answered her."

Hillary looked down and read from a copy of the letter in her hand. "'The more you know about mechanics the better off you'll be.'" She looked up at the audience and smiled. "I guess that's good advice for a pilot."

Laughter filled the room. She continued reading from the page.

"'If your high school has a shop class, take it. Study physics and mathematics. Maybe you could get a group of classmates to visit the offices of an airline or railroad or a bus line.'"

Here, Hillary took a dramatic pause, letting us know that the real essence of the letter was coming up next.

"*'My belief is that work should be done by the individual best suited to do it. Be he a man or she a woman. I warn you that deans, teachers, and possible employers are likely to discourage you from so reasonable a line of thought, but I feel women must hold to it if they are to progress.'*"

Putting down the letter from Amelia, Hillary shared her own feelings.

"Reading that brought back memories of my childhood desire to be an astronaut. I wrote a letter to NASA and got a response back that girls can't be astronauts.

"And then twelve years later came Sally Ride!

"Amelia's letter reminds us that the work of supporting the next generation, particularly women supporting women, is not yet through. Probably never will be.

"That's why it's critical that we all do our part.

"I'm very proud to be at the State Department with such a tradition of mentoring. People here really take their time to do it. I especially want, once and for all, to dispel the myth that women don't support women. Relationships really are the glue that holds life together."

She paused, letting the moment soak in for us.

"I want to close by saying that one of the great privileges of being Secretary of State is to travel around the world representing this great country.

"I started many years ago when I was First Lady with the help of my then chief of staff who is now our first ever Ambassador-at-Large for Global Women's Issues, Melanne Verveer."

Hillary had to stop talking at this point because the applause was deafening. Most of the women in the room recognized that the creation of Melanne's post was the culmination of decades of work to make the advancement of women an official U.S. foreign policy goal. Verveer is the embodiment of victory in this long battle.

When she was able to begin talking again, Hillary waxed poetic as her heartfelt feelings reach a crescendo:

We met with women everywhere.

Women in post-conflict situations

Women in conflict

Women who were struggling to build democracy

Women who had been beaten down and ignored for too long

And women who were leaders in every sense of the word

Everywhere I went I realized that

Talent is universal, but opportunity is not.

Particularly for women.

Right now there is a brilliant girl somewhere in Africa who could be a physicist, a doctor, or Secretary of State. Or even a president. But that girl will never get the schooling that she needs.

Somewhere there is a mother who is struggling to recover from a natural disaster like Haiti's or a manmade disaster like the Congo's. She is wondering whether there will be a future at all, never mind what it holds.

There are so many talented women who will never, ever have the chance that women have in our country.

That's why it's so important for us not to let any young woman ever lose faith in herself, give up on herself, or decide she's not worth it—just because the media says she should look a certain way, or that she doesn't have some other attribute that is exalted the way the content of her character should be.

It's important for all women to stand up for the right and opportunity of every girl to fulfill her God-given potential.

That's what mentoring is really all about.

Thank you everyone!

The response was almost like a rock concert. I half expected the screaming, stomping people to tear down the pricey drapes as Hillary, in her power suit, threw herself out onto the crowd and mosh-surfed across the room. Of course, the reality of her exit was very dignified, but the power was the same. Hillary Clinton, and everything she stands for, meant so much to the women in this room they could hardly contain themselves.

The rest of the program that day incorporated many of the ambassadors present as well as diverse nongovernmental leaders who took turns answering questions posed by the group of mentees. It wasn't a typical luncheon with speakers; Cheryl facilitated a truly interactive, wisdom transference in this magical space. We heard from Maria Otero who had presided over ACCIÓN, a global nonprofit with a microfinance loan portfolio of $3.6 billion. Alexis Herman—the first woman and African-American Secretary of Labor who was a role model for me, Cheryl, and all of the young black women in the White House—shared her mentoring secrets. Even the great pioneering film star, Cicely Tyson, performed a brief, but inspiring one-woman show. Speechwriter and fellow Rhodes Scholar, Lissa Muscatine, told her story about how Hillary Clinton once stood up for her and insisted she be hired for a job even though she was pregnant at the time with twins!

As the program ended and the circulating, hugging, and laughter began in earnest, I reflected on Hillary's impact on women leaders. I understood more deeply why she convened this group, and I felt its urgency and importance. My epiphany was this: what Hillary accomplished at this luncheon couldn't be done by a man.

For hundreds of years men have held gatherings where they encourage and mentor their protégés. They take them out for "drinks with the boys" after work, invite them to conferences, and develop their loyal team of leaders. When men mentor groups of men it goes without comment or specific attention because it's just business as usual.

A man would hardly ever host a luncheon to mentor solely women, and even if he did, it might seem awkward. For our U.S. Secretary of State to bring together women leaders around the world along with the next generation to share their wisdom like this was monumental. And it somehow seemed more natural, more inspiring, and more practical than anything a man would—or could—do. It had been reported in the papers that the "Hillary Effect" was in part responsible for the fivefold increase in women ambassadors in Washington since the '90s.

What I realized here at this luncheon was that leaders who just happen to be women can *choose* to have a profound impact on the women who follow them. The letter from Amelia Earhart reminded me of my own favorite Amelia quote:

Some of us have great runways already built for us. If you have one, take off. But if you don't have one, realize it's your responsibility to grab a shovel and build one for yourself and for those who will follow you.

CHAPTER 7

Wendy Kopp

CEO and Founder, Teach For America
CEO and Cofounder, Teach For All

It was 7:30 a.m. and we were driving up the I-5 freeway from San Diego to L.A. "The 5," as the locals refer to it, spends a good deal of its span right along the Pacific shoreline, offering a clear, unobstructed vista of the emerald-green ocean. We were on our way to interview Wendy Kopp, the dynamo from Princeton University who founded the breakthrough organization, Teach For America, and in doing so, changed education in this country. To be winding my way up the coast on another road trip with Darcy felt great. As always, I loved the opportunity for long discussions, the time to bond, and the feeling of freedom and discovery that traveling brings to our relationship.

"Let's stop at a Starbucks for coffee and muffins," Darcy suggested.

"Okay, great idea," came the smooth New Zealand accent of Grant Deane, Darcy's father, from the driver's seat.

Oh, I forgot to mention, this wasn't going to be our typical mother-daughter outing. My ex-husband was along for the ride, which promised to make this trip a really unusual adventure. Grant came prepared with healthy snacks: yogurt-covered raisins, apples, and granola bars. But alas, no beverages.

"Hey, Darcy," said her dad, handing her his portable GPS device. "See if you can locate the nearest Starbucks."

During the next fifteen minutes, I sat there like a fan at a tennis match, watching the rapid-fire exchange between father and daughter. She threw out options the GPS offered and he responded with answers like, "We just missed that turn-off" or "That's too far away," and she always came right back at him with yet another solution. They had their own cadence—different from mine with her. There was a playful ease to their discourse that signified their deep, loving, spiritual connection. I smiled to myself. It made me happy to see them this way.

Finally they reached an agreement, and our course was set. We pulled off the freeway and navigated precisely to a large building with the familiar Starbucks mermaid grandly displayed on a prominent corner. But something was not quite right. There didn't appear to be a typical entrance to a coffee shop. No inviting tables and chairs strewn around a comfortable courtyard. No friendly, burgundy-aproned baristas eager to take our orders. No colorful signs hawking the latest caramel-laced coffee convection. This place was just an office building.

It was the Southern California Starbucks corporate headquarters! Score another one for the narrow-minded accuracy of our global positioning system.

The three of us laughed hysterically.

Across the parking lot, with no help from the GPS whatsoever, we spied a locally owned café with all the coffee, bagels, cakes, and muffins we wanted. How funny to find a sanctuary like this in the shadow of the coffee-shop royal castle.

Our giggling continued as Grant steered his way over.

You may be wondering how in the world this seemed so easy. Our divorce, according to the mediator, was the most respectful, considerate, collaborative marriage dissolution she'd seen in seventeen years of practice. Though not a painless process by any means, I thank my lucky stars that we could move past all the issues of our marriage and keep Darcy as our highest priority. Since the divorce, Grant and I have cooperated as Darcy's parents in every way we could. We homeschooled her from first through fifth grade while living on opposite coasts. When Grant remarried a few years ago, I met his wife, Noelle, and even shared dinner with both of them a few times. He instantly got along very well with my fiancé, Allen. We, all four, spoke on the phone regularly to discuss Darcy's parenting needs. Riding in his little white car from San Diego to L.A., however, meant being together in close quarters for over twelve hours—something we hadn't done in more than a decade.

> "This is really weird," I said to Mom and Dad. "Seeing you two together in the front of the car...like, my parents. Weird." I had been a little apprehensive about spending a whole day with both of them, but mostly I hadn't thought much about it. I knew they got along well. Whenever they spoke on the phone I could hear how they fall into the kind of comfortable rhythm of conversation you only have with people you've known for a long, long time. But still, in person, it could have been a strange energy. I am such a different person when I am with each one of them, so I wasn't even sure who I would be with both of them together.

Grant loves his daughter fervently. The reason he and I had home-schooled her in the elementary years was so that he could be more directly involved in her life instead of just a weekend dad. For five years, he not only took care of her every other month as a single parent, but he also taught her math, history, reading, and science while she joined him daily in his lab at UC San Diego where he does his research as a world-renowned physicist.

When we agreed that she needed to go to a "regular" school as she approached her teens, Grant gladly would have had her move in with him in California. Only reluctantly did he acquiesce to her entering a school where I lived, three thousand miles away. Our deal, though, was that he would have her with him for all her holiday breaks, and that she would spend her entire summer vacation with him each year. "It's like sending her to boarding school in sixth grade," he once said to me with heart-breaking sadness.

And for so many reasons I felt his pain. My father left my mother before I was born and then died when I was only twelve. I'd seen him only two or three times in between, and then for only an hour or two at a time. Watching Darcy and Grant together always made me feel like the

kid outside a candy store with no money. Nose pressed to the glass and
tummy rumbling, the penniless tyke knows she'll never have what's inside. I would never completely understand the emotions of their, or any,
father and daughter relationship, but I knew I wanted it for my daughter.
I'm one of those parents who wants to give my child everything I never
had. Thus, I hated the thought that our book research was cutting into
his primary time with her in the summer. He'd already let me keep her
on the East Coast longer than usual after school ended to go up to Maine
with Leslie Lewin and to D.C. for the meeting with Secretary Clinton.
We'd also made our abortive trip to Stanford. And he'd sanctioned some
additional trips later in the summer as well: Hollywood and London interviews were already on the horizon, waiting to be confirmed. While
he fully supported all these opportunities, I knew he hated losing even
one of the limited number of days he had with her.

To invite him on our trip to L.A., I reasoned, would be a way to
keep our leadership journey from shortchanging their relationship one
more time. More important, his participation in our journey gave him
a wonderful firsthand glimpse of her strength and enthusiasm about this
project. It was great for him to see her in action: preparing for the interview, asking the questions, and synthesizing the lessons she was learning
about leadership.

> I was excited about having Dad along. I really wanted to hear what
> he would say and think because if anyone is a feminist, my dad is. I
> totally love that, being a feminist myself. I knew he would add inter-
> esting contributions to the conversations.

Darcy gave her father a blow-by-blow overview of Wendy Kopp's astounding achievements. The revolutionary Teach For America program
began as Wendy's senior thesis at Princeton in 1989. She had an idea
that she could enlist recent college grads from a wide variety of schools
and place them as teachers, for at least two years, in low-income communities all across the United States. By introducing such bright, fresh,
enthusiastic minds into these underprivileged environments, Teach For

America could help energize a grassroots movement to bridge the desperate achievement gap between the "haves" and the "have-nots" in this country. Today, over thirty-three thousand dedicated young leaders have committed their lives to create a level of education and opportunity for millions of children who may have been destined to perpetuate the vicious cycle of poverty and deprivation their background would otherwise dictate.

Time flew by quickly, and soon we crested the last rolling hill, dipped into the L.A. basin, and entered the main gates of Loyola Marymount University. We were here on this lovely campus because Wendy had invited us to attend her annual Southern California teacher-training program for the newest crop of Teach For America corps members. This gathering was one of many orientation sessions across the country designed to kick off the preparation of recent top-drawer college grads for their commitment as teachers of at-risk kids in inner city and rural schools. I was eager to see how this training was accomplished; I couldn't wait to wrap my hands around her techniques, look at her data analysis, and understand the vastness of her resources.

"Okay, it looks like you bear to the right at the next corner . . ." Darcy anxiously directed, once again focused on the black-framed GPS screen she held in front of her, "but it's not really clear . . ."

"Well, let's turn here. There's a soccer field over there, so the gym should be nearby," Grant hypothesized. As a scientist, he was used to drawing conclusions from empirical evidence.

"I don't know," argued the right brain of our daughter, "it seems like we have to keep going straight . . ."

We were searching for the Gersten Pavilion, otherwise known as the main gymnasium of the university. The problem was we had never been here before, and our only guide was one of those campus maps with unnamed streets that twist around in circles and then bisect themselves into unhelpful geometric shapes.

"You have arrived at your destination," chimed the lilting, British-accented voice of the navi-gadget in Darcy's lap.

Darcy had set the voice selection of the GPS on "British." She and I love to do this because we have a ball laughing at the mispronunciations—especially in California. The best one is "La Jolla" pronounced with a soft "J" and sounded "L's"—kind of like *"La Jolly"*—rather than the correct, Spanish, *"La Hoya."* Cracks us up every time. Grant, acknowledging his own "down under" accent, especially enjoyed the gag.

We were stopped in front of a tall, white, sandstone clock tower that didn't resemble a gym at all.

"This is *not* our destination, you twit!" Darcy scolded the electronic lass.

"I think we have to turn around," Grant huffed.

After a little more map consulting, a dead end or two, and a few other fits and starts, we finally found a place to park the car and began walking toward what seemed to be the main entrance to the pavilion.

As we approached, the cheering and pounding of a huge, excited crowd wafted out at us from inside the auditorium. Clearly a big basketball game or something was going on inside. Another wrong turn, thought I. This was getting really frustrating. We were now in danger of being significantly more than fashionably late. Wendy had invited us to the event personally. She even promised to save some seats for us. Everything was shaping up as a horribly embarrassing way to make a first impression.

We all stood in front of the giant, modern cement building and reread the instructions. This certainly seemed like the place described. I panicked for a second, thinking maybe I got the date wrong! No, this was the right day and time. Perhaps there was another entrance? Often these big gym facilities had meeting and conference rooms in addition to the forum area.

I decided to brave the tumult and go inside and ask. I pushed through a gaggle of step-dancing college kids in search of someone who could point us in the right direction. Darcy and Grant followed along, a bit bewildered by the throng of sports fans swirling all around us. As we crossed the giant threshold, we were surrounded by enormous bleachers filled with hundreds of college students chanting all kinds of different cheers for their region or team. Thunderous rumbles rose from a multitude of feet pounding in unison on the aluminum planking. The entire room vibrated as if it would explode.

The home team must be winning!

And then we saw it. A vast, raised stage with a fifty-foot banner draped elegantly above it that read: TEACH FOR AMERICA. The thrilling cacophony surrounding us wasn't about hoops at all! It was about expanding the opportunities available to our nation's least privileged kids. This was a rock concert for *education*!

My chest pounded from the thunder. Wendy caught my eye and waved the three of us over to the seats she'd promised to save in the front row. Her slim, fashion-model frame belied the strength and fortitude of this woman on whose shoulders an entire organization rests. With long, straight brown hair and a smile from ear to ear, she glowed from the love she and her brainchild were getting from these inspired young people.

I gazed across the multicolored, multicultural collection of six hundred hollering college grads. These brave new teachers, many who had received their diplomas only weeks ago from the best colleges across the USA, were here with a mission. This group, and ten others like it, would bring aboard over 5,100 of the nation's most promising future leaders. Only one out of twelve applicants was accepted from a field that included 12 percent of *all* the graduates of the Ivy League, as well as significant numbers from more diverse schools including Spelman and Howard. Among their vast opportunities and options, many of the best and brightest in our nation chose, for at least the first two years of their working life, to take on a low-paying job under the most difficult conditions imaginable in order to Teach For America.

Darcy and Grant crammed themselves into the crushing crowd of co-eds on the front bleacher seat. I hugged Wendy, sat down, and tucked my tote bag under my knees just seconds before the lights went out and the crowd fell to a hush.

A lone follow-spot sliced a cone of light through the darkness, illuminating a lonely, single stick of a microphone on the empty stage. A young woman with upswept black hair and freckles stepped up to the mic holding in her hand one of those iconic composition books with a mottled black-and-white cardboard cover—the kind we all used for exams or essays back when we were in school. Bathed in the glow of the spotlight with particulates floating silently in the air above her, she looked straight at the audience and proudly stated: "Good evening. My name is Paige Hendrix.

" . . . And I *Teach For America*."

The whooping and cheering again shook the rafters.

When the fray settled, the lively brunette began to read her story:

"*After three weeks into my second year of teaching, I was suddenly notified that I would be moved to a new teaching placement at Kit Carson Elementary School. Instead of fourth grade, I would have fifth. Rather than specializing in science and social studies, I would have to teach everything. In our first few days together, I learned that my new fifth graders were reading on a third-grade level. I was totally unprepared and already a month behind.*

"*As I was learning the names, faces, interests, and levels of my new students, one of my students, Jose, stuck out to me. A small boy, ten years old, he usually wore a half grin on his round face that was framed by dark brown bowl-cut hair. He always said 'Okay, Ms. Hendrix,' but I began noticing that he never brought back homework and rarely asked questions in class.*

"*When I began pulling kids back for small reading groups, I remember Jose stopped partway through the first sentence and said, 'I can't read, Ms. Hendrix.' It was heartbreaking to hear his little voice shrink as he pushed his head into the gutter of the book.*

"*Jose had a steep challenge: he was reading only thirty-four words per minute when a fifth grader on level should be reading a hundred and eighteen words per minute. This was compounded by the fact that English was rarely spoken at home. In our world of teacher and student, it was 'go time.'*

"*Because I was new to teaching reading, I reached out to my colleagues. In collaboration with the reading strategist and special education teacher, we implemented one-on-one, small group, and other reading practice methods. At home, his sister who spoke English and was successful in school, read with him in the evenings.*

"*With this increased focus came increased confidence: Jose told jokes, volun-*

teered to assist during lessons, and most exciting, he asked to read aloud during small group reading.

"After a year of intense practice, days of 'I can't do it' and 'But, Ms. Hendrix,' Jose was finally ready to battle the timer in class. He inhaled deeply, his confidence radiating in a way that I had not previously seen. With the word, 'go,' Jose pushed through the words, saying them clearly, making fewer mistakes, and following along with his finger. When the timer sounded, Jose had read one hundred words in a minute! When I showed him the test, he glowed! A huge grin spread across his face and his cheeks turned red with a deep blush of pride! He smacked his hands on his face and asked, 'I read one hundred?'

" 'Everyone' I cried, 'Jose just read one hundred words per minute!' Our class cheered loudly, yelling, 'Yeah, Jose!' He told anyone who would listen that day about his success—and word traveled fast!"

Paige had to stop reading for a moment as she became choked up with emotion. She received a rousing ovation from her peers, and fighting back tears, she settled the crowd and forged onward.

"I can see what a challenge it was for all of us. At the end of the year, my students grew one point one years on average. Six of the fifteen students grew an average of one and a half years or more in reading.

"But all of my students will have to continue to push themselves for years to come in order to stay in school and see success. While we all taught Jose how to read, my kids taught me that we don't always get what we expect. Despite the curveballs, it is our responsibility to push ourselves to find the right skills, knowledge, and resources to be the best teachers that we can be."

If there was a dry eye in the house when the story was over, it wasn't mine.

"Jose Mendoza . . . and my fifth-grade class at Kit Carson Elementary School are why." She paused, looking straight at us.

"I *Teach* . . ." Another pause.

" . . . *For America*."

The crowd erupted. I could feel the force of their commitment, their fervor, their eagerness to attack. This was a war on poverty that worked. They wanted to be part of something bigger than themselves, something that truly made a difference in the world, and they knew they'd arrived at a place where they could do just that. Paige was not only helping a small band of disadvantaged kids, she was fighting for civil rights and shaping the course of our nation's future.

One young college graduate who chose to teach in an economically challenged school might be derided as a drop in the bucket, but en masse this crowd of committed achievers exuded real power; they could change the world. Their efforts were reshaping policy debates on education and profoundly affecting the way schools and school systems were set up and implemented. Winning this fight to ensure that all children have the opportunity to attain an excellent education and an equal chance in life was intoxicating.

Wendy and her team were here today to equip their new recruits with enough emotional intensity to take on the long hours and difficult struggles it will take to work within schools that typically don't have the extra capacity and support necessary to help students succeed . . . and to prevail.

Again the room went dark. I felt Wendy get up next to me and circle around the back as the lights blasted the stage and the emcee began her rousing introduction, culminating with " . . . I'm proud to introduce you to our fearless leader, Wendy Kopp!!"

Wendy stepped up to the microphone and, with a wholesome smile that had the audience eating out of her hands at hello, began her address.

"Welcome to Teach For America!"

The blast of love and enthusiasm threatened to, once again, level the building. For ten minutes, Wendy demonstrated the magnetism that made all this possible. I felt weak with awe for the woman who had spawned this incredible organization when she was no older than the enthusiastic young people in this audience. Her stimulating speech, charging them with the task of changing lives and instilling in them the essence of the larger vision, demonstrated her skill at asking—and getting—others to find the superhuman strength inside themselves.

As the crowd dispersed to their dorms and began their preparation for the hard work ahead, Darcy, Grant, and I were ushered into a long, narrow room where we would have our time with Wendy. The walls were a bleak institutional gray with molded plastic chairs and tables to match.

While we waited, Darcy arranged the chairs and set up our trusty digital voice recorders at the best vantage point.

Wendy came in still looking stylish in her purple satin shell under a simple khaki-colored business pantsuit, but visibly exhausted from a very long day. We knew she'd flown in from the East Coast this morning and met with foundations, corporate sponsors, and local education leaders all day. We were honored she was willing to put off sleep to meet with us when her body clock must be imploring her to collapse. We'd better be as efficient as possible.

After congratulating her on the wildly successful kickoff event and her inspiring speech, Darcy dived right in with the first question. "How do you personally define the term 'leadership'?"

"It's interesting," Wendy answered thoughtfully. "We think and talk a lot about leadership at every level of this effort. At the beginning, twenty years ago, only a tiny fraction of our teachers were actually putting their kids on a very different trajectory. So we started spending time with them and were just so struck by the fact that they were operating like the most successful leaders would operate anywhere. So my definition has been shaped by what I saw them doing.

"First of all, they set a vision that's very ambitious, that some people think is a little crazy. Next, they get their kids invested in working incredibly hard to get there—just like all great leaders who motivate others. Finally, they're purposeful and strategic in terms of how they spend their time, as well as completely relentless about overcoming whatever obstacles get in their way."

"Now, do you select people who can already lead that way," Darcy followed up, "or do you train people to lead?" Darcy was going way off the script we had meticulously prepared. I thought, *She's really taking the lead!* Maybe she was showing off for her father? Whatever the reason, I was proud of her. I took a quick glance off to our left at Grant, and I could see he was beaming as well.

"I think it's both," answered Wendy. "After a lot of research we learned that the best predictor of success in this environment was not just the highest grades; we found the people most likely to thrive here are those who have experienced setbacks and recovered from them. Perseverance, being a good problem solver, and the ability to influence others are important characteristics we look for. But the training we give them in both leadership and teaching is also crucial."

I had seen the *Atlantic Monthly* article that talked about TFA's research and how they learned over time to select teachers who have failed at something and rebounded from it. Research has shown that resilience training is what makes the difference for world tennis champions, and I believe the same is true for successful leaders in corporate America—it certainly has been true in my life.

"So what is the relationship between teaching and leading?" said Darcy, still following her very perceptive nose. I was hardly going to get a word in.

> I think Mom could see that I was hitting my stride as an interviewer. After so many of these, I knew more what to expect and got involved in the ideas instead of the details. Okay, maybe having both my parents there at the same time was a special bonus. Bringing together the two sides of my personality felt good. Mom was giving me space to run with the ball.

"Well, I have come to believe that, in very under-resourced areas where the kids are facing so many extra challenges, the only path to successful teaching is tremendous leadership. Working with kids who have given up on the idea that school's a ticket for them, you have to convince them that if they work really hard they'll get smarter, and that it will matter in their life.

"Then you've got to maximize your time during the day and reach way outside of the traditional expectations of the four walls of your classroom for additional resources to truly put them on the level playing field."

"Are you saying that in a more affluent environment you could just teach, but in this environment you have to lead, too?" I jumped into the discussion, fascinated with Darcy's line of questioning on the interrelationship of leadership and teaching. "TFA assumes corps members can teach, but they have to become excellent leaders on top of that?"

"Actually it's very hard to be an excellent teacher, meaning a great instructor, when you're in your first or second year of teaching. How do you teach fractions in the best of all possible ways? It's hard to become really good at that.

"Now, I haven't spent time working with teachers in other kinds of schools, but I know when I gather my best corps members together and ask them what they are good at, they'll say, 'We're culture builders.'

"They're good at figuring out things like, 'How do I get my kids to work with me?' They get the kids so fired up that the students own the goal as much as the teacher. Then, even if you aren't the best instructor for fractions, it doesn't matter. The kids will find a way to learn with you."

TFA wasn't only in the business of creating teachers. TFA is the ultimate training program for developing transformational leaders. TFA teachers, in conjunction with their communities, have discovered a way to communicate a positive vision to a group of kids who are often facing poor nutrition and miserable living conditions. They get those kids on fire about reaching, even surpassing, their goals. And they've created a network to support one another's progress and learn from one another's mistakes. Most of all, these TFA corps members get results regardless of how tough the conditions are by truly inspiring those they lead. Better than any entry-level corporate training program, TFA hones your skills as a leader. If I were a business leader I'd want to hire TFA grads to lead my sales force, run a hospital, or create new products.

We heard a knock at the door and Ella, Wendy's bespectacled, dark-haired assistant, came in and politely asked, "Would you like us to delay your dinner meeting?"

How silly of me to assume Wendy could get some sleep after our interview! Of course she would be off to meet with one more donor, or one more corporate sponsor tonight. She was relentless in her drive for educational change.

"No, we'd better not be late," she said to Ella, and turning back to us, "Sorry, but we've got about another twenty minutes—and we can always talk afterward, on another day if we need to."

Darcy anxiously continued, rising to the occasion and stepping up the pace.

"Does your most recent book, *A Chance to Make History*, explain this linkage between leadership and making excellent education a reality for all?"

"Yes, it goes back to some of the things I said in my speech tonight. It may seem like an obvious thing to say, but it's not obvious to everyone: wherever there is transformational change happening for kids, there's transformational leadership.

"I feel like we have been searching for the silver bullets to fix education. You sort of wish that maybe one curriculum change or one policy change like charter laws will solve the problem. Maybe if we could just have mayors take over school systems or a computer on every desk, then every kid could learn. But there's no way around the fact that to succeed in any sector, it's always about people and leadership. The same thing is true, maybe even more so, in education. Ultimately the real question we all need to be asking ourselves is how do we create the conditions for transformational leadership in schools across the country at all levels?"

"As you look forward to the next decade," I asked, "What do you think you can realistically achieve?"

"We know that classrooms can change and that whole schools can be transformational. But still, we have not created perceptible change on the national level with aggregate numbers. I do believe in a decade we're going to be moving the needle. I really, deeply believe that. It's a big, big challenge, but I think we can do it."

I had no doubt that she was going to help move the needle for the country—even for the world. Modest as she is, Wendy didn't mention that she had helped create another organization, Teach For All, which partnered with groups placing teachers in seventeen countries outside the United States. She had already spread across the globe the TFA vision that every child deserves an excellent education.

"You are a unique example of someone who started young, set out to change the world, and really did it," I said. "Talk to us a little bit about that."

Wendy flashed her incredibly engaging smile. "I don't think there's any one formula. As many challenges as came from my being young and inexperienced—and there were certainly many—there were also huge advantages. I got into many doors of influential folks because the story was crazy enough to be interesting: 'Wait, this person just graduated from college, wants to meet with me to talk about what?' The main thing was that this was an idea whose time had come. I'm glad I didn't wait, because then the time would have passed."

"What advice would you have for somebody in similar shoes, young women stepping up to the plate to take a large leadership role?" posed Darcy.

I was wondering (hoping) that Darcy asked that question for herself—not just because we had put it on our list.

"One of the most important things is realizing that it's not about you," Wendy said, tilting her head to one side. "There's this moment when each of our teachers realizes in a visceral way that it's not about them, it's about their kids. You've got to make that transition. No matter what the cause is, it really has to be about what you're trying to change or what you're trying to accomplish. That's a key point."

"Where your focus is?" Darcy asked, on the edge of her seat.

"Yeah," said Wendy. "What matters is not that you're going to be a leader. It's that you're going to change something."

I had to break the spell of this profound truth because our time was running out. "What are some of the biggest mistakes you made?"

"Oh, gosh." She put her hands on her face. "There were a lot! I mean, it's hysterical now that I think about it, but one of my convictions at the front end was that I was not only going to start Teach For America and reform education, but I was also going to rethink the way organizations work. We had this whole notion that we didn't need a hierarchy.

"It felt like you wouldn't need management systems when everyone believed in the same cause. This became a colossal disaster very, very quickly," she said, making a funny face. "It was pure naiveté, and lack of experience. But we worked through it all, and that's all that matters. Keep your eye on the ball and just keep making mistakes, reflecting, and charting a new course."

"It's great the way you can laugh about it later and not let it crush you," said Darcy. "It makes me wonder, though, is it possible to be too optimistic?"

"Wow, how do I best answer this?" Wendy thought for a beat. "One of the core values of Teach For America is sense of possibility, having a deep sense of optimism about what is possible. But at the same time, you have to have a realistic sense of where things are today. If you're naive about where you are, you make less progress."

"I guess I'm asking," Darcy pressed, "Where do you draw the line with that? Because it sounds like maybe being a little unrealistic is a good thing."

I chimed in, "Delusional enough to think you can raise two and a half million dollars to start an organization?"

Wendy started to answer and then stopped, realizing I was teasing her about the time her thesis adviser had told her she was "delusional" for thinking she could raise enough money to launch five hundred teachers in the first year of the organization. She smiled at me, acknowledging that her own original visionary goal was pretty far out there. "What we say here is you have to set goals that are at the right intersection of feasible and crazy. Where the right intersection lies is subject for debate, but at least having the debate is a good thing."

"So you learned that you must have management systems because not everyone spontaneously does what they are supposed to do. When you're faced with poor performance, how do you deal with finding ways to discipline or to communicate that standards aren't being met?" I scratched at this ticklish issue.

"As a leader, this is obviously one of the most difficult things—easy to answer in theory, but much harder to actually do in practice when you care about people's feelings," Wendy answered. "It's important to depersonalize the situation—make it about the behavior, not the person. At Teach For America, we can easily depersonalize things, and do what's right for the broader mission and cause. You need to think about what kinds of roles maximize each person's strengths."

"What are your strengths?" Darcy continued, moving right along.

"My personal impact, because of who I am and where my greatest value-add lies, is probably more on the entrepreneurial side. I like thinking about things like: Here's where we are now, but where do we have the potential to be? How do we access more resources to get there? My time is generally balanced between managing the external relationships—like my meetings earlier today with funders and community leaders—and thinking about the strategic choices that advance our work; for example, how we can foster greater political leadership among our alums."

"Many of the women we're trying to target with this book, younger or older, have a lot of fear about leading because they could make big mistakes, or they have responsibilities like dealing with those who don't meet standards, or they will have to do something outside their comfort zone, like speak in public. How do you deal with that? How do you overcome obstacles like that?" Darcy prodded.

"Again," answered Wendy immediately, "the important thing is not thinking about your leadership. It's drowning yourself in what you deeply believe and finding a way to have a meaningful impact. That's what enables you to overcome your fears."

"So once again," observed Darcy, "it's where your focus is."

"Do you want to jump into some of our obligatory gender questions?" I asked Darcy, since she was clearly running the show.

"Okay, sure," said Darcy. "Do you believe that women have to lead differently from men?"

"It has never occurred to me," said Wendy, throwing up her hands. "I don't think so. I know a lot of men who lead no differently than the women I know. Every person needs to lead in a way that is comfortable for them."

"For a number of women, there's a concern about work-life balance when thinking about stepping up to the plate and leading," I interjected. "You have children, right?"

"I have a girl and three boys."

"What advice do you have on work-life balance?" I asked.

"Everyone's so angst-ridden about this choice—it is really hard when you have work you love but you also feel passionate about spending more time with your kids. In my case, I didn't really have a dilemma. I never considered leaving Teach For America, but I definitely wanted kids.

"So all of my energy went into figuring out a way to make it work. It's about surrounding yourself with the right supports. Got to marry a supportive man. I have a husband who actually thinks the kids are better off if I'm working, because it's good for their mom to be fulfilled professionally. I think all the time about what I want for my kids and my family."

"Balance wasn't always your strength," I said. "I heard that in the first year of TFA, you actually decided to sleep every other night."

She gave me a wry grin.

"It's true that having kids has forced a new level of balance on me, which has been a very good thing. I have mandatory relaxation, because I've got to (and want to) spend time with my kids getting them to school in the morning, on the weekends, and taking real vacations. I've become more and more cognizant over time that we need to prioritize sustaining ourselves in this intense work, because the long-term broader movement to ensure educational opportunity is better with us running the whole marathon rather than a sprint."

Darcy began to wrap things up. "Our final question: What do you find most rewarding? What is it that offsets all the difficulties, all the dramas?"

"I feel so lucky to have something where every day matters to me. I'm lucky to work as part of a much larger team of people who share all my convictions and ideals, people who are working at least as hard as I am and really keep me going. But at the end of the day, it's thinking about what our corps members and alumni are out there accomplishing that I find most fulfilling."

Darcy paused to let the moment soak in, and then asked, "Can we have a picture together?"

"Sure!" She grinned again. It just never stops. *This woman smiles in her sleep.*

Grant dutifully grabbed the camera and began snapping shots as the three of us squeezed together in a warm embrace.

Then, with one last hug and kiss, we bid farewell to the dynamo that is Wendy Kopp.

We walked out into the courtyard in front of the gym. Grant, who had remained quietly in the background for the entire interview, couldn't hold it in any longer.

"Good job, Little One," he told her, smiling widely and using the cute nickname he's had for Darcy since she was a toddler.

"You have a real talent for getting to the heart of the story," Darcy's dad continued. "I was really inspired by Wendy's commitment to changing the world and standing up for what she believes in. It made me feel like I have to work harder to make a difference on some of the issues that are important to me, like global warming. I think your book is going to inspire a lot of people to do better and to make positive changes in the world."

"Thanks, Dad," Darcy answered with my smile and his eyes. "I'm glad you were here."

"Me, too," he said as he gave her a hug.

After a warm pause, Grant looked at his daughter and asked, "What did you take away from all this?"

"Wow," Darcy exclaimed. "Not only did she create this huge nonprofit organization when she was still very young, but she did it to help other people her age make a contribution. I don't think most young people have that perspective. That's what I admire most."

"Really?" Her dad answered, and continued to dig into Darcy's thoughts and feelings as they began walking toward the car. Despite the late hour, they jabbered ninety miles an hour, still stimulated by the ideas our day had provoked.

I followed a pace or two behind, vicariously enjoying the feeling of fatherly love and support.

CHAPTER 8

Deborah Tom

Founder of Human Systems, Ltd.

As we arrived in the land of Shakespeare and Queen Victoria, the first stamp from our project in Darcy's passport came and went with a lot less fanfare than I had expected. When I asked her if she was excited to step on European soil for the first time in her life, I got little more than a grunt in response. Her blasé mood seemed to come from the overnight flight, time zone shock, and overall lack of sleep.

> I couldn't believe Mom was so excited about walking through another airport. I have already seen my share of luggage carousels after flying coast to coast between my parents ever since they divorced when I was five. Visiting my New Zealand relatives on my father's side over the years, it's not like this is my first time through immigration. I have had a passport since I was two years old. Can't she understand that isn't the point? I wanted to see new places and different lifestyles. Sadly, I wouldn't even get to immerse myself in any foreign languages here, other than cool accents and alternate words like "lift" for elevator and "boot" for the trunk of the car. Culture-wise, however, I planned to soak up every unique custom and colloquial quirk our former colonizers had to offer!

We'd barely dragged our jet-lagged bodies from Heathrow into London before it was time for us to rub our bleary eyes and meet up with Deborah Tom.

I first got together with this redheaded British ball of fire in NYC when I was hired to give a rousing keynote speech to close out a three-day leadership festival she had designed for sixty of a financial giant's most promising leaders from around the globe. During an eighteen-month period, Deb also supervised a phalanx of coaches for a variety of individualized sessions, convened the global group in Hong Kong for a confab midway through the term, and then gathered everyone together in London for the program's culmination. This was typical of the truly global development programs she routinely creates for multinational business leaders from Russia to China, with Europeans and Americans thrown in for good measure.

When I proposed the notion of including her in this book, Deborah graciously invited us to come visit her in London and promised not only to grant us complete access to her business structure and organization, but also to clear her schedule and warmly welcome us into her life for the entire duration of our stay.

And, boy, did she live up to her promise! It all started with afternoon drinks at her London club, Home House.

Originally conceived in 1773 as an entertainment "pavilion" for the infamous "Queen of Hell," Elizabeth, Countess of Home (wife of William Home, the 8th Earl of Home), this gigantic Georgian town house spans three addresses in its affluent, Marylebone neighborhood—19, 20, and 21 Portman Square. Having been the playground and/or home of notable British aristocracy for centuries—it was once even owned by Charles Grey, the 2nd Earl Grey (yup—*that* Earl Grey!)—it exists today as one of the most exclusive private clubs in London. A truly British concept, these lavish, members-only clubs were originally established as exclusive sanctuaries for wealthy, upper-class English men in the late eighteenth and early nineteenth centuries. Much more gender-friendly today, these clubs now provide an elegant social setting for folks, like Deborah, who live primarily in the countryside but want to also maintain a comfortable outpost for frequent visits to the city.

When we arrived at the ancient stone façade to this magnificent building, I felt humbled by the long history of people who had passed through these doorways before us. We crossed under the three-hundred-year-old cream-colored entry portico and stepped into the club's rich décor—stately, high ceilings ornately adorned with gilded neoclassical details, glistening crystal chandeliers that bathed the elegantly paneled walls and opulent antique furniture with a soft, warm glow—it was as if we stepped back in time to an era of candlelit, gracious sophistication. The most striking feature was a grand imperial staircase that rose up from the hardwood foyer floor and split the enormous entry space from side to side. The escalier continued its majestic rise throughout the entire height of the house, drawing our eyes toward a gorgeous crescendo in a brilliant stained glass dome high above us.

"May I help you, Madam?"

The question summoned me from the breathtaking architectural tour de force, and I turned to face the well-stuffed waistcoat of a rather large, round butler, whose job was to keep this "members only" establishment inhabited by *members only*.

"We're here to meet Deborah Tom," I said, looking up to meet his eyes with a touch of defiance.

Was I anxious? I suppose I was. I never feel so *American* as when I'm in England. Despite the four years I spent studying at Oxford—or perhaps because of it—I still often feel that twinge of snobbish condescension from the gatekeepers of upper-crust British society. All they have to do is look at the color of my skin and they assume I am a colonial; but, worse, when I open my mouth they *know* I'm a Yank.

"Yes, Mss. St. John and Deane," confirmed the stuffy, Arthur Treacher look-alike, consulting his guest list. "Please wait here a moment and I'll announce you."

Before he had a chance to take a step, Deb launched herself into the foyer to greet us.

"Bonnie! Fabulous to see you again!" she exclaimed. "And, Darcy, absolutely wonderful to meet you at last!"

We all danced the classic European hugs and double-cheek-air-kiss waltz, with Deborah talking ninety kilometers an hour the whole time.

"How was your flight? Did you get any sleep? Can you believe this club? My husband won't be able to join us much—he's working double-time just now . . ."

We followed Deb and her friendly chatter through the parlor to our left, passing a fascinating juxtaposition of Savile Row businessmen, dignified grand dames, and even a gaggle of young, hip, impossibly thin supermodels taking afternoon tea (Earl Grey?) on the lounge's cushy chesterfield sofas.

Then, as if sucked into yet another time warp, Deborah breezed us into the stunning, contemporary House Bar. The room's gleaming centerpiece—a sweeping, pyrites bronze counter—thrusts out of the polished wood floor with the sleek, sloping lines of a fine Italian sports car. The bar incongruously, yet perfectly, melded into the eighteenth-century room designed by the world-famous (woman) architect and designer, Zaha Hadid.

"Isn't it amazing?" Deb waved toward the behemoth chunk of shining metal. "And this is my daughter, Eliot," she announced, guiding our gaze to the classical beauty rising to greet us.

Eliot smiled warmly, shook our hands, and motioned for Darcy to sit next to her. Though only one year apart in age, Eliot was shockingly mature. Her very short skirt hung on a voluptuous figure; ankle boots ended long legs; and thick blond hair parted on the side fell into her sultry eyes.

"What do you want to do first in London?" Eliot asked Darcy.

> "Shopping!" I answered without hesitation. Friends of mine had tantalized my brain with tales of the chic, cutting-edge stores in fancy London locales like Covent Garden, Piccadilly, and Oxford Street. The idea of rocking a new outfit from London was something I had never imagined happening to me. I felt giddy with the thought of it.

"Topshop!" Eliot said, clapping her hands together with eyes all aglow. Was this some sort of British expression for a peak experience of searching for an outfit, I wondered?

"It's a store," Eliot explained to me, seeing the confusion on my face.

Then she turned back to Darcy. "It's *the* place to nab a great frock," she advised with animated enthusiasm. "Up and coming designers show-case their newest collections, but the prices are absolutely fab since they aren't famous yet."

"Perfect!" I responded gratefully to Eliot. Although I felt a little inse-cure next to this walking fashion page, mostly I appreciated having someone my age to initiate me into British teen ways of behaving, thinking, and of course, shopping. She was the whipped cream on the frappe of my British adventure so far.

Topshop didn't disappoint. Within seconds of our arrival in their flagship store, our youngsters threw themselves into a shopping spree with the gusto of desert nomads discovering an oasis. Their revelry reminded me of one of those movie scenes where the image of the main character quickly cuts from outfit to outfit in a montage of color and fashion.

As I watched the "frocks" on parade, I was beginning to see how my not-so-little-anymore girl might blossom into the frighteningly mature magnificence that Eliot portrayed. First, Darcy chose a series of "don't-bend-over" minis that set my hair on fire, then a tropical-colored maxi with way too much decolletage, and finally settled on a light, shim-mering silver-beaded number that flattered her almost-womanly figure without being so shockingly sexy that I'd have to throw a tarp over her every time she wore it.

"I could get used to this," Darcy whispered in my ear between wardrobe changes.

Although money for our adventure was still tight, we'd been given a free place to stay with friends in London and purchased our airline tickets with the enormous backlog of frequent flier miles I had earned while speaking across the country. So, in this discount designer store half a world away from home, I felt I could still, within reason, make my daughter's dream come true. I just hoped that the glitz and glamour were helping her engage in the quest that brought us here, not derailing her from it.

The following day, we headed to Deborah's house on the outskirts of London to observe her coaching a client from a big multinational firm—we'll call it "Acme Brands." In the past decade or two, executive coaching has risen to become a state-of-the-art, almost essential perk for the corporate elite around the world. These personalized, one-on-one training sessions help focus and strengthen the performance of those highly paid, highly stressed individuals responsible for mega-budget businesses. Coaches guide their clients through a series of detailed, emotional diagnostics of the pressures and problems they face, both short- and long-term, and allow these powerful performers to take a moment away from their hectic, minute-by-minute schedules to reflect, analyze, and clarify their thinking. It's "just in time" learning designed to give a busy leader the necessary tools to make billion-dollar decisions exactly when they are needed.

Deb's house was a converted farm building from a quintessential old English country estate. With low brick walls and an eclectic mix of blue, orange, and purple flowers in the cottage garden, it seemed as if we had stepped back in time to 1852 when the manor house was built. Behind the garden, large barn doors, built in a day when they had to be big enough for teams of oxen to drive through, had been removed and replaced with a twenty-foot-high glass wall that gave the structure an indoor/outdoor feel. We followed a meandering path to one end of the house where a normal-size door led into a large open kitchen area—converted to display all the latest mod-cons and filled with the aromas of sensual European cooking: artisanal cheeses, roasted garlic, and plenty of great French wine. Being there felt like a day in Provence. Once I saw this lavish country retreat, I understood why an important Acme executive would relish the opportunity to escape the bustling city to come here for a few hours of self-reflection and career development time. Not far in miles, it felt worlds away from downtown London.

From my perch on one of the six down-stuffed couches around the main room, I feasted on the blend of breathtaking exterior views, rustic nineteenth-century architecture, and a delightfully surprising collection of ultramodern art. It was amazing how clearly Deb's personality was reflected in this skillful marriage of old, new, playful, and serious.

Our host flashed her wicked grin. "Before my client gets here, I want to show you the office. My commute to work is a real bear. Come along and I'll show you!"

We followed her back out the kitchen door, down another winding path past the rose bush arbor, and across the front lawn to a nearby low-slung outbuilding, which, back in the day, would have housed rows of stalls for animals. Now converted to a sturdy, exposed-brick open workspace, Deb had filled her rough-hewn atelier with oriental rugs, fine antiques, and soft leather chairs with generous footstools. When she wasn't flying around the world training corporate titans and generals, this was her command central, her private think tank.

"Look at this!" She showed us a lovely cabinet full of small drawers. "It's from an old apothecary . . . I use it for office supplies. And this." She posed like Vanna White, arms extended in a large "V" to draw attention to a wall covered with twenty-four-inch-square doors. "This was a set of antique wooden lockers from an old school." As she opened and shut the doors that held her research papers, file folders, and other things one needs to shape the globe's leaders, Deb seemed as proud of this rare centerpiece as if she'd built it herself.

Darcy and I staked out a couple of seats on one side of the office where we could inconspicuously observe the meeting. As we discussed the best place to set up our digital recorders, Deb began her meditative exercises.

"I always do these before a coaching session," Deb explained. "I need to be centered and quiet to offer the absolute best attention."

Right on the dot, Lara from Acme Brands arrived. Her slender, statuesque figure accentuated the fact that she was taller than all the rest of us (which isn't saying much—Deb, Darcy, and I all see the world from the same level). Lara's reddish-brown hair and simple gold jewelry communicated a business-like, yet quite attractive, personal brand.

"It's so kind of you to participate in our book project," I told her after introductions. I imagined it would make me a little nervous to have people eavesdropping into my personal coaching. She was brave and generous to let us sit in.

Lara removed her cream-colored suit jacket and hung it on the coat rack before relaxing into the deep, upholstered wingback chair that seemed to be her usual choice. Deb took the other big chair across from her, and they were off and running. I noticed that despite Deb's enormously friendly nature, she didn't let the small talk and catch-up prattle eat through much time before she got down to work.

"Lara," Deb began, "when I had the check-in meeting with your boss, Danny, I asked him to express what he appreciated about your progress in this Acme Brands Leadership Program we've been working on over the previous eighteen months. He especially noted that you were taking more of a leadership position—not just with your team, but taking a broader perspective developing the wider team beyond your direct reports. Are you aware of that? Are you conscious of that shift he sees in you?"

"Yes, very much so," Lara answered brightly. "I feel it's all for the good. I am working on telling stories and inspiring the team, not just managing the facts and tasks at hand."

"Super!" responded Deb. "Can you share something specific?"

"Danny and I were planning the last leadership team session and realized it could be very dry with the typical facts, numbers, and objectives. We didn't want that meeting to be just a guy standing at the front doing PowerPoint for ninety minutes. We wanted people to feel the passion of the aspects of Acme that we don't, on a day-to-day basis, chew into. We asked ourselves: How do we liven the conference up? I don't mean singing and dancing, but making it real, making it passionate."

"Yes, yes . . . !" Deb was a very enthusiastic listener.

"Whenever we spend even a modicum of time taking appreciation of our heritage—of our brand makeup—it feels brilliant." Lara continued, "The storytelling gets people engaged in delivering for the company."

"It sounds like you've been very creative and it's beyond storytelling. What I'm hearing now is you're bringing the purpose to life." Deb underscored and affirmed Lara's progress.

"The meeting was scheduled for an hour," Lara continued, smiling proudly. "We ran it for about an hour and a half, and it was fantastic! Everyone talked to each other, talked about what matters to them. That was fun."

Nodding vehemently, Deb said, "And you're not hiding behind the slides. Instead of looking at a wall, you're actually looking at each other and thinking... connecting. I like it."

"And I think that is not to be underestimated..."

"Oh, it's not," said Deb. And then she changed gears. "So the other thing that Danny appreciated is in terms of your well-being. He mentioned that you seem happier at work and how that inspires others. You are still very busy and getting a lot done, but the work doesn't seem to get on top of you. What do you think of that viewpoint?"

"When you and I first started talking, everything was balance, balance, balance. I want a good career. I want a good home... and as we moved through the conversation, it became very apparent that I had bad balance in both."

"So we did the Success Walk..." Deb encouraged her to continue.

"When you told me to do it, I thought, *Oh, no!* Every step I take with those papers on the floor, I have to come up with something new on the changes I might make to be happier in my own skin. Actually it was the most fabulous thing, wasn't it? A brilliant, brilliant experience.

"I learned how you can make subtle change to improve and that it doesn't always have to be transformational to be very useful. I used to feel like I can't have my hair dyed every six weeks; that's indulgent. Going to the gym is indulgent. I raced through life guzzling the caffeine and late everywhere. You stopped me at the beginning of one session and asked me whether I noticed the beautiful flowers outside. I hadn't. I know it seems trite, but now I slow down and look more often. This morning two woodpeckers were doing this elaborate dance in my front garden, and I called my husband over to look. Not that I think that watching woodpeckers in my garden is something staggering, but it immediately takes your whole mind-set to a different place. When you step back in, you come back at a slightly calmer level, very subconsciously."

"Yeah, yeah, yeah, yeah." Deb slapped her hand on her thigh. "Exactly."

"Now I go to the gym more often; I see things around me. I am better at taking care of myself," said Lara, glowing with pride about the changes she'd made.

"Yay!" Deb enthused. "Nurturing yourself. Lots of points there. My belief is that if you're not feeling good in your own skin or about yourself, it is impossible to be great. It is impossible to have a breakthrough. I really believe that. Or if you have a breakthrough, it's not going to last. It's not sustainable. So I really work on the well-being thing because then you can go out and engage and commit."

"It seems obvious now, but before it wasn't obvious at all," Lara reiterated.

"Good-O!" Deb summed up the progress so far. "What about going forward? What do you think, heart of hearts, we need to be focused on? I know you've done a lot of work on relationship, on the stakeholders, and on the storytelling. Is there any other aspect of the Acme Leadership Program in which you want to develop?"

"I suspect it's more of the same," Lara answered, "but I think I absolutely need to do more on the relationship side to develop more authentic conversations. For example, I have a stakeholder who I sort of feel isn't on the same page as me. I don't ever really have the right conversation with him."

"Okay, okay."

"Part of the reason for that is because I think he'll just *yes, ma'am* me. Every time we sit down, we're in violent agreement, and then the way in which we operate doesn't sync with what I thought we agreed."

"We could work on that today," Deb offered. "I've got some new toys."

Deb drew out what looked like a pack of playing cards. "Some psychoanalysts have conjured up images on these cards that we use to tap into your unconscious thoughts on things like that problematic relationship. I got these especially for you because they involve storytelling." As she talked, Deb began to deal out the cards with images across the table between them.

"Oh, fab."

"Have a look at the symbols on each one and decide which one describes your relationship with the stakeholder you mentioned, what's his name?"

"Scott. I'm probably going to go with that one." Lara picked up a card and then dropped it again, changing her mind to pick another. "Let me just . . . I think we need to go with this one." She selected a card with a series of arrows and lines in alternating rows.

"Put the others away. Now, just describe what's going on there." Deb pointed at the card Lara ultimately chose.

"So the reason I selected this card was that the arrows show a two-way dialogue going on, but the lines are, if you like, the blockers to the success of that relationship. My sense is that he's only open to what I'm seeking to do in a sort of lip service fashion. Is that the wrong way to do this?"

"No, no, no. That was good. That's fine. There's no right or wrong, you just say what comes to you." Deb picked up the cards and dealt them out again. "Next pick a card that represents you in this relationship."

This time Lara struggled longer, short-listing several cards, then dismissing them and starting over.

"No need to overanalyze. Just pick something spontaneously," Deb suggested. When Lara neatly obliged, Deb said, "Well done. Right."

"I wanted to pick the smiley face," Lara told her. "But instead I went with a more moody face with a furrowed brow. It's not that I'm not happy and smiley with him, because I am. But underneath I know he is unconvinced of where we are going, and my dissatisfaction with him is probably showing in overt or subtle ways. I've already prejudged him."

"Mm hmm. Which then has what effect on him?"

"I would imagine it has an effect whereby he places more barriers up in the conversation. I'm *assuming* he's disengaged, which actually *makes* him more disengaged."

Darcy and I watched avidly as Deb gently peeled back the layers of Lara's feelings and showed how they shaped her relationships. The pictures worked beautifully to pull Lara out of the logical mind-set she normally habituated and to connect her with the subtext of her own attitudes and behaviors.

By practicing different phrases and approaches, they explored ways to initiate a new conversation and to create more common ground in the tricky relationship they were addressing.

Lara brainstormed, "I could say: 'I am genuinely passionate about us doing the right thing for Acme, and at the same time, embracing what's success looks like for me and what success looks like for you.' "

"Yes, and then you might want to focus on exactly where you share values around that. Is he taking the Acme Leadership Program? Has he ever been on it?"

"He's done it. He was one of the first to go through it."

"Perfect then, perhaps he could share some of the things he worked on to declare his values and purpose in that course. Is that something that would help you both in the exploration of how you're going to work together going forward?"

"Yes, yes. It could."

Deb helped Lara to transform situations in business and at home by altering—in small but profound ways—the energy and approach she brought forward. The time flew by, and too soon it was time for Lara to pack up her things and drive back to the big city. And I'd bet my digital recorders she took time to smell the roses on her way out.

After watching her in action, we peppered Deborah with questions.

"Is what Lara is working on very typical of the leaders you coach?" I wanted to know first.

"Becoming an inspirational leader is a common development need. Poor things, someone says, *'You are now a leader,'* and suddenly you have to inspire the team that you used to work with, a team you don't know at all, or even a team that might be spread across the globe. If you ask most leaders, *'Do you think you're getting enough out of your team?'* almost everyone will say they're definitely not.

"To be a great leader you have to have a vision and be able to communicate it in a way that inspires others to put in effort toward that better future. A leader also needs planning and organization skills. But the biggest challenge, I believe, are the people-management skills, because they are less easily learned. You saw that was a big part of what Lara wrestles with."

"What are your core values?" Darcy asked next, one of her favorite questions.

"My absolute number one priority is my daughter, Eliot, but I don't think that's what you mean. I'd say my top three values are: warm hearted, considerate, and zest. Although I'm tough minded, I feel for people and have compassion. I believe in the goodness of people. By considerate I don't mean kind and cooperative. I mean that I have a considered point of view. I'm a bit of a mad reader. It's important to me to learn constantly and to make better judgments.

"My third core value, 'zest,' is about joie de vivre: energy...passion...action. I'm not really frightened or flattened by anything, because my parents died so young. Mum died when I was twelve and Dad very shortly after. When something terrible like that happens, nothing can be as bad again." There was a pause as the pain revisited her for a moment. Pushing it back, she continued, "I don't go out as a miserable misery or a bland thing to people. I start the day cheerful, realistic mind you, but still cheerful."

"Deb, since you coach both men and women, what do you see as the challenges unique to women leaders?"

"Women do have added issues, different from the men I work with. There's the obvious one: more intense pressure around balancing family. A less vaunted challenge though, is how to get the right visibility. Sometimes women are written off more easily than the guys. There's the whole conception of the glass ceiling, but there's also a glass cliff. Rather than giving them a development opportunity, women are often put into important positions as a last-ditch attempt in a bad situation. But many of them rise to the occasion and make it a success regardless."

Darcy followed up with a great question also leveraging Deborah's bird's-eye view. "How do the pressures on women executives vary from country to country?"

"Germany is relatively egalitarian for women who go to work there from abroad, yet not many middle-class German women who are married with children work. They have a great deal of social pressure to drop out and bring up the children. Then they miss years of career development, so it's very hard to come back in. It's also the same in Japan. I know because I've lived and worked in both of those countries.

"Russia's a very educated country and used to women working. Nearly all my clients from Russia had mothers who actually worked. In Russia there are a lot of female scientists, engineers, and doctors. I don't actually know the statistics, but it seems somewhat more progressive about women working with children.

"The Chinese women in our programs who work at an American or an English firm are expected to have a voice, to be edgy, and to be challenging. Then they go back to a family life where their uncle, their brother, or their father expects them to shut up and never second-guess them simply because they are male. A Chinese woman may be very talented, but if she seems timid, she won't look like a leader to us in the West.

"The women I work with in America are very ambitious. They have quite a lot of help and are very organized on the home front. But my goodness, they work hard on every level of their life!"

"What do you think is changing about developing future leaders?" Darcy asked next.

"In the future, we will have to lead people differently because we can't expect them to want to do the long-hours culture that the previous generations have done. We can't just give them money when they've seen how volatile the markets are. The younger generation are interested in ethics, the environment, and social aspects that our grandparents never expected from work. So we need leaders who are prepared to have a dialogue about meaning and be spiritual mentors in many ways.

"Another way that we are growing leaders into the future is by helping them to become more global. A lot of my clients tell me how hard it is to make something work in one country the same as it's worked elsewhere. Firms want international consistency, but to be effective, you need customization to what's happening in each country and an appreciation of what the cultural mores are."

"What do you find most rewarding about what you do?" Darcy asked our favorite closing question as the rays of sunset refracted their way through the quintessential British evening drizzle.

"Helping people make changes in their lives for the better," she answered zestfully. "Many start out jogging along a little dissatisfied, or perhaps nearly depressed. They've given up on their dreams, hopes, or goals, and I'm actually opening them up. Suddenly they're feeling more alive, daring to set goals again, and feeling excitement about going after them. They blossom with confidence. I get such joy when they come back with their stories about what they've done: 'You're going to be proud of me!' It's just fantastic."

"Yet you've told us," Darcy said, "that you spend most of your time managing the forty-six coaches in your organization, researching, writing client proposals, designing curriculum, and so forth. It makes me sad that leadership often means not getting to do what you love most."

"Alone, I can only affect tens of people per year. By leading teams of coaches, we can together impact hundreds of leaders at once, which means actually having an impact on the entire human system in the organizations where we work. My joy at helping people to engage fully with their lives is multiplied a thousand-fold by rising to the leadership challenge."

CHAPTER 9

Amy Pascal

Co-Chairman, Sony Pictures Entertainment

Hey, Mom, what's this?" Darcy asked as she pointed to the stack of mail haphazardly strewn across my desk. Opening snail mail is not one of my strong suits, so I hadn't even noticed the unusually large envelope perched on top of the pile.

"It's really cool," she continued, handing me the heavy black pouch.

I immediately recognized the classic lady-with-a-torch logo of Columbia Pictures elegantly embossed across the crease at the top of the outer cover. Just below, also in silver but with an even more expensive texture treatment, were four, huge block letters: SALT.

Last I heard, Columbia Pictures hadn't ventured into the food additive business, so I was pretty sure this wasn't an advertisement for a new product. Still, I was about to dismiss the whole thing as direct mail garbage, when I noticed it was addressed to "Bonnie St. John and Darcy Deane." Not the usual junk mail.

"Open it," I urged Darcy.

In typical teen fashion, my daughter tore through the fancy outer layer and yanked out a thick card, also embossed in glistening silver calligraphy. Darcy's jaw slowly fell open as she read through the sterling message: "You are cordially invited to attend the World Premiere of *SALT*, starring Angelina Jolie..."

She stood there with her face in a frozen gape, like that famous Edvard Munch painting. At first, no sound whatsoever emerged from the great hole in the front of her face. Then her entire body began to shake and ...

"Aaaaaaeeeee!" ... she let out a squeal so piercing, I feared for the safety of my collection of crystal wineglasses in the hutch behind her. "Omigosh . . . I can wear that new dress I got with Eliot in London!"

Through his connections in show business, my fiancé, Allen, had helped us secure a chance to get together with Amy Pascal, the Co-Chairman of Sony Pictures Entertainment. Amy presides over the movie studios of Columbia Pictures, Tri-Star Pictures, Screen-Gems, and Sony Classics, plus Sony Animation, Imageworks, and Sony Pictures Television, making her one of the most powerful women in the entertainment industry.

In the course of investigating how we might get a real taste for what it was like to run a movie and television studio, Jim Kennedy, Sony's delightfully charming head of public relations, suggested, as one option, that we might like to accompany Amy to a movie premiere. Of course, I agreed this would be a great idea, but I didn't really hold out hope that such a thing would be possible. Invitations to movie premieres are coveted in Hollywood, and I doubted we would be granted such an honor.

I grabbed the invitation from Darcy's manic grip and read it for myself. The excitement welled up inside me just like it did for her. We were invited to Grauman's Chinese Theatre to attend the gala opening of Columbia's mammoth "tent-pole" summer film, starring Darcy's favorite actress. We'd be walking with one of the biggest stars in the world down the red carpet into the most famous theater in the history of the movie business as guests of the head of the studio! Glamorous to the nth degree! Now I lost it, too. I grabbed my daughter by the arms, and we screamed and danced around like a couple of whirling dervishes.

Six weeks later, I was sitting in a tin can with wings helplessly watching the clock tick away our dream of a big Hollywood night.

"This is the captain speaking to you from the flight deck. I have some good news, and I have some bad news . . ."

As you may have surmised by reading this book, I spend a lot of time on airplanes. And in all the miles I've flown, I have rarely, if ever, heard a message like this from the cockpit that made me feel all warm and fuzzy. I was pretty sure this whole good news / bad news thing was going to play more like bad news / cataclysmic disaster. Our airplane jockey didn't disappoint.

"The good news is that we are cleared to leave the gate and taxi to the runway..." she squawked into the microphone.

Yeah, and...?

"The bad news is there are about eighteen planes ahead of us, so it may be a while."

Oh, no. We had already been perched on the tarmac at Kennedy Airport for over two hours. From what I know about ground control patterns at JFK, it takes about five minutes for each plane in a runway lineup to actually get into the air. Even without a calculator, I totted up at least ninety more minutes on the ground.

I looked over at Allen in the seat next to me. I was sure he had made the same calculations and was already figuring how we could alter our timetable on the other end.

"Are we going to make it?" I asked hopefully.

"Hmmm..." was all I got in response.

This was not good. Normally Allen is one of the chattiest people you could ever want to travel with. We had run into delays together many times before, and he always had this uncanny ability to come up with some sort of alternate scheme or clever shortcut he could immediately put into play to keep our schedule on track. When he gets quiet, I get nervous.

In a few short hours, Angelina Jolie and her hunky husband, Brad Pitt, would be making their way along Hollywood Boulevard with or without Darcy Deane and Bonnie St. John. And we still had *a lot* to do. We were flying into San Diego because Darcy was staying there with her father, Grant, for the summer. We had to pick up Darcy, drive 120 miles up the California coast to Los Angeles, check into our hotel, change into our fancy party dresses, do our hair and makeup, and get to the theater in time to join the grand festivities. This three-and-a-half-hour delay was tying my stomach into a knot any sailor would be proud of.

Fortunately, once we got off the ground our pilot put the pedal to the metal and made the typically six-hour flight in about five hours and fifteen minutes! Thank goodness for small favors.

As soon as we landed in San Diego, Grant and Darcy met us at the airport. We threw Darcy's luggage into our rental car—being careful, though, not to crush the elaborately beaded bodice of her sparkly silver Topshop gown, and hit the So-Cal freeway system.

Now it was Allen's turn to drop the hammer. We ticked off landmark after landmark of Southland tourism as we ate up the distance to our goal as fast as possible. The fake-snow-covered peak of the Matterhorn Bobsled ride at Disneyland; the tacky spires of the Medieval Times dinner-jousting arena; the cute, Snoopy-themed directional signs to Knott's Berry Farm disappeared in the rearview mirror as the skyscrapers of downtown L.A. gradually appeared on the horizon in front of us.

And then it happened—5:30 p.m. on the I-5 freeway in Los Angeles. Solid bumper-to-bumper metal gleaming in the hot sun as far as the eye could see. We had barely an hour and a half before the curtain rose on our magical night, and we were stuck on a parking lot. I could see the famous, crooked white letters spelling out our destination across the hillside in the distance. So close, yet so far.

"I think I know a shortcut," Allen whispered as he slipped the car along the shoulder of the road toward the nearest exit.

I looked all around. Burned-out buildings and gangland tags were the only landmarks I could see. But Allen had lived in L.A. for more than twenty years.

"When the freeways are jammed, you have to take the surface streets," he explained as we zigged and zagged across blocks and blocks of hot, sticky asphalt. "This will get us around all sorts of traffic."

I saw the sign for Fountain Street as Allen swung our rented wheels hard to the left. Parallel to its much larger, legendary boulevards with names like "Hollywood" and "Sunset," this little artery is, and always has been, well known by locals as a primo thoroughfare to avoid traffic while crossing through Hollywood. When the "First Lady of the Silver Screen," Bette Davis, was once asked if she had any advice for young actors coming to Hollywood, she took a moment, slowly lifted the darkest, most smoldering eyes in American cinematic history, and replied in her classic, smoky slur . . . "Take Fountain."

I could see our hotel coming up: the Hollywood Roosevelt, a newly renovated hotel adjacent to the "Hollywood and Highland" complex, home to the Kodak Theater where they hold the Oscar ceremony and, just next door, Grauman's Chinese Theatre!

It is by now 6:15 p.m. Show starts at 7. Can an adrenaline-infused one-legged ski racer, a giddy blond teenager, and their middle-aged companion whip themselves from haggard travelers to glamorous sophisticates in forty-five minutes? The next few moments played out faster than one of those time-lapse film sequences where they take footage shot over a long period of time and run it in herky-jerky superfast motion—everything flew around so quick the eye could hardly follow the action. Sooner than seemed earthly possible, we were on our way to the crisscrossing klieg lights on Hollywood Boulevard.

Darcy let out a strangled sound of dismay as our feet hit the processional rug laid out over the "Walk of Fame," where luminary after luminary throughout entertainment history is enshrined with a bronze, star-shaped plaque buried in the sidewalk. For the premiere of *SALT*, the high-energy, action adventure thriller starring Angelina Jolie, the "red" carpet was black. Go figure.

> I felt robbed of the opportunity to say that I have walked the red carpet. Hey, I love black—but why here? Why now? But my happy exhilaration soon overwhelmed any disappointment about the color scheme. Here I was on the same walkway with my favorite star of all time. The first time I saw Angelina as Lara Croft, I was seven years old. It was like a revelation of the anthropologist I wanted to be. In the *Tomb Raider* movies, Angelina was adventurous, globe-trotting, omni-lingual, and able to spew out nerdy facts concerning obscure cultures while looking gorgeous and saving the world. Who wouldn't want to be that? Since then I studied languages from ancient Greek to Chinese, took martial arts classes with my dad, and imagined being the brilliant, strong heroine of the world. Silly maybe, but a girl's gotta dream.

"Angelina, over here. Over here! Brad, *BRAD*!"

We turned around just in time to see Hollywood's hottest super-couple emerge from a long black limo to face an army of hungry paparazzi champing at the bit for a big-money photo. A chorus of screaming fans who'd lined the barricades for hours hoping for a fleeting glimpse of their cinematic idols cheered with a deafening roar.

The "Bradgelina" duo stopped often along the black carpet to shake hands and sign autographs. In the grand tradition of Gable and Lombard, Bogie and Bacall, Tracy and Hepburn, and so many other successful Hollywood love teams, this pair of white-hot stars took almost humble, gracious care with their adoring admirers. It was delightful to see.

They also paused for the gauntlet of media representatives jockeying for position to get a word or two they could use for that night's entertainment news. It was fun to watch the Sony public relations team deftly guide their stars through the mob, stopping for different measures of time with each correspondent, depending on their stature and influence. The whole process reminded me of traveling the rope line with President Clinton back in my White House days.

When Darcy turned around again, I thought her face was going to explode. There, less than three feet in front of us, my soon to be intrepid anthropologist came face to face with her hero: the one and only female Indiana Jones, *Lara Croft*!

Both Brad Pitt and Angelina Jolie were now strolling right next to us, with their cadre of publicists, agents, and assorted other handlers following dutifully behind. The entire entourage paused one more time for a few more pictures, this time with the producers, director, and studio heads—including, of course, Amy Pascal. And then in a flash, they were all gone—whisked into Sid Grauman's elegant pagoda for more gladhanding before the actual movie starts.

Attending these galas is a big part of the job for studio executives. To the average, star-struck fan (i.e., *us*) this whole enterprise looks like one big perk—a chance to blow off steam and have a big party after a long, hard batch of work to put a movie together. But it's more than that. The premiere is a huge, splashy way to remind audiences that a film they've been hearing about for months is finally about to open. It costs over a hundred million dollars to release a major studio film these days, so a lot is riding on how well it is received—particularly in the first weekend. This kind of bash, and the attendant publicity surrounding it, is a crucial part of the marketing campaign. It gives the filmmakers, the stars, and the studio execs a chance to include the audience in the enthusiasm they all feel about the project they've just spent the last several years of their lives bringing to fruition and, thereby, help generate excitement about going to see it.

We had a few moments before the beginning of the show, so we lagged a bit to gaze around one of the most famous courtyards in the world. Right under our feet were the concrete slabs where the biggest and brightest stars in Hollywood's firmament have, for almost a hundred years, traditionally knelt on the ground to forever immortalize their hands, feet, and assorted other body parts (Al Jolson's knees, Betty Grable's legs, Bob Hope's nose . . . etc.) in cement. Thousands of tourists each year flock to this free, open walkway and compare the size of their hands and feet with yesteryear's movie idols like Rock Hudson, Elizabeth Taylor, Jimmy Stewart, John Wayne, and Ava Gardner, as well as more recent stars like Tom Cruise (very small feet), Whoopi Goldberg, John Travolta, Denzel Washington, and Johnny Depp. Darcy was particularly taken with the imprints of *Harry Potter*'s Daniel Radcliffe, Emma Watson, and Rupert Grint—complete with their magic wands!

Once inside the grand auditorium, we were enveloped in the fiery red glow of the most famous movie house in Hollywood. Built in 1936 by theater impresario Sid Grauman, this historic cultural landmark boasts a huge main theater, grandly decorated with gigantic Chinese dragons, Ming Heaven Dogs, and elaborate gold-leafed depictions of various oriental landscapes. Darcy enthusiastically translated many of the Asian words that dotted the architecture all around us. Those Chinese classes were really paying off!

As the lights dimmed and the movie began, I looked up and saw the face of the lovely Ms. Jolie, now twenty feet high—a face I had seen in the flesh just minutes before. It was a strange feeling. The close-up encounters of the past few minutes made it hard for me to suspend disbelief and immerse myself in her character on the screen. In the beginning of the movie, she's all beaten and bleeding, having been tortured in a North Korean prison camp. *No she's not,* my mind told me definitively, *She's right down there, a few rows in front of us, in that pretty little sparkly black dress . . .*

> I thought I might explode with excitement sitting in that huge movie theater for the first screening! I could hardly believe I was actually there with the stars when they get to see the movie for the first time. Brad had walked in with Angelina and seated her in a gentlemanly way. I liked the way he was with her. Of course he was comfortable being the big star in his own movies, but here he supported her being the center of attention while still keeping his own swag and suave style. To be honest, I wasn't a big Brad fan before (he's pretty old for me), but watching him rock those sunglasses on the "red" carpet I was starting to see the appeal. Angelina herself—not just Lara Croft—is a pretty cool character, too. A bit of a rebel pushing the limits with the tattoos and all, she has worked hard as a UN Goodwill Ambassador to focus attention on refugees around the world.

After the screening came the enchanting after-party. We walked next door to a ballroom elaborately decorated with thirty-foot-high screens running scenes from the movie, gorgeous ice sculptures featuring the SALT logo, and several lavish buffet tables that tantalized us with a wide variety of culinary delights, including a cornucopia of sinful desserts—all of which we felt obligated to try. After all, someone went to a lot of trouble . . .

A huge dance floor opened up in the center of the room, almost daring us to join the crowd flailing around to the thick, pounding music. Darcy couldn't resist the temptation to strut her stuff, and soon provoked both Allen and me out into the fray with her. All three of us boogied on down until well into the wee hours, soaking up every bit of the glitz, glitter, and colorful characters around us.

By the time we finally spilled into our hotel rooms, the three of us collapsed, reeling from the thrill of it all, and drifted to sleep with bliss-ful exhaustion, capping a day and a night none of us will ever forget.

The next morning, a bit bleary eyed but nevertheless filled with nervous energy, we headed straight to the Culver City headquarters of Sony Pictures Entertainment for our meeting with Amy. But before we sat down with her, another thrill awaited us. Jim Kennedy had arranged for us to take a private tour of the studio lot—an experience that yielded a fascinating slice of Hollywood history.

Probably the most elaborate of the remaining old Hollywood facilities, the Sony Pictures studio is the former home of the legendary Metro-Goldwyn-Mayer motion picture company. Yes, this was the place where Judy Garland clicked her sparkly red heels and tripped along a yellow brick road in *The Wizard of Oz*, where Gene Kelly happily splashed down the street in *Singin' in the Rain*, and where, with a touch of movie magic, the entire city of Atlanta succumbed to one of the most spectacular cinematic conflagrations ever filmed in *Gone with the Wind*. Esther Williams's swimming pool still lurks under the floor where the *Wheel of Fortune* spins today, and you can almost hear echoes of Busby Berkeley ring throughout the walls of the largest sound stages while Spider-Man now swings from their rafters. Around one of the corners we saw a tiny schoolhouse where young Mickey Rooney, Shirley Temple, and Elizabeth Taylor learned their multiplication tables. And we had a quick bite to eat in the commissary where, according to Louis B. Mayer, the mogul of all moguls who ran this place with an iron fist for over forty years, you could see "more stars than there are in the heavens."

One of the most impressive structures on the lot is the Irving Thalberg executive office building, named for the wunderkind production chief L. B. Mayer hired to run the creative aspects of MGM from 1925 until his untimely death, at age thirty-seven, in 1936. This beautiful art deco structure sits regally just inside the studio's main gates and still houses the offices of the big-wigs who run the place.

"Did you have fun last night?" Jim Kennedy's voice boomed from around the corner as he greeted us in the gorgeous, wood-paneled Thalberg lobby.

"Oh, it was amaaaazing," Darcy gushed as we all profusely offered our gratitude.

Before we knew it, Jim had escorted us up to Amy's large, tastefully decorated office suite. Comfy pastel fabrics and delightful artwork radiated an easy, inviting feeling throughout the large space. And that was just the waiting room!

Amy's inner sanctum was like a huge living room, with a beautiful central fireplace and several seating areas—reminiscent of an elegant drawing room in a grand New England mansion. The soft, warm color scheme continued to wrap us in a homey, welcome vibe. Amy was in the center of the room, standing behind an exquisitely carved antique desk covered in movie scripts and . . . *books*! I immediately knew she and I were kindred spirits.

"This was Mr. Mayer's office," Jim whispered to me as Amy finished her call. I was struck by the history of it all. For almost a hundred years, Hollywood's elite powerbrokers have sat in this very room to make the decisions that yielded some of the most memorable entertainment events in motion picture history.

"Hi, I'm Amy."

Years of misconceptions about the stereotypical "Hollywood studio head" immediately flew from my mind. Far from the gritty, cigar-chomping narcissists that established the movie business in the early days, Amy Pascal is charming, friendly, and completely delightful. Dressed tastefully in a simple turquoise shift over a cream camisole, she is the anti-mogul—a woman whose strong convictions and obvious business savvy are well shaped into a smooth, easy demeanor.

"Anybody want anything? Espresso, tea?" she graciously offered as we all sank into the plush sofas around a sturdy, dark wood coffee table.

"I'm fine with lemon water," I demurred. Jim, Allen, and Darcy shook their heads to say they were fine, too. "Thank you so much for taking the time to do this interview. You know that Condoleezza Rice, the Chairman of Deloitte, and the President of Liberia have already agreed to be featured, right?"

"I don't get how I fit in that group." Amy laughed. "No one ever interviews me about leadership . . . they usually just ask about the movies and the celebrities!"

"We want to include all different kinds of leaders," I explained, "and we also want to get across the idea that leadership isn't boring. You can lead in whatever area is your passion!"

"Since leadership takes so many different shapes and forms," Darcy said as an impressive segue into our interview questions, "we're curious how you define leadership."

Amy tilted her head, taking a careful moment to think this over.

"The most important kind of leadership I do is getting very talented people to put forward their best work. In a creative world like this, that means I have to understand who people are, understand human behavior, and get them to find the inner part of themselves that provides their inspiration. I need the people I work with to get in touch with what they're best at. I help them draw that out."

"What would you say are your core values?" I continued.

"My single-most core value in what I do is *authenticity*. People only do good work here in Hollywood when they are being honest and authentic. From the outside, people think the movie business is all plastic and fake personalities, but there are phony-baloneys everywhere. When people go to the movies they want to see something that moves them; and the only things that can move you are things that are true. Remember that a plot and a character are the same thing; that how a person behaves is also what the story is about. Whether it is someone to look up to or someone to avoid, it has to be *true*. The explosions in an action movie or the musical numbers in an event movie are only good inasmuch as they advance the character, which is also advancing the story. Those things are completely interrelated.

"When it's working and the product is authentic, that kind of invades everything. As a leader, my job is to create the environment where people can be authentic, agree or disagree, and do their best work."

"Can you tell us a little bit about how you lead to get authenticity out of people?" Darcy asked. No one else we'd talked to had raised this issue.

"We try to get 'stuff' out of the way," Amy answered. "Stuff that can block honest, creative work. For everyone at the studio we pay attention to a pyramid of needs with physical well-being as the foundation. Mental, emotional, and spiritual needs are layered on top of that. You can easily work twenty-four hours a day here if you want to . . . and many times you *do* want to. You get stimulated, you fall in love with what you're doing, and you love the people you work with . . . so you can just disappear into your project. There are supports at the studio for physical health like walking pathways, a beautiful commissary where the healthy foods are subsidized, a fantastic gym, and a daycare center across the street so that moms and dads can go spend a whole lunch hour with their kids.

"I'm also a believer in 'No Fingerprints' leadership. I don't need to take the credit for everything. If I want things to come out a certain way, I need to get people there without them thinking that I got them there. People want to be seen and to feel that there is consequence to their actions—that what they do and what they feel matters. It's like being a parent. They want to be validated and recognized. I think that if you allow people that and you're not constantly taking away everything, I think you have a good company."

"So your ego doesn't take front and center," I said, nodding. "You let others express themselves more."

"I can almost go too far the other way, though. I have a tendency to give up the credit for success and then take all the blame when things go wrong. I want to take it away from them so much; it is very hard for me to allow people to own their own blame. But they can't have an authentic experience that they did something well if you never let them fail."

"What made you want to make movies? When did you fall in love with movies?" I asked.

"I fell in love with movies because I loved my dad. He loved movies—so of course, I loved movies. We went to the movies every weekend at the Encore Theatre, which showed art movies and black-and-white movies. It doesn't exist anymore. Back then my dad watched more movies than anyone I know. Still does."

Darcy asked, "Can we hear more about your childhood and how you grew up?"

"I had a lot of learning disorders including dyslexia—I still can't spell anything," Amy told us with a stunning frankness. "Growing up in a Jewish, working-class, intellectual, academic family, I always thought I was pretty stupid. I think everyone in my extended family is a professor or a teacher of some kind.

"I had a crappy couple of years as a teenager where I was super insecure and felt really ugly and dumb. Can we talk? I was an alcoholic; I was a drug addict; I was bulimic; I smoked cigarettes; and it all started at about twelve years old. I wanted to be beautiful and tall and thin and Christian and blond and have all the things that everybody says make you beautiful."

> I leaned forward, horrified and fascinated at the same time. Although Mom had raised me in Protestant churches, I had plenty of Jewish—and even a few Muslim—friends. I couldn't imagine them wanting to trade in their rich cultural heritage. "Why Christian?" I asked.

"I wanted so much to be like the girls in the Palisades. They didn't have curly hair, big hips, or all the other things that we Jewish girls have. I wanted to look like a cheerleader, and there was nothing I could do about it. I was so lost. I hated myself."

"How did you pull out of it?" I asked.

"I finally went to a special high school with alternative methods. I learned to figure out what I was good at, value myself, and build out from there. It saved my life."

"We heard you started as a secretary in the movie business in the eighties and worked your way to the top," said Darcy.

"It's true. I got my first job as a secretary for a wonderful man named Tony Garnett who taught me all the good things that I know today. He was a producer from the BBC who has since gone back to the UK. He is brilliant. I got the job just by looking in the 'trades'—the industry newspapers—which I hadn't even heard of before I started looking for a job. I just wanted to get into the movie business.

"Back then, the writers were the only ones who would talk to me because I was so low on the totem pole. They taught me a lot about storytelling. The writers who I built relationships with back then are still the ones I work with today. People say the writers in Hollywood don't get enough respect, but I have a lot of respect for writers. When you make a movie without a good script it's like having an alcoholic parent. You never know any day what it is going to be like. There is no center, no gravity—you're re-interpreting it all the time. You are constantly trying to make it okay. That isn't a good way to work."

"So you found good mentors early on. What advice helped you the most?" I inquired.

"One of the most important pieces of advice in my career came from a man named Barry Hirsch who was one of my very first lawyers. He said: *'Don't ever compete and you will end up in a class by yourself.'* One of my best friends, Donald, and I turned that into a phrase we often say to each other: *'Stay inside your triple axel.'* It started when we were watching the Olympics ages ago. One of the top skaters totally flubbed it. When the reporter interviewed him, he asked, *'Triple axels are your thing. Why didn't you do it?'*

"*'Well, I was watching the guy from Russia and he was doing it great. And I saw the French guy do it in practice, too, and I just choked,'* the skater answered. *'You have to stay inside your triple axel. You just have to or you'll lose.'*

"What that means to me," Amy continued, "is that you have to completely stay inside of what you're doing, what you're good at, and who you are if you are going to succeed. That is the only way that you will be any good at anything. You have to figure out that thing that you do that makes you different, the thing that you know, and the thing that you have that is your gift (and your curse, probably—it's the same). But it is the thing that you can hold on to. It's the only thing that's *true*.

"It's the place where all the good stuff comes from. Don't try to be somebody else." Amy switched abruptly from adamant to angst. "Oh, I've tried, I've tried! Wearing designer suits, the shoulder pads, everything. I tried being somebody else. It just didn't work for me. I wasn't any good at it.

"They put blinders on racehorses because if you look this way or that . . . you screw up! It's the hardest thing in the world, let's be honest. All of us are really competitive, but if you are worrying about how other people doing it, you aren't doing it yourself.

"When you see a Rothko painting, that stuff is real; you know he felt it and you feel it when you are looking at it. You know it. You can't create art when you are wondering what other people think about you. You have to be inside your own triple axel. You have to be in the doing of it and not outside it.

"That's the high, right? That's the adrenaline that we all get when we are in the moment of what we are doing. It's a visceral thing. It's so exhilarating when it's happening in a meeting, or in a movie . . . It's like ahhhhh! There is nothing like it. It's what you live for."

I knew the feeling, for sure. Looking at Darcy, I wondered whether she had any inkling of it. "It's hard to be a teen, isn't it?" I said to my daughter. "You still probably spend way too much energy worrying what other people think about you or what they are doing."

"That is the worst part about being a teenager," she agreed with chagrin.

"But you know what?" said Amy. "The truth is, you can never do anything creative if you don't have a little part of that desperation still with you. You have to understand what it feels like to be tempted by all that stuff. We're not monks. The struggle of life is dealing with all our demons, walking a straight line, and knowing that in two seconds you can go right back there. In two seconds you can go to that place of insecurity. The struggle is to stay in your triple axel. Stay in touch with who you are that is valuable. It isn't easy to do, even when you are supposed to be grown up."

"Okay, let's switch gears," I said to both Amy and Darcy. "We've asked other women how they have the most impact. You've talked about relationship building a lot. Is that where your impact is?"

"Relationships are so important. I invest a lot of time in that because—Wait!" Once again the lightbulb appeared over her head, but this time it burned up and exploded.

"I get to pay for movies!" Amy said as if she just realized it. "The movies themselves certainly have the most impact. If I can influence anything, it's because I get to help decide what movies can be made."

"You've green-lighted movies that enrich and inspire women, like *A League of Their Own*."

"I know my impact isn't limited to women, but that is important to me. And I'm not embarrassed for it to be important. I am very much a feminist and it matters a lot to me. I didn't have many role models for what I wanted to be when I was growing up. I didn't see people that I wanted to become.

"So I have always wanted to make movies that are role models for girls, movies that are about being the protagonist of your own life. Whether it was *Girl, Interrupted* or *Sense and Sensibility* or *Little Women* or *Charlie's Angels* or *Julie and Julia*—any of them that would have helped a mixed-up young girl like I was.

"When Penny Marshall and I were working on *A League of Their Own*, we were proud because women don't get so caught up in the other stuff when they're doing sports. They feel their bodies are working for them and that their bodies are strong and their bodies are capable and their bodies aren't just the property of somebody else. When we made *Charlie's Angels* one of the things that Drew Barrymore and I really wanted to emphasize was that the girls ate all the time. And they were eating hamburgers and they were eating real stuff because girls shouldn't starve themselves. In *Charlie's Angels* it was important that women took care of themselves *and* they can kick your butt. There wasn't a choice that had to be made that either you are beautiful or you are tough. Those things should go together."

Amy walked across the room to get herself another espresso while Darcy and I quickly conferred on our question list to choose the next direction.

"What does being the co-chair at Sony Pictures entail? There's the movie side, television and entertainment, plus the accounting, reporting to the shareholders and business side. How do you do it all?" Darcy asked.

"Part of the reason all this works so well," Amy offered, "is because I have a very unique partnership with Michael Lynton who is my co-chair at Sony Pictures Entertainment. I believe in the law of competitive advantage—everybody should do what they're best at and then you win. I clearly am most interested in the creative process. Michael went to Harvard Business School and is well read. He's super cheap and I'm super extravagant. It balances out.

"We don't do anything without each other. We actually have an office that is in between our two offices where we secretly meet and say, *'What do you think, what do you think?'* He is probably one of the people I am closest to in my life, now. Our children are even friends.

"I think because we're a man and a woman, we actually run the company *together*. There are no power struggles, ever. No one has to win the way it is with two men; we don't do that. We are not afraid of each other, which I think is an advantage.

"One of the reasons that our company does well consistently is because of the give and take between the creative process and the need to make money. We understand that the creative process is making money, and making money has to be part of the creative process. You don't get to be creative if you're failing. You only get to be creative and take risks when you're making money.

"I can say things to Michael that probably a man wouldn't feel comfortable saying to him, or if they did he would get his back up. That is one of the things about being a woman in business in general: you can say a lot of things that men can't say. Right or wrong—men are willing to hear it from you in a way they can't hear it from other men. And there are advantages in that. Sometimes I say to him: *'You did not want to behave like that. You need to call that person and say yes or say it differently.'* "

"Whose idea was it to be the co-chair?" I was curious how this unusual relationship had emerged.

"Our partnership was Michael's idea. I didn't know him at all. I was told Michael was being brought in to work over me and I said, *'No, thanks, I'm leaving.'* So Michael said, *'Well, then, make her my partner.'* That says a lot about Michael. He was so open and generous to set the table for our relationship."

"Building a sense of trust takes time, though, doesn't it?" Darcy piggybacked on my question.

"The truth is that in the beginning we took a leap of faith. It was a shotgun marriage that we really wanted to work. It does take time, though. You can't pretend you're in love with somebody that you're not; you have to actually let it happen. In the beginning we were hoping it was this great partnership. We were careful with each other because we knew we had something really special, but it was fragile. We put in the work. Like the summer of 2005 when movie after movie failed, but we stuck together and built it back. Now we really trust the bond because we have been through enough failure and success and wrong decisions and better decisions.

"And the decisions get more complicated all the time. People even twenty years ago didn't have to know about DVD markets, international markets, or financing the way that everybody does now. We are no longer just a domestically focused business."

Jim was signaling that we had time for only one more question. Darcy and I both pointed to the last question on our page.

"What do you find most rewarding about what you do?" Darcy asked.

"Making movies!" she said with childlike glee. "I just love making movies. I love the product. I love helping people find what they want to say. It is thrilling when people love it. There is nothing like it."

"Tell that story about Paul Haggis," added Jim.

"Paul, who wrote *Casino Royale*, and won an Academy Award for directing *Crash*, works with Father Rick in Haiti on a project called 'Little Hollywood.'

"Right after we made *The Pursuit of Happyness*, Paul was with Father Rick in Haiti driving in the middle of the night to the worst slum he had ever been in. Children there hadn't ever seen a flower or anything like that. Paul said he was a little scared. They took this big sheet and hung it up on a rope for a makeshift movie screen.

"All of a sudden from the alleyways and over the mountains came these hoards of children who were in their best clothes with their hair brushed back, and wearing shoes if they owned them. They showed *The Pursuit of Happyness* way out there. It makes me cry. And they didn't even understand the words. It didn't matter.

"They got to see a story and smile. And dream. That really happened in Haiti. And I get to be, in some small way, a part of that. What could be better?"

CHAPTER 10

Lt. Col. Nicole Malachowski, USAF
First Woman Thunderbird Pilot

Unlike our most recent calls, this time Lieutenant Colonel Nicole Malachowski, USAF, call sign "FiFi," picked up on the first ring.

"Hi, Nicole! How are you doing?"

"Not so good actually," the colonel answered with a weary tone, surprising for this combat veteran supersonic F-16 fighter jet pilot.

"What happened?" I asked, almost afraid to hear the answer. Images flashed through my mind—a plane crash? Shot down by the enemy? What could knock down this extraordinary soldier—the first woman ever selected to fly as a member of the U.S. Air Force's elite precision flying squadron, the Thunderbirds, as well as a former White House fellow who worked to obtain the first official recognition for WWII's Woman Airforce Service Pilots (WASPs) by writing legislation that awarded this all but forgotten legion of American heroes the Congressional Medal of Honor?

"Well, since I last talked to you, I found out I'm pregnant . . ."

"That's great news!" I exclaimed. I remembered those days of morning sickness.

" . . . with twins!" she finished. "Omshgna!—Excuse me! Hold on!" Nicole made some unearthly noises and urgently left the phone. After a minute, she came back breathing heavily.

"About three weeks ago I started going into contractions periodically, so the doctor has me on total bed rest. Unfortunately, I can't take you to an air show like we talked about . . . I can't even get out of bed!"

I was too stunned to talk. This more than explained why I had no luck reaching her for the past few weeks. She was so genuinely interested and supportive in that first conversation that the "radio silence" to my subsequent calls was surprising. She had even proposed that we join her for a Thunderbird air show, and I had been trying to reach her to lock in a date that fit her schedule. Now I understood. Our book project paled in comparison to her difficult pregnancy.

"No problem! I can imagine you are a little distracted!" I said, hoping to add some levity, but with genuine sympathy.

"I asked my friend, Sean Gustafson, if he would give you the air show tour I promised. He flies with the team now, Thunderbird #4, and he's a great guy. Is that okay with you?"

"That's amazing. I can't tell you how much we appreciate this, Nicole," I replied, thinking I'd better get off the phone and let her rest. With a mountain of her own problems, she still thought about me, my daughter, and our project. I hung up the phone and immediately closed my eyes to pray for her continued strength and for the safe delivery of her babies.

As instructed, we soon followed up with Maj. Sean Gustafson, who exceeded Nicole's description of a "great guy." He deftly put us in touch with all the right people who made our arrangements and took care of the complicated military clearances we needed in order to join him at an airshow. Within about a month, on a crystal-clear Sunday over Labor Day weekend, Darcy and I ferried our faithful Ford to the Martinsburg Air Force Base in West Virginia to get our "Top Gun" guided tour. We were on our way to experience what it felt like to go to work every day strapped into a supersonic rocket ship!

Created back in 1953, the Thunderbirds represent the crème de la crème of our nation's military aviators. This team travels the world as official goodwill ambassadors of the United States, performing a spectacularly choreographed ballet of the most incredible airplane flying stunts you have ever seen. The pilots fly in perfect synchronization, at close to the speed of sound, often upside down, with mere inches from wing tip to wing tip.

As if that's not amazing enough, every Thursday of the tour, these American heroes turn their rehearsal flight sessions into a private show for the kids of the local Make-A-Wish chapter in the area they're visiting. Not only do they fly for them, but the pilots and crew also sit and connect with each of the kids one-on-one. Can you imagine the kind of impact they make with these visits? Picture a young boy, his body riddled with cancer, having just seen the Thunderbirds flying overhead in a thrilling display of aeronautic acrobatics. The planes land with a booming roar that pounds his little chest. Cockpits open in perfect unison, out climb the pilots . . . and they head straight for him! His face is still beaming. They smile, hold his hands, and regale him with glorious tales of soaring among the clouds. And next week, they do it again. And again. That's what it means to be a Thunderbird.

And since 1953, every Thunderbird pilot has been a man. Until Nicole Malachowski.

Our point person for the day in Martinsburg was press representative Sgt. Pamela Anderson, who had graciously arranged for us to get the full VIP treatment. Our tickets were waiting for us, along with "all access" passes and instructions to contact her as soon as we arrived.

Once inside the chain-link gates of the air force base, Darcy and I flowed into the enormous sea of people who descended upon the several acres of asphalt that comprised the infield taxi area immediately in front of the hangars and flight control tower. Lots of families, *lots* of kids, lots of senior citizens—a real slice of Americana. Many of the families were clearly military—some in uniform, but most in "civvies." Even absent their USAF attire, the hard, fit bodies and conservative hairstyles told their tales. Many of the older folks proudly sported their WWII, Vietnam, or other vintage veteran paraphernalia—hats and jackets adorned with colorful patches and pins depicting designations of service in various theaters of war. We felt proud to be in the presence of these noble protectors of our freedom.

The atmosphere was like a carnival. From the wide variety of antique aircraft on display, to the various activity centers (even a climbing wall!), everyone—young and old—seemed to be having a wonderful time. Old-fashioned bi-planes buzzed overhead, scoffing at gravity with their barrel rolls and loop-de-loops. The scene reminded me of trips with my family to the Del Mar State Fairgrounds in the summers of my child-hood. Melding aromas of flame-broiled hot dogs, hamburgers, BBQ, and buttered popcorn wafted from a series of mobile concession stands that dotted the tarmac. All sorts of artery-choking confections taunted us with temptation—ice cream, sodas, red-white-and-blue slushies, kettle korn, and my personal favorite, funnel cakes—those globs of dough, deep fat fried and smothered in powdered sugar.

Darcy and I threw caution, common sense, and cholesterol to the wind. Like a couple of six-year-olds on a bender, we indulged until our tummies begged for mercy. It was, after all, the last gasp of summer.

Via rapid-fire text messaging, Sergeant Anderson directed us to a huge, white big-top tent right along the flight line labeled VIP PAVILION. There, the electronic typing told us, we were to meet up with everyone on the team. We waved our credentials to the camouflage bedecked gatekeepers and were admitted to the inner sanctum.

"Bonnie! Darcy! It's so great to have you here!" Pam Anderson laid out the welcome mat and began making introductions for us to her staff and other fascinating folks collecting under the white canvas. We each grabbed a cool drink and happily chitchatted for a few moments with friends, family, and other special guests of the Thunderbird team.

And then, the stars arrived. All eyes seemed to move in unison to the rear canopy entrance. One by one, the six United States Air Force Thunderbird pilots bounded into the tent with gleaming smiles and in-fectious energy. The razor-edge creases in their dark blue one-piece jumpsuits split the air as they smoothly moved through the swarming crowd. They were each incredibly attractive, with just enough swagger to exude strength and confidence, but without ever crossing the line into cocky pretension. These guys were *polished*.

I was a little sad that none of the pilots in the show today were women. I imagined if Nicole were there among them, even though she would have been the only woman, she would have blended in with her own brand of strut and confidence. I could totally see her holding her own here.

One of the stunning aces made a beeline for us. From the pristine, white embroidery emblazoned on his chest, I was immediately aware this was Maj. Sean "Stroker" Gustafson. The epitome of poise and charm, you just knew Stroker belonged in this milieu. He owned the room, yet in a way that immediately invited you into his aura. His impossibly square shoulders, twenty-eight-inch waist, and thousand-watt smile didn't hurt, either.

"Bonnie, Darcy, it's such a pleasure to meet you both. Thank you so much for coming," he called as he closed the gap between us and grabbed our hands.

> I don't usually think uniforms are attractive, but that tight little jump-suit was working for Major Gustafson *Big Time*! He was sleek and slender; he moved like a cat—strong and bouncy. Even though he was way too old for me, I could see that he had a powerful effect on the women around him.

"Did you hear?" he excitedly announced, "Nicole had her babies! A boy and a girl!"

"Wow! That's wonderful news!" Darcy and I chimed together. I had been so worried since our last conversation with Nicole that I literally let out an audible sigh of relief. This was the best moment of the day. So far.

For the next half hour or so, this delightful young man gave us his exclusive focus and attention. He explained every aspect of life as a Thunderbird, with an emphasis on how honored and rewarded he felt to have the opportunity to represent his country in this way. I felt like I was talking with one of my fellow Olympians. He was filled with that same kind of extreme pride and sense of humble accomplishment and achievement.

Far too soon, the energy in the room shifted again. These pilots are so in tune with each other, communications seem to pass between them by telepathy. Though the process was ethereal, the message was clear: it was showtime. With another big, shimmering show of his pearly whites,

Sean snapped dark aviator sunglasses onto his head and bid us farewell, promising to meet up with us after the performance to get our reaction to the show and give us a close-up tour of his airplane. Then he was off—into the wild blue yonder!

"C'mon you two," Pam Anderson said as she grabbed us and hustled us into an official looking golf cart. "You're going to have the best seats in the house." And she wasn't kidding.

I assumed we'd stand outside the tent with the other VIPs and watch the show. But no.

Pam drove us through the main crowd, past the roped-off area for military guests, and kept going right out to the middle of the runway to the command post for the show! We were further stunned when she handed us each a pair of headphones so we could listen to the radio broadcasts between the pilots and the ground crews. These headsets would allow us to hear everything they said to each other as they flew around, right over our heads, at just under the speed of sound! Way beyond the level of garden-variety VIPs, we had been granted entry into the Thunderbird's inner circle.

The huge crowd—it had to be over a thousand people—had now gathered, with rapt anticipation, along the blue barricades that spanned the entire length of the flight line. This was the moment they had been waiting for all day long. Every eye was fixed on the six gleaming, red-white-and-blue F-16 Fighting Falcon aircraft parked in a precise single line along the taxiway. Aaron Copeland's glorious "Fanfare for the Common Man" blared from huge loudspeakers as the 100,000-horsepower engines exploded to life with a chest-pounding, thunderous roar.

I was drenched in a rush of emotions. Patriotism as an American, concern for the safety of the team, and an overwhelming sense of awe and gratitude wrestled for supremacy against giddy excitement and childlike wonder. Knowing Sean and Nicole made the experience so much more personal.

The narrator welcomed the crowd and, in perfect time to the music, began the show by introducing the pilots, one by one, and then plugging their cockpit microphones (the ones we were listening to over our headsets) into the loudspeakers, allowing each of them the chance to give the audience their own special, personal welcome.

When the MC got to #4, Darcy and I got a yet another shock.

"This is Major Sean 'Stroker' Gustafson from Homestead Air Force Base in Homestead, Florida," the scratchy voice bellowed. "And I'd like to welcome Olympic ski racer, Bonnie St. John, and her daughter, Darcy, who are visiting with us today . . ."

Darcy and I looked at each other and screamed.

> It was so cool! Each of the pilots was mentioning his children or wife—someone very close. So we were totally surprised when Major Gustafson talked about us from the jet! It made us feel special in a warm and fuzzy way. We liked him so much and it seemed that he really liked us, too. We'd formed a really cool bond in a short period of time.

But then came a more emotional moment. In a true testament to the courage and commitment these brave individuals accept to be a part of this team, pilot #5 gave *his* speech: "This is #5 Captain Nick Holmes, from Nellis Air Force Base in Las Vegas, Nevada, and I'd like to announce the birth of my first son, James Nicolas Holmes, born at 07:36 Mountain time this morning . . ."

The cheering from the crowd was so deafening, it obscured even the sound of the twenty-five thousand pounds of torque blasting from the turbofan jet engines on the runway. This man couldn't be by the side of his wife during the birth of their first child because this team can't function without him—an extraordinary sacrifice for his country. An extraordinary sacrifice for *us*.

The sun glistened off each fuselage as the F-16s rolled down to the far end of the runway, almost out of sight. I could feel the tremendous suspense building all around us. Then, like a rapid succession of uncorking champagne bottles, the magnificent machines came hurtling down the runway and one by one launched their way into the perfect, blue West Virginia sky.

As the narrator guided our gaze, the sextet of our USAF's finest aviators ripped through the crystal-clear skies above us, perfectly executing formation after thrilling formation—upside down, side-by-side, impossibly close, unbelievably fast, incredibly exciting.

"Roll left, and *rolling* . . ." the voice of the "boss," #1, Lt. Col. Chase Cunningham, crackled in our headsets. The pilots take their cues from this leader's directions, but it's not just his words they heed. His almost musical cadence sets the pace and structure of every move they make.

"Smoke . . . on . . . and . . . *pull*," groaned Commander Cunningham as his body tightened under the strain of pushing against the earth's gravitational pull.

When the team landed, again in rigid, military formation, the jubilant jet jockeys vaulted out of their rides, high-fived each other in celebration of a job well done, and then immediately headed straight for the flight line. There, straining against a rope stretched as far as the eye could see were their adoring fans anxious to meet and greet their heroes. This "grip and grin" was the encore performance of every Thunderbird show. The pilots and support officers spent over an hour signing autographs, shaking hands, posing for pictures, and soaking up glorious adulation.

Each of these crisp, clean, marvelously skilled leaders probably sat in a show just like this years ago—as wide-eyed kids staring up to the heavens in petrified awe of the gleaming steel and heart-pounding roars of a previous team of heroes crisscrossing the skies. They dreamed of a day when they would wrap themselves into a cockpit and punch a hole in the sky with all the skill and grace of those magnificent flyers before them.

What did it take for a young *girl* to look up at this show and dream that dream? How did Nicole have the courage to believe she could become a combat pilot in the air force when none had ever been allowed before? What did it take for her to believe she would be allowed to take up the mantle of a Thunderbird and assume the public face of the U.S. Air Force when no women had ever been given this honor? We couldn't wait to find out.

Five months later, Darcy and I were finally scheduled to interview Lt. Col. Nicole Malachowski, and we could hardly contain our excitement. In addition to being the first woman Thunderbird pilot, a highly decorated combat fighter pilot, and a distinguished White House Fellow, Colonel Malachowski had just embarked on the perilous endeavor of mothering twin babies.

As Darcy and I prepared for the interview, I recalled those first few months of motherhood—bottles, burping, round the clock vigils, sleeping in shifts, and so forth. They were the most wonderfully rewarding yet grueling and challenging times of my life. When Darcy was born, I thought I had it all planned out perfectly. I read all the books. I got all the stuff. I was ready. Of course, the moment she came home, all hell broke loose and every scrap of planning went right out the window. I looked at that little face and realized I was responsible for her every need: feeding, sleeping, cleaning, dressing. She couldn't do anything on her own but breathe, and I felt responsible for that, too! It was daunting, invigorating, wonderful, and . . . . exhausting. I couldn't imagine doubling it with twins.

Of course, I had no idea back then how hard it would be to birth an adolescent into adulthood, either. There were definitely days when I would trade the fear of a toddler falling down for the fear of this teenager crashing a car as she learned to drive. I certainly hoped that this book would hone her judgment and increase her sense of responsibility so that she could reach escape velocity from childhood while still in one piece.

We'd put off the interview repeatedly out of deference to Nicole's complicated life: recovering from her pregnancy, going back to work in a top-secret desk job, and the "twinado" as she called it. We finally decided that a phone call would be the least intrusive option, a disappointing outcome since we had been following her life for these past ten months.

Then Darcy had a stroke of genius. "Why don't we Skype her?" said my computer-savvy teenager.

Nicole already had a Skype account. Military folk often use this electronic technique to communicate with their friends and family back home while they're deployed overseas. So, on a chilly day in January, we fired up Darcy's computer and logged on. *Blooop* went the connection tone, a sound rather like a cute, electronic bubble bursting. The bright smile from the most beautiful and charming colonel the military has ever seen filled our computer screen, and our first and only "Skyperview" began.

We saw Nicole awkwardly move around, making adjustments to her position as if she were having trouble getting comfortable in her chair.

Then, tiny fingers began gingerly crawling up her neck, and wisps of fine, blond hair appeared at the bottom of the screen.

"Who's that?" I asked with a smile.

"This is Norah . . ."

The delicate yellow locks gradually pushed into the picture, giving way to a creamy forehead, followed by the sweetest, biggest baby eyes you could ever imagine. I longed to wrap a cuddle around the precious bundle and breathe in her fresh, sweet, baby smell. Darcy and I remotely sent giggles and coos as baby Norah entertained us with that unabashed infant wonder and curiosity. *Who are those new people in Mama's picture machine? They look interesting. But so do these funny, wiggly things at the end of my arm. Look, I can move them. I wonder what they're for. Oh, they must be for poking Mommy in the nose . . .*

> I found Nicole's existence as a fighter pilot completely alien, especially since I haven't had any family members active in the military. The intensely strict, authoritarian absolutes I see portrayed in movies made military life seem pretty scary. It was much easier to relate to her as a mother with her cute babies on her lap because I *have* been around kids—that's familiar. Seeing her as a mom made it more comfortable for me to connect to her as a person. "What made you want to become a fighter pilot?" I asked.

Her charismatic, homespun smile flashed across the screen. "I went to an air show in Las Vegas when I was five years old," Nicole answered, "and a plane called the F-4 Phantom was flying. It was loud—it was fast! When it came by, it shook your whole body and rumbled your chest. An air show, as you know, is a real sensory experience. You can see it, hear it, taste it, smell it, and feel it. It was powerful and graceful technology. What kid wouldn't want to be a fighter pilot after they saw that? It was just cool. I was bit by the bug that day at the air show and told my dad: *'I want to be a fighter pilot!'* He looked down at me and said, *'You're going to be a great fighter pilot.'*

"I was really fortunate. My parents never said, *'No, girls don't do that'* or *'It's too hard to become a fighter pilot.'* I always just knew I was going to be a fighter pilot. Little did I know that the laws against women in combat wouldn't change until I was in college, but it turns out I was born at the right time."

"What does it mean to you to be the first woman Thunderbird pilot?" asked Darcy.

"I was blissfully naive about it when I applied. Women had been flying fighter planes for more than a decade. Dozens of women had been in combat in all of the services. In fact, it wasn't until after I applied to the Thunderbirds that someone mentioned to me that they hadn't had a woman yet. Didn't even occur to me that it mattered. But once it got out in the public, that's when I realized it really did mean something. I was proud to put a face on the eighteen percent of the air force that is women. I consider that a huge honor . . . and a big responsibility. When you put on a Thunderbird uniform, it doesn't matter who you are or where you come from, you turn into Superman. Trying to live up to that—not just in the jet, but also in your interaction with the public and what you do in your private life—was something I took seriously.

"I don't think there's any way to be prepared for the media onslaught that happened. Luckily, it was a feel-good story, so I was given an incredible platform. I came to the Thunderbirds directly from combat and I wanted to brag about my air force family—Americans only eighteen, nineteen, twenty years old, away from their families, serving their country. I also saw it as an opportunity to talk about how long women have been flying for the military. In World War II, the WASPs, or the Women Air Force Service Pilots, were flying bomber fighter aircraft for training, testing, and maintenance—non-combat missions. A lot of Americans had absolutely no idea that women had been flying military planes since the forties. When I learned about them as a teenager, their example gave me the inspiration to keep hoping and dreaming that I could do it, too. I studied them at the [Air Force] Academy. It meant a lot to me to know that women like me had gone before.

"The most powerful—and the most humbling—thing I learned once I became a Thunderbird was how much it also meant to other people to see someone who looks like them succeeding. When I saw little girls line up as far as my eye could see to get an autograph or a picture, it hit me that this is not about me. Being the first woman Thunderbird pilot was all about them. I had this opportunity to be that person who said, *'Hey, I think you're going to be a great fighter pilot,'* just like my parents did for me.

"I would get these letters from young boys of the same age: ten-, eleven-, twelve-year-olds who would draw an airplane—usually in hot pink—and write something like, *'I think it's cool girls fly jets.'* I thought, Holy cow, just by doing my job I am changing a whole generation's paradigm of what women are capable of doing.

"But I'll never forget the very first time I walked up to the autograph line, after so many combat missions and then earning my place as a Thunderbird. It was my first air show and there's all this media attention that, as I said, I didn't anticipate. I get out of the jet after the performance, and I see a group of ninety-year-old women standing there on the autograph line wearing the trademark blue WASP scarves.

"They wanted to thank *me* for my service. They wanted *my* autograph on a glossy picture. I said to them, *'This is backwards!'* Here were these women who made it possible for my dream to come true. I was so grateful for *their* service. When I saw all the media for me, and I saw them standing there, that's when I became determined to make the story about them and how they built the runway so I could take off."

"Gaaaaaaa," came a powerful voice from somewhere to Nicole's left.

"Sorry, there's Garrick," Nicole said as her husband, Paul, made the switcheroo and deposited Norah's twin on his mother's lap. "You going to sit here for a second?" she said to her baby boy. To us she said, "We have a boy who wants to eat and he's getting feisty."

We watched Paul quickly place a bowl of mashed bananas and a spoon on the table in front of Nicole.

Darcy asked the next question: "Since you didn't realize what this path would be like before you went into it . . . why did you apply to become a Thunderbird?"

Garrick popped his toothless mouth wide open, ready to receive his food. Of course, his pilot mommy made an "airplane" circle with the spoon before smoothly landing it in the hangar as she replied, "The message for applications usually comes out a couple of months in advance by e-mail to the whole air force every year. And every year since I was the right age to qualify, I deleted the message. Finally, my squadron commander said, *'Hey, have you ever thought of doing this?'* And of course, I laughed, because it's so competitive and I hadn't thought of it really. Then, three days before the deadline for the application, I woke up in the middle of the night—this is really weird—because I dreamed I was flying as a Thunderbird. I remember waking my husband up telling him, *'I'm dreaming about being a Thunderbird.' 'So why are you waking me up?'* he asked. *'Do you think I can do it?'* I wanted to know. *'Yes,'* Paul told me, before he rolled over to go back to sleep. The next day I thought, What the heck? I'm going to try this."

Just then, Garrick had enough of the spoon thing and launched both of his tiny paws right into his lunch. At eight months, solid food was probably still something of a novelty. In a matter of seconds, the yellowish mush was all over his face, his bib, and the table in front of him. This little guy was fast! Another Malachowski fighter pilot in the making . . .

"Oh, sorry about this! Paul! Can you take him?"

"No," Darcy insisted, "don't give him away! He's adorable!"

"Yes, he is, isn't he?" the proud mommy gushed, placing a joyfully wet kiss on his puffy cheek.

"Is your faith important to you?" I asked. "Do you think that dream was a message?"

"That's interesting," Nicole answered, wiping the schmutz off her face. "I don't think it was a sign saying 'This Is Your Destiny.' I think it was just encouragement to not be afraid to try. What's the worst thing that was going to happen if I don't get selected? I'm going to be flying F-15Es in the greatest fire squadron with my current friends. I'm going to be doing what thousands of people wish they could be doing and that's flying to serve their country. There was nothing to lose.

"One of my core values is that we should have faith in ourselves, in our inner compass. Listen to that little voice that wakes you at two in the morning and says, *'Hey, you can do this.'*

"You bring up faith," said Nicole, kissing the top of Garrick's head. "There's no medical explanation for why my kids are here. They're miracles—period. If I wasn't a person of faith before that, I am now!"

"What do you mean?" I asked.

"Well, there's a little more to the story than I told you before. After two ultrasounds, they still said it was only one baby—one healthy growing baby. Paul and I were very excited. Then fourteen weeks into the pregnancy I slipped and fell down a flight of icy stairs outside at work and tumbled head over heels—Hollywood cartoon style—all the way down. When I hit bottom, I was in an awkward position with my back on the stairs and my pregnant belly sticking out. I tried to sit up and move my knee, and that's when I saw that my shin was completely broken in half. My left ankle was actually ninety degrees dislocated, too."

Darcy and I exchanged looks of concern . . . we hadn't heard about the broken leg before!

"Luckily, there was a guy behind me who called an ambulance. I was in pain because of my leg, but at the same time, I was more scared about my baby. They were going to put me into surgery right away, so they had to do another ultrasound to check on the baby first. The medical technician said, *'Your babies are fine.'* I kind of freaked. *'What did you just say? I heard an "s" on that.' 'Your TWINS,'* the med tech clarified, *'They have two strong heartbeats.'* She was smiling and trying to mollify the injured mother on her table, but I said, *'I'm not having twins.' 'Oh, yes, you are! Look.'* She turned the ultrasound screen toward me and all of a sudden my broken leg didn't hurt anymore."

We watched her on our Skype screen look back and forth between her two gorgeous children, one off camera.

"Can you believe it!" she continued, "in the next few hours I also found out that I had a triple fracture of my leg and a complete dislocation of my ankle. The doctors put in a lot of pins and metal. Using crutches was causing Braxton-Hicks contractions, so I was put on strict bed rest at home, which stopped the contractions. My mom came out to take care of me because Paul was still working.

"Then, about two months after the accident, things got even stranger. It's another one of those things—faith, if you will. I just didn't feel right. I was totally zoning out. I felt like I was having an out-of-body experience. I wasn't contracting. I wasn't bleeding . . . I just didn't feel right.

"We went to the hospital and in the forty-five minutes it took to get there, I started contracting and actually dilating. It was very scary. All the doctors came in and told me, *'You're going to deliver these kids in the next twenty-four to forty-eight hours and they're not viable at twenty-one weeks. You're going to lose your babies.'*

"The chaplains were brought in . . . lots of tears. I remember asking the doctors, *'Well, how many weeks do I need to make it to?'* *'Twenty-eight weeks at a minimum. At twenty-four or twenty-five weeks they might live, but have serious disabilities like cerebral palsy,'* they told us.

"If we'd had two children with disabilities, we would love them anyway. But these are conversations you never thought you'd be having. We went from, *'I'm having a baby'* to *'I'm having two babies'* and the excitement of telling everybody. Then all of a sudden your whole dream is going to be snatched away from you and you have no control over it. *'Twenty-eight weeks?'* I said, *'Okay, I'll make it.'* *'You're dilated,'* the doctor said, feeling sorry to have to say it. He thought I was out of my mind with grief. *'You're going to deliver these babies now,'* he said. *'No, I'm not.'* I insisted.

"I just started focusing on twenty-eight weeks. I just closed my eyes and zoned out as best I could. Thank goodness my husband was there and my mom was there.

"One of my mentors from my Thunderbird days was e-mailing me at that time, too. It was great to have e-mail so I could communicate with friends between contractions. He was a retired general, but at one time spent seven years in the Hanoi Hilton as a P.O.W. He knew a lot about focusing and how to block things out while being tortured. He saw what I was going through was very painful physically and emotionally, so he shared a few key sentences about how to meditate and how to focus. Here's this Vietnam prisoner of war who was helping me—across generations, across genders, across completely different situations.

"I went into a meditative state and got hyper-sensory. I couldn't be really touched. I didn't like sound. I would say to myself, *'I'm in control of my body and I'm stopping these contractions.'*

"And I just said that over and over while I contracted every three to twelve minutes for fifty-four days. I think the G-Force training we have as fighter pilots helped, too. We learn a lot about controlling our bodies. I got *with* the contractions, to the point where they almost didn't hurt anymore. I just rode them. I don't know how to explain it. I would close my eyes and ride them like waves."

I had to pause to digest this. "Let me get this straight." I laid it all out, still not quite believing what I heard. "You were having contractions. You were dilated. The doctors told you the babies were coming in twenty-four hours. But you said, *'No.'* You stayed in labor and willed your offspring to stay inside you for another fifty-four *days*! You conquered one of the strongest forces of nature by sheer focus, strength, and determination—along with tactics of survival from a prisoner of war."

Nicole smiled proudly. "So, I made it to twenty-nine weeks and three days and my babies, as you can hear, are very healthy." As if on cue, Norah let out an impressive off-camera screech. "At twenty-eight weeks all the doctors and nurses brought me presents and threw a big celebration—they couldn't believe it. For eight weeks they had checked on me every day. I actually went into the active labor side of the hospital four times. Each time they would tell me it was all over. I'd say, *'No, it's not. I need twenty-eight weeks.'*

"I'm still friends with all of them. I depended on everybody—and that was hard for Ms. independent fighter pilot, Thunderbird, and White House Fellow. I literally had people taking care of all of my bodily functions with bedpans and sponge baths."

Nicole hugged Garrick close to her face and smiled. Her baby boy started pounding his miniature fists on the table, with a hearty "bah, bah, bah" as accompaniment to his drumbeat. Paul swiftly and smoothly transferred boy for girl, and made off to give Garrick something else to bang on.

"He's proud of me," Nicole said as she watched her husband disappear into another room, "He's never jealous or intimidated or anything like that. He's such a complete, confident person that he's able to be married to someone like me and cheer me on. He just giggles at my faults, too. He loves me just the way I am. Marrying the right guy is the best thing I ever did."

"Let's go back to the air show and flying. How does it feel to be strapped into a plane pulling nine Gs?" I asked.

"Physically speaking," Nicole answered, "it's extraordinarily demanding to be a fighter pilot. Nine Gs is not comfortable. It's very tiring and puts a huge strain on your body."

When the huge jet thrusters kick in their afterburners and accelerate toward the stratosphere, the pilots are pulling up to nine Gs (nine times the force of gravity) on their bodies.

"When you pull heavy G-forces, the gravity takes the blood from the top of your body and pulls it into your feet. Clearly not having blood in your brain would lead to incapacitation, which you don't want when you're two hundred feet off the ground upside down at over five hundred miles an hour! You really want to stay conscious. We do what's called an anti-G straining maneuver: you bear down and flex your lower extremities—your thighs, your gluts, and your abdominals. That literally puts the blood back up in your head and keeps it in the upper half of your body. If you can imagine just doing these big isometric muscle contractions the whole time, it's exhausting."

Recent medical studies, by the way, suggest that women are better at withstanding high G-forces than their male counterparts. Apparently, due to the fact that the blood vessel routes from the heart to the brain tend to be shorter in women, we are far less likely to "gray out" (begin to lose consciousness) or "black out" than men given the same level of positive-G pressure.

"When I'm flying a Thunderbird air show or in combat, I don't have time to really think about how I'm feeling," Nicole continued. "I am at work the whole time. Every millisecond there is a decision that's being made. Every millisecond your mind is thinking, What's coming next? What's coming at me? Where are my hands? Where's the throttle? Where's the stick? What are teammates doing?

"In a lot of ways it's even more of a mental marathon than a physical marathon. Am I excited and exhilarated while I'm actually doing it? Not so much. I'm just too busy to think about it. As I'm getting in the jet, or when we taxi and take off, you're waving to the crowd, and they're waving back. That's exciting. The crowd fires me up."

"It was fun when we saw Major Gustafson taxiing out," I told her. "He had us on the com listening to all the pilots. He greeted us on the way out from the cockpit. He was absolutely fabulous to us."

"I'm so glad you guys got to listen to the communications. It's very unique. Everything that the commander leaders said—the rate—the tone—the inflection—those little subtle things mean something to your hands, to the stick, and to the throttle. Just ever so slight things. You're flying inches away from other people, so every millisecond matters."

"The commander's voice is almost like singing, isn't it?" I asked, remembering the otherworldly chanting we overhead during the show.

"I hear it in my sleep, still. I dream it," she mused. "The littlest change in his voice means something to the maneuver. When we're out there as a six-ship, we really think of ourselves as one plane. We're just an extension of the boss. I'm his right side. Someone was his left side. We're just an extension of each other."

"What's the difference between being a leader among leaders in the Thunderbirds, versus leading in combat?" Darcy asked.

"As a flight commander I am responsible for leading people less experienced than I am. I had responsibility for career development and mentoring of eight people on a long-term basis. And then when I flew, I would be leading a different set of eight people, depending on the nature of the mission.

"People relied on me to help them make decisions in combat that are going to be the best for not only our formation, but for all Americans and our ally partners on the ground. My team looked to me for advice and guidance in mission planning and debriefing, as well.

"In combat there is no place for ego. It is a life-and-death situation and I'm not just talking about our squadron. It's about those men and women with boots on the ground. We're there to help them. When there's an American on the radio calling for your help and you can hear bullets flying in the background, it becomes very serious and very personal. Our formation of airplanes is dedicated to one very clear mission.

"When you're able to help, we land, look at each other, and think, *Wow, I don't even know who that guy or gal on the ground was that we helped today* . . . but talk about a fulfilling sense of mission! There's tremendous job satisfaction in helping other people."

"Thank you so much for your service," I choked out.

"In a different direction." Darcy saved me from my emotions. "I want to know if you got hassled a lot by the guys when you first started. You were in the first wave of women coming through flight training, right?"

"When you are on the forefront of a cultural change, it's not only difficult for the women coming into the group. I had to remind myself that it's also difficult for the people who have to accept change. I didn't look at them as the enemy. I asked myself, what could I do to make this change more comfortable for all of us?

"The wonderful thing is that the aircraft is a great equalizer. We video-record everything, so when we come back and debrief the mission, it's very measurable. There is nothing subjective about putting bombs on target. There is nothing subjective about how you dogfight. For the people who weren't sure about women in planes, it very quickly becomes obvious whether or not you can do the job.

"The socializing took more adjustment time. Does having women around mean that we can't have fun and sing macho fighter pilot songs? Does that mean that we can't swagger around, beat our chests, and call ourselves the brotherhood?

"It takes time, but the responsibility lies on both sides. I believe in giving people the benefit of the doubt, not reading a lot into what people do that might upset me or catch me off guard. That's not fair to them.

"I've been around nothing but men since I was seventeen and started at the Air Force Academy. So I know for a fact that women and men are different. When I'm around women I communicate differently than when I'm with men. I feel like I have two personalities.

"Women are very good at nuance. We communicate with other women nonverbally using body language, tone, and inflection, even acts of omission. Men don't. Men mean exactly what they say. They're so much more direct. When a woman says, *'No, it's fine. You don't need to come by,'* that means I need to come by.

"As far as integrating culturally with the men, not reading into the things they did kept me from blowing things out of proportion. Guys don't remember the next day what they said or did yesterday. They really don't."

A bloodcurdling scream came from the other room.

Norah snapped her head around to see what the heck her brother was going on about. She seemed totally content, though, to just sit there and pull on her mom's hair. "Sorry, we have a minor meltdown going on with my son . . ." In no time, the crisis in the other room seemed to dissipate. For the moment.

"Do you have a motto?" Darcy followed. "Words you live by?"

"I always tell people to dream big. I'm not afraid to dream big because that's the only way things get done. Somebody has to think outside the box. Somebody has to be not afraid."

"What's next for you? What are you dreaming big on now?" I asked.

"Right now I am dreaming about getting back in the F-16 and flying. I didn't really tell you how debilitating my pregnancy was. I had the broken leg, but with all the bed rest I never got to do any rehab. They told me I might not ever get back on flight status again. I couldn't believe it."

We held our breath as she continued . . .

"Three weeks ago, I got back on flight status."

I think we cheered even louder over the Skype connection at that moment than we did at the actual air show. We felt an overwhelming sense of joy because we knew fighter jet flying was such a passion for Nicole. Once you had the ability to fly like that, having it taken away would be devastating. I could imagine how exciting it would be for her to get her wings back.

"I'm back as a fighter pilot on the front lines, and I'm back with my air force family. I enjoyed being a White House Fellow and being outside of it for a while, but I've been wearing air force blues since I was seventeen. It's nice to be back in my community, my original family."

"It's really an honor to be in your presence," I said. "Thank you for your service to this country. Thank you also for giving us so much of your time. We'd better let you get back to your babies and your husband."

"It looks like he just got both babies to sleep," said Nicole. "Now we can do the dishes, the laundry, pay the bills..."

"Don't say that!" I said earnestly. "Here's my advice to you: Grab your husband and give him a big kiss. That's much more important."

"I will. I will." Nicole laughed as her husband nodded vigorously.

Blooop! Skype out.

CHAPTER 11

———————

Marin Alsop

Musical Director and Conductor
Baltimore Symphony Orchestra

Since September 2007, the Baltimore Symphony Orchestra has been under the musical direction of Marin Alsop, the first female music director of a major, full-time American orchestra. This pioneer is the reason Darcy and I were sitting in the parking lot of Baltimore's Joseph Meyerhoff Symphony Hall on a rainy afternoon in October.

With Darcy back in school now, the pace of our adventures had slowed. I was happy to be on the road again, but I could see there was slightly more tension in Darcy's demeanor. To traipse about on these adventures in the summer was one thing, but putting her studies on hold, even for a day, was something else altogether.

> I was a totally different person, sitting in my high school classes after having met women like Hillary Clinton, Amy Pascal, Wendy Kopp, and the others. They aroused my competitive instincts, but made me a bit afraid, too. Knowing there were people out there my age all around the globe who were preparing themselves to take on really big challenges made me wonder: *Are they reading more than I am? Are they working harder in school? Are they already taking on leadership roles?*

From our car, we were eyeballing the backstage entrance and hoping against hope that the rain would let up for just a moment so we could run in. And this wasn't the kind of drizzle where you dance around a few puddles with a newspaper over your head. This was a monsoon! The water was coming down in sheets—*sideways*.

Through our foggy windshield, we saw musicians running at forty-five-degree angles into the wind, using their bodies to protect the black leather cases that held their precious instruments. When the little guy carrying the impossibly large tuba slipped, I gasped. If he went down, I envisioned, the torrent of water rushing by his feet would wash him down the hill and right into the Chesapeake Bay, tragically leaving one less oompa-doompa from the brass section in that night's performance.

Having been in orchestras for the past several years, I have a strong sense of pride as a cellist. This made me especially anxious to meet Marin Alsop because of my respect and affection for the conductors I have worked with.

We'd put Marin Alsop on the list from the very beginning; her name was in every version of our book proposal. Then, after going for months and months with no positive response to our requests, we'd almost given up hope. Finally managing to get a "yes" seemed like finding the gold pot at the end of a very long rainbow. This was one of the meetings I most wanted to do. While the downpour *was* torrential, I didn't want to miss a second of this opportunity because of a little water.

"We'd better get in there," I urgently said to Mom. "We don't want to walk in while they're in the middle of practicing something."

We jumped out of the car and made a mad dash across the fifty or so feet to the door. Well, Darcy dashed. My prosthetic leg and I can cover ground, wet or otherwise, rather quickly, but "dash"? Not so much. She arrived at the door several beats before me.

We were totally drenched when we crossed the threshold. Standing there sopping, we announced ourselves to the receptionist, who sat inside a little booth that resembled a movie theater box office.

Darcy and I had been invited to attend the orchestra's last afternoon rehearsal session before a gala performance to be held that evening. We were ushered into the grand concert hall and took a couple of seats just in front of the stage. An impressive arena, modern in style, with all the latest acoustics, this stunning theater was one of the most pleasant venues I could imagine for enjoying an orchestra concert. Warm blond wood enveloped the plush seating area. A comfortable loge surrounded the back third of the auditorium, insuring an excellent visual as well as auditory experience from every one of its almost twenty-five hundred seats. I was struck by the flowing design of the architecture. The entire space was completely round. There were no flat walls or ninety-degree angles anywhere.

On stage, the musicians of the Baltimore Symphony Orchestra slowly meandered onto their individual folding chairs. Velvet-lined instrument cases snapped open, revealing hundreds of thousands of dollars worth of finely crafted wood, strings, and brass. It was odd to see the performers in street clothes rather than the usual elegant black and white apparel at performance time. They chitchatted, compared notes on their giant scores of music, and assembled their instruments. Slowly, but deliberately, a cacophony of musical tones and muffled chatter rose into the baffles high above the stage.

As I gazed over this assembly of immensely gifted performers—every one a prodigy or shining star in their own right—I was struck by an interesting dilemma: how do you corral such a mass of talent and ego into a mellifluous musical meld that does justice to the composer's wishes, yet allows every performer to assert their genius at interpretation? Such is the challenge of the one who stands on the box and wields a baton.

> For the first time on our journey, we were entering a world that I understood better than my mom did. I was so happy that this example of leadership—the one I knew best—was to be included in the book. I felt a more intimate connection with Marin than I did with any of the other women we'd met.

Suddenly, from the stage-right wing, a hidden door opens and she emerges. Immediately, the dissonant scratching, blowing, and pounding of the last few minutes turns into a much more specific collection of instrument tuning. Elegant yet comfortable in a vibrant pink shirt and simple black trousers, the maestro quickly and deliberately crosses to center stage and mounts the podium with an air of casual, but composed ease. There is no wasted effort or flourish in her presence. A definite economy of movement seems to exemplify Marin Alsop's demeanor. Her close-cropped blond hair almost suggests the mane of a lioness, and she moves with catlike precision.

She nods to the concertmaster in the first chair of the violin section, wishing him a cheerful "good morning," scrutinizes a section of the score, and then it's straight to business. The players already know what piece they are starting with. It is the "Lenore" Overture no. 3 from Beethoven's one and only opera, *Fidelio*, with a brilliant arrangement by another legendary composer and conductor, Gustav Mahler.

In an instant, the immense theater fills with the romantic phrases of Ludwig van's spectacular melodies. Our souls seem to float in the air, buoyed by the harmonies that careen around the circular hall. I close my eyes and let my entire body feel the glorious, wistful early themes that gradually build upon one another, adding instruments to finally swell with an intensity that vibrates deep into our bones. And then, just as my skin tingles from a huge crescendo of horns and clarinets . . . everything stops!

It was as if all my senses were simultaneously slammed into a brick wall.

I leaned over and whispered excitedly to Mom, "These musicians are really disciplined. In all the orchestras I've been a part of, everyone will keep playing a few bars further than the conductor tells us to. It's always tempting not to stop. These guys slam on the brakes in an instant!"

Some people think conducting is easy because you just stand there and wave a baton, but I have a unique appreciation for what it takes to be up there. I had experienced being conducted for years and I knew how it makes me play better and makes all the musicians more cohesive. While different conductors have different styles, I had immense respect for the job they all do. Conductors have a relationship with the music that is more intense than any of the musicians. They have to hold in their head all of the instruments playing at once in perfect pitch and tempo. They imagine the way the composer intended the music compared to the way they want it played.

"I think that second note of the slur needs to be more on the short side, okay?" comes the voice from the podium. "Pick it up from measure twenty-one. And..."

The maestro raises her arms and instantly engages the one hundred plus virtuosos before her. She guides them through the rest of the piece, occasionally taking a pause to again pick at a minute detail completely lost to my ears. A hold here, a note there, they massage the performance to perfection. With every movement of her body, with every glance, even with the slightest shift of her eyes, she communicates her direction, moving the entire orchestra as if it were one, single, euphonic organism. A giant musical instrument that responds, shifts, and adjusts precisely as commanded by the subtleties of her touch.

> I wondered what it was going to be like to meet the woman whose face was twenty feet high on the signs outside. I'd met many conductors before, but not world-famous ones. Will she be scary and intimidating? In only a few minutes, she'd come down off her podium and I'd be talking with her face to face. I could feel my heart beating faster than the pace of the music.

Once she was satisfied with each piece in the repertoire for the evening, Marin retreated to her private office / dressing room neatly tucked away off the stage-right wing. Decorated in soft, pleasant, almost pastel tones, this private sanctuary was clearly designed to provide her with a peaceful place to gather her thoughts, rest, and prepare for the daunting task of not only performing the music, but running the day-to-day operation of a major symphony orchestra. She was performer, muse, and guide to the entire operation. And, today, she had a snoot-full of a wicked cold.

"Sorry," she sniffed as she welcomed us into her inner sanctum, "I can't seem to kick this rotten thing." With the same direct, no-nonsense tone that she demonstrated on the podium, Marin Alsop welcomed us with warmth and caring, yet clearly focused on the business at hand. As if directed by her wand, we immediately launched into our questions.

"We've heard that both of your parents were professional musicians and that you started playing both piano and violin before the age of six," Darcy began. "And we love the story of how you first set your sights on conducting at age nine when your dad took you to see Leonard Bernstein. Tell us more about the journey from there to here."

"It certainly was no easy task. I tell students all the time: you need to invest in yourself, educate yourself, and work really, *really* hard. Even when I was ten years old, I would study the entire arrangement of the pieces I was playing in the orchestra, not just my part. I knew I wanted to be a conductor, so I learned the whole score."

> I was surprised at how comfortable I felt with this larger than life woman. Her voice was low and husky, probably because of the cold, but it felt easy to lean in and listen to her flowing words. I could imagine her as an adorable ten-year-old, earnestly planning to be a conductor.

"Then gradually, I started forming little ensembles to conduct, to try things out. It was all about becoming my own teacher. I think that's what really successful people do. They're able to self-scrutinize all the time. Constantly, objectively assessing where I am, how I could be better, what I could do. Luckily, video was in the mix, so I videotaped everything I did in those days. I would watch it. I would change things. I would change the way I spoke to the orchestra. Let me get a tissue, sorry."

Her deftly articulate hand reached out to pluck a tissue from the ornate box on the table between us and blow her nose with a perfect F#

honk. Her nose now sufficiently un-stuffed, she continued, "It's tough because you don't have an instrument. You need at least forty people to work on your craft. I got all my friends to play and kept trying to talk them into creating a group. My backup plan was to become a rock 'n' roll violinist, and I was trying to find somebody to write some music for this imaginary ensemble when I met a guy who agreed to provide some swing music. I didn't really know what swing music was. So I said: *'Sure, that sounds good.'*

"I had told the composer I had this ensemble, which I didn't have, but I called all my friends and we played through this music he wrote for us. This was long before classical groups played swing and rock music. We didn't know we had to swing it; it sounded horrible! When the composer came and heard it, he was laughing so hard...they all thought I was crazy. It wasn't easy to keep them from going home right then and quitting.

"Gradually, I talked them all into practicing in a church basement at eleven o'clock at night after our gigs. It was six violins, three violas, three cellos, bass, and drums. Then people started coming to hear us— it was a fantastic sound and there was nothing like it. Oh, and then I got us a gig at a jazz club. Which was funny since I'd never been to a jazz club!

"One night at the club I was giving quarters to this guy and playing Pac-man with him, and it turned out to be Phil Ramone, the producer who discovered Billy Joel and others. Long story short, our ensemble started playing on Billy's albums.

"Then, my swing band, called String Fever, played at a wedding for a Japanese businessman named Tomio Taki. The flowers at that affair cost more than I'd ever earned in my life! So I called him up after the wedding and asked him to have a drink with me.

"I said to him, *'Look, you don't know me at all and I don't really know you, either, but I need help. I want to be a conductor. I want to start an orchestra. I have no idea really what I'm doing, but it's the only thing in life I want. Would you help me?'*

"And he said, *'Absolutely, I'll help you.'* "

Darcy and I were utterly stunned by the story. Just as a breathless "Wow" escaped from Darcy's lips, I blurted, "You're crazy!"

"I am crazy," she agreed, nodding. "That's an important quality for a conductor!"

All three of us laughed, and she continued, "Mr. Taki single-handedly supported the orchestra, which we named Concordia, for eighteen years. Essentially, I started a not-for-profit business. I hired my core of string players, built a board of directors, and expanded from there.

"Both Concordia and String Fever were incredible leadership development opportunities for me. At the beginning, I had to convince the thirteen other members of String Fever to stick with something they thought was really without a future, with no pay, and late-night rehearsals, but it was worth it. Not only did we get really good, but we ended up playing concerts all over the world. We played together for twenty years.

"It changed the way people thought of string players. Now you often see string players in rock bands. We were on the cusp of crossover music—like Queen and Fleetwood Mac—everybody loved it. We all loved each other and we loved doing it. Of course that group gave me the experience that allowed me to build my larger orchestra, Concordia, and begin to get auditions to conducting even larger orchestras.

"Mr. Taki is still a very, very close friend of mine, and he is very proud of what I have achieved. He said, *'Well, we wanted to get the first woman conductor out there. We did that. But now, how will we keep women conducting?'* That's what led me to think about starting a fellowship for women. I named my conducting fellowship after him: the Taki Concordia Conducting Fellowship."

Darcy broke in with another question. "We heard that when they first offered you the job as conductor here in Baltimore, there were some problems and you almost didn't take it. What actually happened?"

"Well, the appointment here was very, very badly handled. The whole organization was in a state of frantic crisis—not just crisis, but completely over-the-top, hysterical crisis. The musicians had been kept out of the loop for the last couple of decades. They weren't involved in many decisions, so they were an angry bunch, really angry. Plus they had huge debt, sixteen million dollars of debt. They had only sixty percent audience attendance. Oh, it was a terrible disaster.

"When the board decided they wanted to make me an offer, they didn't really get enough buy-in from the musicians. The musicians said, *'That's ridiculous! How can you just hire her without our involvement?!'*

"Then, it blew up in the press. It was horrible. You work so hard to get to this point in your career, and then the front page of the Washington Post had my picture with the caption: MOST MUSICIANS BALK AT AP-POINTMENT OF MUSIC DIRECTOR. All the papers kept saying that ninety percent of the musicians opposed my appointment. Well, nobody ever polled anybody, but somebody said it and they kept repeating it, so it became 'fact.' I didn't really think it was true, but I had a decision to make.

"A lot of people advised me: *'Don't take this job. The way they've treated you so far is terrible. Everything about it is terrible. Don't get anywhere near them.'*

"I was talking to my two managers. I talked to executive directors of big orchestras. Debra Borda, Executive Director of the Los Angeles Philharmonic and arguably one of the leading managers in the world— probably the most powerful woman in the management field—said, *'Marin, you can't take this job.'*"

She paused.

"I find advice so interesting . . . because I often do the exact opposite. That's not to say that the advice isn't extremely helpful. I weigh everything and think it through from every perspective, but ultimately I follow my instincts."

The three of us laughed again. This was one of those ironic insights that rang very true.

"Do you ever notice that? When someone tells you something, and only at that moment do you realize you violently disagree? I find that advice is really critical in galvanizing me to my belief, my own personal truth. So that was a big leadership moment, figuring out, well, okay, what do I do now?"

"I heard that you met with the musicians separately," I said to Marin, "and actually told them, *'I won't take the job if you don't want me to.'*"

"Right. I did," said Marin, shrugging as if it were the simplest thing in the world. "I called up a colleague of mine who was guest conducting the BSO and asked, *'Could I have ten minutes of your rehearsal?'* He said, *'Oh, my God, are you really going to do this?'* And I said, *'Yeah, I need to talk to them.'*

"The board of directors and the management wanted to be there when I met with them and I said no. I wanted to talk to them myself. Just the musicians and me. When I came in, they were surprised to see me, believe me! I talked to them for about six or seven minutes and basically said, *'I have no idea what happened here and I really don't know if I can recover from this. It's just horrible what's happened.*

" *'But,* I said, *'I don't think you understand what kind of vision I have for you. I see enormous potential with this orchestra. I think you're wonderful artists, but there are serious problems here.'*

"Because I had worked with them before, I knew a bit about them. So I went through everything very quickly, just an overview. I went through recordings, debt, audience development, everything.

"And I said: *'The reason I was considering this job is because I felt I could really impact all of these areas positively, but I can't do it if I don't have your support. I won't sign the contract unless I have your support.'* Before I even left the stage, they called me back; they said: *'You have our support.'* I'm not sure they meant it at that point, but they said it.

"It was the head of the player's committee who communicated directly with me. She had been the one who had been quoted in all the papers stating that ninety percent of the musicians opposed my appointment and now she said, *'We will support you one hundred percent.'* She also said: *'We'd like to apologize on behalf of our management.'* So, I took that as an apology from them, too.

"I called my friend and colleague, Debra Borda, back and I said, *'I'm really sorry to tell you this. I'm going to take the job.'* "

"But you didn't take the job. You created a different job," I said. If you had taken it as it was offered, it would have—"

"It would have been a disaster," she agreed. "I think it would have been a disaster."

"You changed the framework," I pointed out. "You transformed the job."

"There was an element of liberation in going into a job where I couldn't have cared less whether anybody liked me. Do you know what I mean? Usually when you go into a new job, you're trying to be all nice and saying, hi, how are you? It wasn't like that after all the negative press and problems. At that point, I really felt I had nothing to lose."

"Nothing you did could make it worse!" said Darcy, throwing up her hands.

"So I decided, I'm just going to work their tails off. Just work, work, work. I rehearsed and really went after everything. I also decided that I would always try to communicate with them openly and transparently. Then and now, I will take just five minutes here or there at the end of a rehearsal and say: *'Listen, I wanted to just bring you up to speed on a couple things. I'm thinking about a vision I have about this and that.'* "

"What would you say are your core values?" Darcy queried.

"Honesty would be number one. I'm not afraid to be myself. I don't change much when I'm on the podium or off the podium. I'm not afraid to stand up for what I believe in. I'm willing to say I'm wrong. All those things are really important.

"I believe in leading by example and investing in things I believe in. You can't ask people to do something you won't do. I'm a big believer in philanthropy, community, and making a difference by being a citizen of the world. Everyone does it in her own way.

"I'm really proud of the BSO. Nobody stood up on the podium ever before and said, *'How are we going to make a difference here in Baltimore?'* Up to this point, I don't think it ever even occurred to them. Now they're willing to stand up and be counted as community members as well as musicians."

"How do you actually define leadership?" Darcy asked.

"Leadership is the ability to galvanize people and motivate people— bringing out the best in people. It's a perfect manifestation of what I'm doing. I'm trying to enable everybody to be at the top of his or her game. It's leading, but also listening while you're leading. I think the best leaders are great followers, too. You balance when you assert yourself and when you don't; when you listen and when you stop the dialogue and move it in a certain direction. For me, it's all these things."

"Have you studied the discipline of leadership apart from music?" I wanted to know.

"No, I never have, but people have always said that I have it innately. When I was a kid, even if I was not very good at a particular team sport, I was always the captain. You know what I mean?

"My managers, both of them, are always yelling at me for being too accessible, but I think to be a great leader you have to be, to a certain degree, accessible. People have to be able to relate to you and understand where you're heading and what you're trying to do."

"Can you tell us a story about a pivotal point where you grew as a leader?" I asked.

"It took me a long time to not care so much what people thought of me and also not to worry about everybody's feelings so much. I used to always be thinking: Is everybody okay? What's wrong? Somebody's got a strange look on their face. Is it something I'm doing?

"I spent nearly a decade learning to stop trying to make everybody happy and content. When I need to, I can still turn on my perceptive abilities, but I had to be stronger. I had to almost shut down some of my sixth sense, my intuition, in order to really focus on the mission: the music.

"If it's not about the music, I can be sympathetic, but not susceptible. Instead of micromanaging details, I stay focused on the big idea: it's about the music. It's always about the music. *'I'm sorry you had a problem on the way to work, let's get back to the music.'* If they have a problem, they'll have to deal with it. I assume it's their issue, not mine.

"It was hard at first. I even used to always apologize when people made mistakes. If an oboe played a wrong note, I'd say, *'Oh, oh, I'm sorry.'* I don't think men do that."

At that moment, a man leaned his head in the door and gave Marin the look that said . . . time to move along.

"Can you give us five more minutes?" Marin said generously.

"Sure, sure," said her handler smoothly.

"Quick," said Darcy, poking me in the ribs. "We'd better get in the most important question. We almost forgot!!"

"We've heard that a woman conductor can't make the same gestures as a male conductor. What exactly does that mean?" We had already asked a male conductor about this and he told us it was true, but he couldn't explain it. It bothered us for months. Isn't a gesture a gesture— no matter who makes it? Why couldn't she move her baton exactly like the male conductors?

"Of course, gesture is everything for a conductor. That's how I'm communicating with the orchestra," Marin replied. "But I have to think about it more because of how people interpret female gesture as opposed to male gesture."

She jumped up and picked up her baton—it was the moment we had been waiting to see for so long! "For example, if a man does *this*..." She held the baton with two fingers raising the other three into the air like a British person drinking tea in a fancy way. "...musicians think he wants the music to be delicate. But if I do it, it looks girly. Even smiling too much can be interpreted as a giggly girl. Luckily, I'm not a giggly person.

"In the same way, if a man looks strong like this..." she scrunches up her face, balls up her fist as if she's commanding the orchestra to play fortissimo "...he's strong and effective as a leader. When a woman makes the same movements and facial expression, she's scary, a witch, or overbearing. I'm always careful to be very neutral. I try not to do anything that could be seen as girly. When I'm strong, I try not to clench up and be tense. I'm strong in a relaxed way without any excuse, apology, or attitude.

"It's a lot of working in the mirror and to figure out how others are reading your gestures. It's a two-step process for women. It's easier for a man. He walks up to the podium and they're not seeing him, they're just seeing the music. For a woman they have to get past seeing her. Like, what man gets criticized for wearing the same suit every time? I actually have to talk to my female students a lot about what clothing to wear."

"Well, what advice do you give them about what to *wear*?" Darcy had mastered the art of the follow-up question.

"You have to find your own style. At the same time, you have to look in control, in power, and not have anything that draws attention to your female attributes. You won't believe this, but I've had to take a few students aside and say: *'What you're wearing, it might be little too revealing or too tight.'* It never occurred to them. And meanwhile, the men are all, like, mesmerized the whole time as the woman conductor leans forward over the podium—and not by the music!"

The image of what she was describing broke us up in chuckles once again.

Knowing our time was at end, Darcy asked our favorite wrap-up: "My last question is—What is most satisfying about what you've achieved?"

"Oh, everything satisfies; I'm thrilled," she answered easily. "To have a dream, and then realize that you're able to live your dream . . . it really doesn't get better than that. I feel fortunate every day."

The door opened a slit, and her handler's head appeared again. This time we could see all the way to his neck where he made slicing motions.

"We're done," said Marin. "He's like my pit bull."

That evening, Darcy and I were set to attend the gala performance featuring the unfinished symphonies of Beethoven, Gustav Mahler, and, in a fascinating selection of Marin's, seven songs composed by Alma Mahler, the much celebrated, Viennese-born siren who famously cut a seductive swath through late nineteenth- and early twentieth-century artistic scene by marrying, successively, Gustav Mahler, architect and Bauhaus movement founder, Walter Gropius, and the controversial novelist, playwright, and poet, Franz Werfel.

The virtuosos we'd seen earlier laughing in their jeans and sneakers were now acting as serious as the tuxedos and evening gowns they wore. The soloist, who we saw in her glasses and ponytail at rehearsal, had gone totally diva with professional makeup, a fancy up-do, and a purple outfit with so many layers, drapes, and frills it looked like she could hang-glide with it.

When they finished the first piece, Beethoven's Lenore Overture, the whole orchestra expressed their pleasure at getting it right—they wore cat-that-swallowed-the-canary grins, subtly high-fived each other, a few even left their seats to offer their compatriots a well-deserved spot of congratulations. In the rehearsals they had worked hard to perfect this music more than any of the others, and they were thrilled with the results. Marin most of all.

Perhaps her potent inspiration is why BSO attendance numbers are climbing, their donations never dipped during the recession, and classical music venues across the country are looking to Marin Alsop for answers on how to stay relevant and vital to a new generation.

CHAPTER 12

Geena Davis

Women's Rights Activist
Movie Star

EXT. DESERT—DAY
The turquoise blue, 1966 Thunderbird convertible stops
abruptly. Ahead, the vast expanse of the Grand Canyon.
Behind, a wall of police officers with an entire battery
of artillery trained on the heads of the two fugitives
sitting in the car. The women look at each other, really
hard.

                    THELMA DICKERSON
          OK, listen; let's not get caught.

                    LOUISE SAWYER
            What're you talkin' about?

                       THELMA
              Let's keep goin'!

                       LOUISE
              What d'you mean?

                       THELMA
       (nods toward the canyon ahead of them)
                   . . . Go.

LOUISE
(smiling a nervous smile)
You sure?

THELMA
Yeah. Hit it.

Louise grabs her dear friend's face, plants a huge
kiss on her lips, then mashes a well-pedicured foot
onto the accelerator. A cloud of dust spews from the
rear wheels as the car lurches forward. The girls clasp
hands, giving each other one last look before they fly,
in slo-motion, right over the edge of the magnificent
cliff . . .

With this most unusual of happy endings, *Thelma & Louise* sailed into
Hollywood history and into the hearts and minds of millions of women
all over the world. The Academy Award–winning actresses who played
these roles, Susan Sarandon and Geena Davis, still remain cultural icons
of female rebellion twenty years after the movie's release.

I was excited to learn that Geena was slated to deliver the closing
address to the United Nations Economic and Social Council meeting
on "Engaging Philanthropy to Promote Gender Equality and Women's
Empowerment." Darcy and I had been encouraged to attend this international forum on progress of women's empowerment throughout
the world by Sharon Allen, the chairman of Deloitte we profiled in
Chapter 5. The conference was a key colloquy to investigate issues,
identify needs, and support initiatives and partnerships to achieve gender equality in public and private sectors across the globe. Opened by
Sarah Ferguson, Duchess of York, it featured presentations from Michael
Patsalos-Fox, the vice-chairman of McKinsey & Company; Zainab Salbi,
the founder and CEO of Women for Women International; and many
other fascinating advocates for women.

We hustled through the crowd of international dignitaries and scrambled to get a seat in the huge lecture hall of the UN Headquarters in New York. Amidst a beautiful mélange of Indian saris, traditional African dress, and western European suits, we found two spots near the middle of the auditorium. Darcy's eyes lit up as she grabbed the personal language translation headset hanging in front of her seat and played with the controls.

As soon as the meeting began, my little language connoisseur vigorously flipped the round black switch back and forth through every dialect available. The smile of pure joy on her face was immutable as she savored each delicious tone and phrase.

"Oh, my gosh!" Darcy whispered a bit louder than she meant to, since her ears were muffled by the large "language-lab" headset, "I'm listening to this in *Swahili!*"

> As soon as I put the headphones on I was addicted. For a lingophile, an extreme lover of languages, it was like a toy that I couldn't put down; a toy that I would never find anywhere else. I imagined myself as one of the simultaneous translators working rapid fire with complex words and ideas. It fascinated me, yet almost gave me a headache to imagine having to speak, listen, and translate all at once. Pretty cool that the translators get to listen in to all of these multinational meetings, too.

I looked up just in time to see the elegant movie star take her place on the dais. Her long dark hair draped softly over a lovely ecru ensemble adorned with a simple, silver beaded necklace. But to me, her most exquisite fashion accessory was a perfectly round dark mole on the cheekbone just below her left eye.

I nudged Darcy out of her linguistic reverie and pointed toward the front of the room where the blue-and-white United Nations flag was stretched across the stage—a constant reminder of the august location for this gathering.

"Hey, that's . . . *her!* That's Geena Davis!" Darcy said again, louder than she meant to. I grabbed the earphones off her head so she could hear herself again. I think the people next to us were becoming annoyed by the noisy Americans.

"What's *she* doing here?"

Attending this event had come together at the last minute, so Darcy hadn't had time to completely scour all the material about what we were going to see and hear. She immediately snatched up the program and read about the Geena Davis not too many people know. Beyond her brilliant portrayal of wide-eyed, often goofy, but ultimately redeeming characters on screen, this Mensa member has an astonishingly eclectic curriculum vita. She is an archery champion who participates in international competitions and almost qualified for the U.S. Olympic Team in 2000. Through the Woman's Sports Foundation she established the "Geena Takes Aim" campaign in support of the landmark Title IX legislation that insures balance in women's athletic programs at educational institutions. She is also the mother of a nine-year-old daughter and seven-year-old twin boys.

One day, while watching television with her daughter, Geena noticed what seemed to be an acute disproportion in the number of boy characters versus the number of girls. She did a little research and uncovered some alarming statistics: the ratio was almost 3 to 1. Her crusade to rectify this imbalance ultimately led to the establishment of the Geena Davis Institute on Gender and Media, which sponsored the largest research project ever established on gender in children's entertainment, and has pioneered an effort to insure more equitable portrayals of women throughout the entire entertainment industry.

After hearing this famous mother and women's rights activist give her impassioned speech about the importance of gender representation in the media, Darcy looked at me and said forcefully, "We *have* to get her in the book."

"Absolutely. She'll be in the book," I promised.

What was I thinking? How in the world was I going to do this? Did I expect to just call her up, tell her about the project, and she would jump right in?

Well, that's kind of how it happened.

A mutual acquaintance gave me a contact phone number and e-mail address to Geena's office. I composed my most fervent e-mail invitation, sent it off, and hoped for the best. After a week or so with no response, I decided to try the phone number—just to see if the right person actually received the letter.

"Hello?" The voice was unmistakable despite background noise.

"Um... Geena?" I felt a lump in my throat the size of a small asteroid. This wasn't an office contact number. This was Geena Davis' cell phone!

"Yes?"

"This is Bonnie St. John. I sent you an e-mail..."

"Oh, yeah, the thing with your daughter. I think that's so cool! Tell me more about it..."

Within two weeks, Darcy and I again found ourselves basking in the warm, Southern California sunshine. Geena asked us to meet her at a lovely little Pacific Palisades café for lunch. We got there plenty early and scoped out a quiet outdoor table in the corner under the shade of a tall palm tree. What a treat to be outside, sitting in the warm sunshine in early November!

"The Palisades," as it is known by the locals, is a beautiful, affluent bedroom community perched high on the cliffs of the Santa Monica Mountains in the northwest quadrant of Los Angeles. At the area's center is a charming, Mediterranean-style village full of quaint shops and excellent restaurants, along with the usual upscale suburban amenities. The famous Sunset Boulevard runs directly through the center of the village as it winds its way down to the beaches of the Pacific Coast highway below. Multimillion-dollar estates dot the western facing hillside, taking full advantage of the calm, cool sea breezes and stunning Pacific Ocean views. It was easy to see why a movie star, especially one with a family, would choose this happy area for her home.

When Geena Davis enters a room, everybody notices. It's not just that she's famous. It's not just that she's gorgeous. It's not just that she's poised and carries herself as if she's in complete command of herself and her life. Geena Davis is also really, really *tall*. Even in flats, she's over six feet!

Darcy and I are both only five foot three. We didn't stand up. What would be the point?

"Hi, I'm Geena. Great to meet you guys."

She immediately made us feel like we were just sitting around, hanging out with one of our best girlfriends. Clad in soft, simple jeans and a cotton sweatshirt, no makeup, and no pretensions, she chatted, laughed, and munched on fresh green salad and designer pizza with us like we were pals. Maybe it was the whole "mole on the face" connection?

"Who were your early mentors, or people who influenced you?" Darcy began.

"Wow, I grew up in a town so small and plain it could have been Amish. Nobody in my family had *ever* been anywhere on a plane. The only movies we watched were from Disney," Geena answered in between bites. "It was my aunt Gloria whom I looked up to. She had lived in Boston. She wore real suits with a flouncy skirt and said things like, *'Let's go scuba diving! The coast of Portugal is very nice this time of year.'*

"In my world that was like saying we'd go to another planet. My aunt was the only one who understood that I wanted to act, and she encouraged me. She took me to my first play. It was a dinner theater show in Framingham, Massachusetts. Dinner theater now is considered kind of tacky. But back then I thought it was so glamorous! You could eat *and* watch a show. Aunt Gloria ordered a glass of wine. I thought that was so sophisticated because I had never seen anyone drink any alcohol before.

"I signed up to be an exchange student junior year in high school because I just wanted to go somewhere else and be someone else. When I got selected to go to Sweden I thought, *great!*, until the minute they closed the door on the airplane and I saw my parents looking forlornly through the window of the terminal. Suddenly it hit me I wouldn't see them again—or anyone else I knew—for one whole year. I'd never been anywhere, and now I was going someplace where I didn't know anyone and I couldn't even speak the language. I was terrified. It was hard at first, but I learned Swedish quickly."

Switching to our main topic, Darcy asked, "How do you define leadership?"

"Oh, that's tough." There was a long pause. Our genius IQ companion seemed to be stumped by the question.

"She chewed and thought," Geena said, mocking herself.

"What does leadership mean to you personally?" I asked to give her a helpful jog. "As the head of your own Institute on Gender in the Media, what qualities do you draw on to make a difference?"

"Oh, you meant me? As a leader?" Geena seemed genuinely surprised to think of herself as a leader.

The United Nations had no problem seeing her as a leader. Amy Pascal, the head of Columbia Pictures and Sony Entertainment, had all but insisted that we include Geena in our book because her groundbreaking research and creative leadership was having a tremendous impact on what is understood about gender images in media. There was no question this talented woman had leadership in her blood.

"I didn't really start out trying to lead anything," Geena said, poking the air with her spoon. "But being in the movie *Thelma & Louise* changed everything. Up until then, I'd made some unusual career choices like *Beetlejuice* and *The Fly* and *Earth Girls Are Easy* just because I wanted to do unique kinds of parts—not just the girlfriend or the wife. I was selfishly, for my own amusement, picking parts that would give me something to do that was challenging.

"*Thelma & Louise* was a whole different experience. When we were making it, nobody had any idea what would happen when it came out. It was a very low-budget movie, so we just hoped someone would show up to watch it and that they wouldn't hate it when we drove off the cliff.

"From the opening weekend it was like night and day as far as the people recognizing me in the supermarket or on the street. Before, they'd say, *'Do I know you?'* or *'I liked* The Accidental Tourist.'

"But afterward, women would get in my face, grab me by the lapels, and say, *'Oh, my God! You have no idea. That movie! Oh, my God!'* Every woman would tell me all about her experience in watching it and what it meant to her. It was a huge lesson for me. I had never seen anything like it before. Their reaction to it, their feelings, and their excitement taught me about the power of media images. It also made me realize how few opportunities women have to react that way to a movie—to feel exhilarated and empowered; to be cheering and get excited."

"Yeah," I said, leaning forward to share her emotion, "I was definitely cheering when you blew up that oil tanker!"

"Yeah!" said Geena with a grin so big that made me think she really would enjoy blowing up a tanker.

"Oh, yeah, I loved that, too," chimed in Darcy with the kind of enthusiasm that proved the movie still worked its magic with a whole new generation.

"I know. I know," said Geena, beaming. "So ever since then, I chose parts differently. I still wanted roles that were interesting and had something challenging for me to do, but now I had in the back of my head: women are going to see this. I wanted women to be able to react or get something for themselves from it. What are women seeing in this character when I play it? It wasn't just about being a role model. In *Thelma & Louise* I was certainly not a role model."

We all laughed really hard over the idea of Thelma and Louise as role models.

"Well, what don't we do in that movie?" said Geena, the comedienne. "Sex with strangers, driving drunk . . ."

"Armed robbery," I interjected.

Geena ticked off on her fingers the sins of Thelma and Louise: "Armed robbery, killing ourselves, killing someone else . . ."

"You have quite a laundry list."

"Yeah, yeah, but the ultimate effect was empowering. It really colored everything after that. I became hyper-aware of women's portrayals in the movies. After that, my work and my life experiences informed the kind of issues that I got involved in.

"For example, after I did *A League of Their Own*—that was when I became a trustee of the Women's Sports Foundation. It was such an eye-opening experience to learn about baseball because I hadn't really played sports as a kid at all. Even though we only played 'movie baseball,' I still gained a new respect for myself and felt better about my body. I realized how important sports are and the importance of Title IX. I joined the WSF because I wanted to help girls realize when they're kids what I didn't learn until age thirty-five. It wasn't that I wanted to lead something. But suddenly, because I had a lot of public goodwill, I wanted to spend that capital on causes that I care about."

"So you're an accidental tourist in the land of leadership?" I quipped.

She laughed and continued, "The same thing happened when I did *Commander in Chief*," she said, alluding to her TV show where she played the first woman President of the United States. "I ended up getting involved. Have you ever heard of the White House Project? It was founded over a decade ago and their slogan is: 'Add women, change everything.' They work on many fronts to increase the number of women leading in all sectors of the economy.

"The White House Project had been lobbying for years to get somebody to make a movie or a TV show with a woman as the president—they know that what people see matters. So they were very excited when I got to play the Commander in Chief. Meeting them and learning about the organization made me realize that everything I really care about has adding women as the goal. So now I serve on their board. *Earth Girls Are Easy*, on the other hand, didn't spur me on to any pro-social action—"

We were still laughing when our waitress with that bright, scrubbed So Cal cheeriness I always find refreshing, asked, "Cappuccino? Coffee? Latte?"

"Sure," said Darcy, "Cappuccino with extra foam, whipped cream, and a cherry on top." Her order captured exactly how I felt about our gabfest with Geena. This was a whipped-cream-with-a-cherry-on-top kind of day.

Geena continued to tell us about the White House Project. "In the political arena, now, they focus on finding women at the grassroots level and encouraging them to run for office. They found that women tend to run if you ask them to. Men will usually nominate themselves. Their first reaction is *'I'd be great.'* Women tend to think *'I can't do it,'* so you have to encourage them."

"One of my best friends from college just got elected to Congress," I shared proudly. "Terri Sewell is the first woman to represent Alabama on the federal level. Not just the first African-American woman, but the first woman at all."

"Wee! That's good," said Geena.

"Sad that's she's the first woman," I said, "but good that she's the first woman."

"Why do we have to keep having firsts?" she said. "It's ridiculous that we would have the first woman anything in the twenty-first century. Unbelievable. Anyway, but here we are. A lot of people think that women leaders are everywhere now so we don't have to push for equality anymore. That's why the White House Project did a major benchmarking study to determine where women really stand in leadership positions across ten sectors of society. What they found is that women have stagnated at eighteen percent on average across the board for years, and in many areas, women leaders are an even smaller percentage. Why eighteen percent—isn't that bizarre?

"Some of the research I've read says that getting to one-third women makes a big difference. For example, if there are only one or two women on a board of directors, they get treated as the women in the room. Once you get up to a third, gender becomes less salient. They get treated more equally and as individuals, not representatives of the female species. They move from 'gender' to 'agenda.' Things that used to be considered women's issues become everyone's issue.

"We need to make a big jump forward—gradual progress is not working. Do you know that if women continued to be added to Congress at the rate they have been, we would achieve parity in five hundred years? If female characters were added to family films at the rate they have been, we'd achieve parity in seven hundred years. Waiting for things to get better isn't working."

As our coffees arrived, I brought the conversation around to her organization. "You mentioned in your speech at the UN that you were watching TV and movies with your two-year-old daughter and started to see big problems in the way women and girls were being treated in programming for kids. How did that lead to creating the Geena Davis Institute?"

"When I first talked to my friends at the studios about how few women and girls appeared in shows and how stereotyped they were, most of them simply didn't believe it. They thought all that had been fixed at some point. I figured that I needed research and hard data to prove what I knew from watching the screen.

"I got ten of my girlfriends together, and we formed a committee to put on a fund-raiser luncheon. In the end we got four hundred women to come—everybody used their connections and got people to believe in this thing when we didn't even know whether it would work. With a live auction and a silent auction we actually raised enough money to fund two huge studies in partnership with the Annenberg School for Communication at USC. Once we had the proof, it was like night and day in terms of getting influential people to listen.

"So the next thing was getting the nonprofit started. I got advice from people I knew at the Women Sports Foundation. It took a while to get all the paperwork done, but it's worth it. Having an institute is better than just saying 'Geena wants to talk to you about something.' We keep the research going and monitor whether anything has changed. We have very high-level meetings with the studios, and they all come out to join us when we announce new findings. Over three hundred people attended the last symposium we hosted."

"I have another question on that—" I began before Darcy cut me off.

"Oh, hey. No, no, no," Darcy looked at me sideways. She'd been trying to get in a question for a while and I wasn't picking up on her nonverbal cues. I was amused by her comfort and forcefulness. She was really getting the hang of interviewing!

"I'd like to get more of an idea of what your leadership style is like. What would you say are your core values?"

Geena thought for a moment. "I would say my approach is to be collaborative. I want to present myself as a partner and use encouragement as a tool rather than berating or hitting people over the head with the issues. The institute never calls out a particular movie or a particular studio. The message is that *'I'm in the industry; I'm on your side. I work with you guys all the time; here's something I know; and how can I be part of addressing this?'*

"I get a lot of comments from people that they like that style—it's not threatening. Every studio we've ever been to said: *'Please come back.'* Some of them we have been to three and four times, so it says to me that the message is getting through.

"Humor, I am told, is part of what works well for me. At the last Sundance Film Festival I spoke about our research, and afterward quite a few women came up and said, *'You have a really winning kind of style. You put humor in there and it really works.'* I didn't invent this approach, but I guess most people talking about women in the media come off as angry. My style is more collaborative and lighthearted. But it works."

I jumped back in with my next question. "I'm wondering if you could wave a magic wand, where would you like the institute to go? What's next?"

"We will definitely continue our research. The main goal is being able to measure a change, an actual increase in women shown in children's shows. The institute is also starting to work on the behind-the-scenes side. There is a direct correlation between the number of women who end up on the screen and the number of women who are directors, producers, editors, camera people, etcetera. Another area that I am interested in is school textbooks."

Darcy let loose an emphatic groan. "It's so lame!" my proud high school student protested, "when they try to jam women into the stories in my American history books, it's so deliberate and contrived. Then there's English. This year, all of the books assigned—all year—were written by men. My teacher assigned only one short story by a woman. That's all. So I brought it up with my friends in the class, and they pointed it out to our teacher. He just said, *'Well, I like to teach the books I'm passionate about. Besides, most of the classics are written by men.'* I really like my English teacher, but what about Jane Austen, Charlotte Brontë, George Sands…"

"That's nuts!" Geena concurred, a bit wound up, too.

"He couldn't find one book written by a woman?" I added. "That's sad."

"Do you want a cupcake for dessert?" It was just as well that the waitress interrupted our group rant. It could have gone on for hours.

"Are they known for their cupcakes here?" I asked Geena.

"Oh, they're really good," my new gal-pal promised.

"I'm just so full from all of that pizza," moaned Darcy. "I don't know if I can do it."

"I'm going to have a cupcake!" said Geena.

"I'll just bring out the tray," obliged the waitress. Nobody argued.

Darcy asked Geena how she has balanced work and family life.

"I always feel very privileged because actors can bring their kids to the set. It's completely unfair because the second assistant director or the dolly grip can't bring their kids to the set. But the actors can—if you're high enough up on the call sheet. It works partly because there's so much downtime while things are set up.

"When I was doing *Commander in Chief*, my boys were one year old and my daughter was three. I was working fourteen-hour days, but the nanny could bring them to be with me for a good part of that time every day. I'm lucky that I've really been able to balance things pretty well. If you're the chairman of a board you can't have your kids run around under the table while you're having your meeting. For actors, it's not as bad as people think."

The tray arrived with cupcakes in a rainbow of colors. The waitress leaned in and pointed out the flavors.

"Red velvet, coconut, Oreo, mocha, chocolate, vanilla..."

"I'm having the green one." Geena dived in.

"Let's split the coconut and red velvet," I suggested to Darcy so I could taste both.

"Will you encourage your daughter differently than your sons, when it comes to leadership?" asked Darcy, keeping us cupcake mongers on track.

"I want my sons to be aware of the issues, and to care about them, as much as my daughter," said Geena without hesitation. "I'm trying to raise all of them to be champions of women. They are being raised to see that what affects women is important. They know that Mommy cares about it, Daddy cares about it, and we do things about it. My husband was the one who insisted that Alizeh go to the UN meeting with me. He wanted her to see me making a difference for women."

"With all the challenges and negative programming, how do we encourage young girls to seek more leadership opportunities?" Darcy asked, not letting go of the upper hand in the questioning.

"It's like what we said earlier about political candidates. If you ask women, they'll run for office. I think if you ask teen girls to step up, if you explain to them and point out the limitations that society is trying to put on them, they will be more likely to rise above it and seek to break that stereotype."

We continued to munch cupcakes until we all wound down in a fog of post-feast bliss.

As I looked across the table into Geena's eyes, I knew in my soul this was a woman whose strength, intelligence, and courage could inspire anyone to follow her anywhere. Even off a cliff.

Good thing they don't rent '66 T-bird convertibles in the Palisades . . .

CHAPTER 13

Noemi Ocana

*Nicaraguan Director of Microfinance Loans
for Opportunity International*

The cane-backed chairs of the tranquil outdoor café in downtown Granada reminded me of Mexican bistros we visited when I was a kid growing up in San Diego. But these furnishings were much nicer, with ornately carved spines and comfortable, burgundy-covered cushions that made us want to lounge around there all day. The rich, dark Central American espresso was just what we needed after our long flight to this land just north of the equator.

Darcy and I had just arrived in Nicaragua for the next episode in our mother-daughter expedition. It was Thanksgiving break, so the tropical air was a delightful change from back home where the autumn chill was in full swing.

We gazed around the central village, soaking up the ambiance of a country so far from our own. Darcy's eyes went wide as tortillas as they fell upon the exquisite pastel pinks, yellows, and blues so prominent in the town's ancient architecture. Horse-drawn carriages still provide some of the local traffic in Granada, so if you close your eyes, you can transport yourself back in time with the *clomp-clomp-clomp* of hooves dropping slowly onto cobblestones—just as their ancestors did to ferry the Spanish conquerors of this region over five hundred years ago.

Nicaragua delivered on all the promises of foreign travel: vibrant colors, ethnic markets, spicy smells, appealing textures, and conversations in strange, exciting accents. Walking through the main square, our ears were tickled by the trill of handmade flutes calling like exotic birds. On the surface, everything about this charming town pulled you into its piquant embrace.

Yet, there was another side to it. If we hadn't done any research into the history of battles and invasions—burning much of the city to the ground at one point—you could easily miss the layers of cracked paint, rebuilt areas of the city, and other souvenirs of enormous suffering. Similarly, since I was aware of the intense poverty (Nicaragua is the second poorest country in the Northern Hemisphere), I felt a pang knowing that the whistle trills were coming from young children, not in school, but instead carving and selling these and other trinkets to rich white tourists. Granada was a flavorful town, but peppered with stark realities.

Concerned about finding food Darcy was willing to eat in this part of the world, I was thrilled to see a restaurant with pizza on the menu. In this steamy climate, most places had pleasant outdoor chairs and tables where dinner was served so we grabbed a comfy corner for our al-fresco meal. Even this simple fare felt magical as we surveyed the easygoing community of people around us out and about in the warm evening air.

"Look at those little boys over there," Darcy said as she dove into the surprisingly tasty tomato pie.

"They're adorable!"

The boys smiled and waved at us when we looked at them. We waved back.

I couldn't finish the whole pizza, so I decided to wrap it up and take it home for a late-night snack like I always do. As we left the restaurant and began to cross the central square, I happily looked forward to some mother-daughter bonding time over a movie we could watch on her computer. At 8:30 p.m., lots of people were still strolling, sitting, eating, and chatting outside—I felt comfortable and upbeat even though I was in a strange place.

In front of us I saw the same boys we had waved to earlier. One of them, a skinny eight- or nine-year-old, walked straight up to my mom and pointed at the bag with our leftover pieces of pizza. It was obvious what he wanted.

My instinctual reaction was, *"No! Don't take away my vision of a pizza-film evening."* But it only took a second to realize I did want to give the food to this hungry kid in front of me. He must have been waiting outside the restaurant hoping we wouldn't eat it all. Mom was already handing him the bag when the second barefoot boy stepped up and said, *"Para dos?"*

Mom understood immediately and nodded, smiling, holding up two fingers to indicate, that yes, they could share the pizza between the two of them. But, as the other boy reached for the bag, the first little guy pulled it back, took off running, and disappeared around the fountain. The second boy pursued him, yelling. Funny how you don't have to understand Spanish to know he shouted: *"The lady said to share!"*

For a split second we chuckled at what looked like two cute young boys jostling each other for a soccer ball. Harsh realization, though, soon cut short our involuntary laughter: these were malnourished kids in the park asking strangers for food and *fighting* over it. That is serious. I stopped and let the weight of what we witnessed sink in. At that moment, I desperately wanted to buy more pizza for them, but they were already gone. Looking around at the numerous other urchins playing in the evening shadows, I knew that bringing out more pizza might just start a bigger fight. I felt hopeless as we trudged back to our room.

We were in Nicaragua to interview and job-shadow Noemi Ocana, the regional director for Opportunity International, and their Nicaragua microfinance initiative. Noemi oversees more than twelve hundred women clients and the programs that provide them with money, training, and support to develop their own small businesses. Opportunity International is a nonprofit corporation based in Chicago that has helped people in twenty countries around the world break the cycle of poverty by giving them the resources to create, own, and run successful, profitable businesses for themselves. Through programs that issue microfinance loans, encourage savings, finance insurance, and administer all sorts of other assistance, groups like this have supported effective and sustainable economic progress in developing nations for over thirty years. Particularly with regard to women-owned businesses, these resources have saved the lives of millions of people in distressed areas by giving them the hope, the strength, and the resilience to rise above their hardships and lead proud, fruitful lives.

Early the next morning, we met Racquelle, our contact person, guide, and translator from Opportunity International's office in Manaugua, Nicaragua's capital city. Racquelle told us it would be a two- to three-hour drive up the rough, craggy roads of the Mombacho Volcano to reach Noemi's village.

"I am proud to work for Opportunity International," she told us as we ventured up the steep hillside. "I am from the Western region of Nicaragua...there is even more poverty there. My mother struggled to get basic schooling for me, and then I earned a scholarship to study at college in the United States." Racquelle's lilting voice carried echoes of the Caribbean coast—an almost Jamaican melody. Her skin was a darker, more chocolate color compared to the milky caramel of most people in this area. She wore her hair in hundreds of tiny, long braids pulled back into a bountiful ponytail. Her maroon golf shirt was plain except for the OPPORTUNITY INTERNATIONAL logo emblazoned on the left side.

"Opportunity International," she explained, "was one of the first organizations to see the importance of lending money in developing countries and training people to start their own businesses. We are a Christian organization, so I love working for them because I can be open about my faith—I don't have to hide it at work."

As we continued to climb the treacherous hills, the roadways became more rural with every mile. Macadam streets gave way to single-lane, broken gravel surfaces, which eventually reduced down to hard-packed dirt and mud paths. Around every corner, the dense, tropical canopy fanned out for miles in every direction like a soft green blanket draped over the hillsides. Occasionally we'd pass through a small village—a ramshackle collection of flimsy looking dwellings, right along the road, packed next to each other so tightly their corrugated metal roofs seemed to connect into one, long, wavy strip of smudged, splotchy steel.

At one point, the road had been completely washed away in a recent storm. Our driver, Manny, picked his way one by one over rocks and deep, scary potholes that looked as though they would swallow up our minivan in its entirety. Even as we traveled along the edge of a series of incredibly steep cliffs, Manny seemed to take it in stride. But we were slopping around the interior like rag dolls on a bucking bronco.

I looked over at Darcy. Skin should not be that color green. "Are you okay?" I asked.

"I don't feel so good," she answered. "Maybe I should lie down."

"Umm, Racquelle?" I said, "let's stop the car for a minute."

Manny quickly found a rare flat spot between the boulders and pulled over. "C'mon honey," I said to Kermit the Frog, "let's walk a little; get some air." Darcy stepped gingerly out of the car, then immediately ran for the bushes. Doubled over into the thick brush, her body rejected its breakfast in heaving convulsions. I was at her side instantly letting her lean on me for support, yet a wave of helplessness settled over me. My child was sick in a third world country, on a dilapidated stretch of road, hours from any kind of medical help.

Racquelle came over to us with a bottle of water from her cooler and a paper towel. She was prepared. She wetted the paper towel for Darcy to wipe her face and gave her a cool drink.

"I'm okay," Darcy insisted bravely. "I'm okay."

But Mama knew she was far from okay. My baby looked woozy; her eyes were glazed over. Still, I reminded myself, Darcy often has trouble with carsickness. This wasn't the first time I had to stop and let her get some air on a long drive. Normally, it would pass after she got out of the car for a few minutes. Once we got to our destination, I reasoned, she'd be up and at 'em for the rest of the day.

Just then, she exploded with another shuddering blow. Wow. I didn't think she ate that much for breakfast...

After a while longer in the fresh mountain air, Darcy seemed to recover well enough to continue the journey. We sat her in the front passenger seat where she could hang her head out the window.

"Not far now," Racquelle said soothingly.

We'd risen mighty early so that we would arrive in time for Noemi's morning devotional with her staff. In a Christian organization, particularly in a part of the world where the majority of the population is Catholic, starting the day with morning prayers doesn't raise eyebrows the way it would in most American corporate environments. In addition, as a person of strong faith myself, I was excited to experience how this special woman blends her leadership with her faith. "I'm really looking forward to the morning devotional," I said to Racquelle. "Will we miss it?"

"Oh, no!" she replied with a smile, dismissing my concerns. "We're fine."

We arrived at Noemi's office—a low, cinder block building toward the end of a dusty dirt road. The façade was painted a soft pink with muted lime-green bars covering the windows that surrounded a small patio on the side. We went inside and passed an open area with several desks covered in files, loose papers, and the usual office paraphernalia, before heading down a hall to a meeting space large enough to fit the whole team.

Small and compact, yet with a presence that filled the entire room, Noemi wrote on a whiteboard in the middle of fourteen loan officers who sat in a wide circle around her. Compared to the pink walls on the outside of the building, this area was quite bland: off-white linoleum flooring complemented by light, putty-gray walls. Everyone sat in the kind of generic metal and plastic chairs you see in a public school library or classroom. There was no carpet, no decoration on the walls, and no color at all. Where glass windows would normally be, cinder blocks had been turned sideways to let in light and air. These concrete blocks, possibly the only interesting design element of the whole building, had unusual decorative patterns—not the traditional domino shape—evoking fans, florals, and seashells. This far south, direct connection with the elements is a blessing—as long as you like to be warm. No heating or air conditioning system was anywhere in sight. It was a clean, pleasant, but not particularly interesting space.

But we were not here for the architecture. The scene was transformed by the warmth and beauty of the women sitting around the room. These were Noemi's charges—the women Noemi trained to go out into the farms and villages in the area to disseminate the Opportunity International funds and resources. They all wore the uniform golf shirts with simple jeans and sneakers. Neither plain clothes nor colorless walls could dim the brightness of the *almas*—the souls—of these Hispanic women. Their powerful, colorful, Latina heritage seemed to be magnified by the austere background. Some were short, some tall. Some were thin; others more rounded with ample hips and bosoms. I love the energy that springs from being with any gathering of women, and I could feel something special about the spirit of this particular group of brown-skinned, dark-eyed, dark-haired mothers and daughters who spent their lives working tirelessly to uplift others.

We found seats and settled in to observe Noemi talking and writing on the board. Her lecture had been going on for quite a while and showed no signs of stopping. I leaned over to Racquelle and whispered, "We *did* miss the devotional."

Racquelle looked at me with brows furrowed. "What do you mean?" she whispered back. "This *is* the devotional."

I had assumed that a morning devotional would be a time of prayer or perhaps a reading from the Bible. Even with a brief commentary or discussion, I wouldn't expect it to last more than fifteen minutes or so. Between a struggle to recall my high school Spanish classes and the whispered translations from Racquelle, I began to understand the nature of this meeting. This was really a workshop for her team—much like leadership training sessions I had both participated in and delivered myself all across the United States. The topic was the importance of integrity and the consistent modeling of the values you want to impart. The only difference was that Noemi's seminar was entirely based on biblical principles.

Written across the top of the board was the following:

We are the body of Christ.

What do you do to feel God within you . . .

. . . at home? . . . at work?

. . . on the street? . . . when no one is looking?

Noemi led an engaging discussion about how we all can strive to be a better example and become a better person by improving ourselves everywhere; not just to earn a higher paycheck, but because we are children of God. Under each heading on the board she wrote examples volunteered by her team members. This "devotional" was not a precursor to the work . . . it *was* the work!

While I was happily soaking up these lessons in character and stretching my Spanish vocabulary to its limits, I didn't notice that Darcy was still feeling uncomfortable until I heard her lean over and whisper to Racquelle, with a hint of desperation, "Where is the bathroom?"

Montezuma had, once again, come for revenge.

When the meeting ended, Darcy still remained shut in el baño. I mingled with the loan officers and learned more about Noemi's background while I waited for my daughter to return.

"When I talk to my clients," a woman with long, wavy black hair told me, "they are so passionate about Noemi because they knew her when she sold seafood to tourists. They remember her catching the bus with a big bowl of fish on her head!"

She smiled and mimed walking with a giant basket perched atop her noggin.

"Noemi isn't just a branch manager with a desk job telling other people to try harder. She herself received a loan and built up her business. Her story inspires others to do the same."

A number of people also talked about how much they love their jobs; how they felt such joy from being able to make a difference for others. One woman put it this way:

"We are not just giving them economic help, we are creating social change. We teach them the desire to be better every day, just as Noemi instills it in us. We are agents of change."

Darcy finally emerged looking a bit tired, but with at least a little color back in her face. She actually smiled at us. Although the jet lag, carsickness, and unfamiliar food had rocked her boat with a perfect storm, Darcy seemed to be back in control of the helm.

Racquelle found a Sprite for her to drink, hoping to settle her stomach. "Are you hungry?" she asked.

"Oh, no!" The last thing Darcy wanted at the moment was food.

"Do you think you can get back in the car?" Racquelle asked her gently. "It's a short ride. We are going to follow one of the loan officers to meet with a trust group that they supervise. Noemi will come, too."

Darcy, trooper that she is, climbed aboard and took her seat up front next to Manny. Racquelle, Noemi, and I piled in the back of the van. As we drove, Noemi shared more about her life before Opportunity International. Racquelle translated for us as she spoke.

"I was very good in school," she told us. "I liked school a lot. I began selling fish when I was eleven or twelve so that I could pay the fees and not have to drop out. I had to watch my younger brothers and sisters, sell the fish, and do my homework, but it was worth it.

"I earned a technical degree by the time I was eighteen; then I got a job in the government doing bookkeeping and accounting. At twenty-one I married my husband, and our first son was born when I was twenty-three. Three more girls came after. I moved up in my job to become a manager. After fourteen years I was the second highest boss there."

"Wait," I said. "I thought you were selling fish when you got a loan from Opportunity International . . ." I had no idea that she was educated and so experienced as a manager.

"That was when I lost my government job—after fourteen years. The government changed and the economy went downward. There was no way to find another job. Suddenly I had no way to support my family. And my husband's job as a mechanic just wasn't enough. I couldn't believe it. All I could do was go back to selling fish like when I was a child."

As Racquelle gave me the English on this bit, I shook my head in disbelief. We always think that working hard and getting an education is the

universal panacea for poverty. Not so. In a country with so many political and economic ups and downs, even someone so highly skilled and
highly educated can be thrown back down to the bottom in an instant.

"Opportunity International invited me to join a Trust Circle, receive
training, and then get a small loan. With the loan I was able to buy
shrimp in addition to fish and increase my profits. Later I graduated to a
Solidarity Circle with only five women in it. The loan was a little bigger
and allowed me to buy a small freezer for my seafood.

"I was doing well enough, but then I was invited to train and become a
loan officer myself. I liked being in the leadership role again. Eventually,
I was chosen by the other loan officers to be the regional director."

Our bumpy burro of a van continued on to the next stop. We had
seen the powerful impact of Noemi's role as regional director in both
her teaching and in the numerous testaments to it, but I was excited to
be able to see one of her trainees in action as well. For most people back
in the USA, microfinancing is a check in the mail or the click of a button
beside a two-dimensional stock photo of a borrower online. It makes us
feel good for a moment to contribute, but soon we are off to our busy
lives and that moment fades away. But here a donation, that probably
reflects a sacrifice of only a couple of dinners in a favorite restaurant,
makes the difference between starvation and a full belly; between sickness and health; sometimes even between life and death.

The trust group we were about to visit was one of about sixty under
Noemi's jurisdiction. Meetings were held weekly with one of Noemi's
loan officers presiding. Each of the twenty or so women in the group
would arrive to pay their loan payment out of their weekly earnings and
then stay for the training sessions the officers presented.

As we approached, we could see that the meeting was being held in
a long, skinny, covered patio that resembled a baseball dugout—sunken
halfway into the ground so it stayed cool. Women lined the benches on
both sides of the shelter, leaving only a few feet to separate their knees.
Young children sat on most laps—adorable babies and toddlers patiently
biding their time as Mama's meeting carried on.

Again, the fashions were plain comfortable cottons, but the brightness and beauty behind the trappings shone through with a glorious light. These women were making something happen in their lives. They were earning a living and paying off their debts. They were not beggars. They were strong, proud entrepreneurs.

A folding card table at one end of the dugout displayed a logbook to record the payments. We'd missed the financial portion of the meeting; the group's loan officer was already in full swing with today's lesson on customer service.

"To sell more fish, jewelry, or anything, you must give good service. Who do you serve in your business?" the loan officer asked them. A chorus of Spanish voices answered her: *"El cliente!"*

The loan officer was good at getting them involved in the discussion. Members of the group shared their own customer service secrets of success.

"I try to make my food so tasty, people want more."

"Everything is served with love."

"I keep a positive attitude. I pray."

The loan officer used small role-playing games to teach good service habits. She stressed the importance of looking nice, wearing clean clothes, and even admonished them to make sure they take a shower before going to work. As we were in some pretty close quarters, I noticed some of the women needed this advice more than others.

Escucha dos veces y habla una was written on another poster that she pointed at.

"Listen twice and talk once," she told them. "Listen carefully to your customers and answer quickly as you can. Don't make them wait."

I was surprised by the extent of the training. The talk back home about microfinance usually emphasizes how a small loan can allow a family to start a business and change their lives; it is about giving money. But there is so much more going on down here. When life is already so hard, finding the courage to work a little harder and to hope a little more is not easy. I saw women with a tough subsistence life support one another, boost one another's confidence, and create a clear vision of what was possible.

I asked Racquelle whether Opportunity International loans always involved so much Christian training all over the world.

"Oh, no!" she was glad to explain. "We do whatever is appropriate in the places we go. There are even trust groups in Africa with Muslims, Jews, and Christians all working together. Here, the groups rely on Christian teaching because they want to."

We left the dugout, humbled by the power of women pulling together. Noemi wanted to show us a tortilla factory that had grown to several times its size—a real success story. It was like we were going downstream and seeing the effects of Noemi's leadership. She teaches the loan officers, they teach the entrepreneurs, and now we would see the impact on an actual family.

First, though, we stopped for lunch. Racquelle treated us to sandwiches she had packed in her cooler with chips and sodas. We parked the car alongside the road with the windows rolled down for a little breeze to relieve the hottest part of the day.

As most of us noshed (Darcy stuck to potato chips and Sprite) I asked Noemi, "What have you learned that is most important about being a leader?"

"A lot!" She laughed. "I learned how important it is to model good values. I work hard to teach others to take responsibility for themselves and for making their lives better. People need to do what they say they will do. Then they can accomplish anything.

"I have learned," she continued, "about developing the loan officers and other people who work in the office. Some you have to hold back; some you push forward. I have had to learn patience . . . and flexibility in different situations. Everyone reacts differently, especially in emotional situations. I listen carefully to them. The loan officers and the clients have taught me as much as I have taught them," she finished humbly. "Without them I can't do anything."

We packed up the remnants of our lunch and headed for our next stop. Darcy was looking much healthier and regaining her disposition as we arrived at the "tortilla factory." I expected a warehouse space and a sanitized kitchen—my Western, industrialized perspective—and was surprised to see that the production process took place in the backyard of the family's three-room house.

The entire "factory" existed outdoors on a hard-packed dirt floor. Everything was open-air, covered overhead with corrugated iron panels hung hurly-burly from poles and trees, and attached precariously to the house. The sales counter area, where a long line formed in the morning for fresh tortillas, had a roof of loose palm branches, giving it a more festive air. Chickens clucked around our feet, running wild and chasing each other through the yard. The whole family pitched in— Mom, Dad, Grandma, all the kids—making tortillas was a real family affair.

As we entered the small space for a tour, I had to step sideways to avoid a five-year-old girl carrying a baby so big his head towered over hers. Still staring at the adorable pair, my prosthetic foot stepped on a cat that hissed its displeasure, causing me to jump back—which startled a chicken, sending it flying up in my face squawking and flapping at me. The girl rushed her baby brother to safety as my arms flailed and threw my entire body off balance. Nice entrance.

Our hostess, the entrepreneur, steered me out of the center of things and put me in a corner, probably in hopes that I wouldn't cause any more commotion. Racquelle and several other adults who weren't immediately on task gathered around me sociably. We all had a good laugh as the family continued their tag-team production process.

"Darcy," said Racquelle after a few minutes, "you better make yourself useful."

Darcy happily joined the other kids at the table—some older than she, some younger—and began pounding out tortillas. New at this, Darcy seemed to take eons to make her first, ugly, misshapen circle while a young girl who was only just tall enough to reach over the table could pound out the dough with firm whacks and precise shaping to create a perfect new tortilla every thirty seconds.

A continuous thumping sound of dough being smacked and whacked into submission throbbed in the background all day long—like the heartbeat of this ultra-low-tech food factory. When one family member tired and moved away, another would slip in and take their place to hammer out the product.

Once a perfect pancake was produced, whoever was closest reached back and placed it on the steel plate over the wood fire. Flames licked at the bottom of the griddle, heating the metal to the perfect temperature for toasting the dough lightly on each side. The smell of the burning wood and the roasting corn-meal batter was irresistible.

I bought the deformed tortillas that Darcy made. We could eat them quickly, I thought, and thereby protect the reputation of the family business from her irregular output. Folding the warm, fresh tortillas in our hands and popping them in our mouths was a fantastic taste experience. The plastic-wrapped slabs we have in the grocery store at home couldn't even remotely compare. We were on a whole other planet tortilla-wise!

"How many tortillas were being produced before the loan?" I had Racquelle ask them.

"Only a few hundred a week," she reported back. "They used the loan to stock up on wood and get through the rainy season." Without any irony she added, "With the loan, they have more raw materials so they can make more dough every day."

Now, with the help of Noemi, her team, and the generous donors of Opportunity International, this family-powered assembly line produces hundreds of perfect, fresh, ready-to-eat tortillas every day.

Our last stop was to drop by Noemi's house and meet two of her daughters—teens about Darcy's age. As the heat of the day began to ease off, Noemi, her girls, Racquelle, Darcy, and I sat on the back porch to talk. Some of us had chairs; some just sat on the stairs at the back of the house.

"What do you admire about your mother?" Darcy asked the girls.

As Racquelle translated, Maia, the oldest, immediately began to choke up.

"My mom developed the courage that makes her greater and greater," she said with difficulty, fighting back her tears. Her high regard for her mother was profoundly emotional.

"To become a leader you need to grow as a person and reach a stage where you can make your own decisions and reach your goals."

"Does your mom ever spend less time being a mom because she is a busy leader?" Darcy asked.

The daughters looked at each other and laughed. "It isn't always that way, but there are times when it's *work, work, work*! When that happens, she tries to control us from afar. Through neighbors, family . . ."

"They are girls," Noemi said in explanation. "I need to have them controlled."

"Ain't that the truth," I let myself say in motherly unison with Noemi. "And, your girls are so beautiful! You certainly have your hands full keeping them on the straight and narrow."

We all laughed. Some things cross all cultural barriers!

Noemi continued to talk about work-life balance. "You have responsibilities on both sides, but they are different. My daughter, Maia, helps when I am not around. The struggle for me is to find the moments to spend with family. Sometimes I come home, but I am just too tired and want to rest. They would like us to be all together and talking. It is hard, but God gives us the strength."

After a full day, we were fading as fast as the daylight. On the way down the mountain, exhausted and overwhelmed by our experiences, Racquelle told us one more story. "A woman came to her trust group meeting and explained that she could not pay her loan payment because her husband had taken all her money and went drinking at the bar.

"En masse, the group of women marched into town to knock some sense into this worthless man. He tried to sneak out the back when he saw what was coming, but they already had both doors covered! They formed an angry circle around him and demanded the money back.

"'I only took what was mine,' he said, laughing and breathing his boozy breath in their faces. Traditionally in this Latin, male-dominated culture, whatever the wife earns is automatically the property of her husband.

"'Oh, no!' their leader shot back. 'What you took did not belong to your wife. It belongs to us!' Since they receive their loans as a collective, there is a collective responsibility to repay.

"I am not exactly sure what happened next," Racquelle said, capping off our day perfectly, "but I know they got their money back and none of the husbands ever bothered any of them again."

For more information, or to make a donation to Opportunity International, please go to: www.opportunity.org.

CHAPTER 14

———————

Eileen Fisher

Fashion Designer
CEO and Founder, Eileen Fisher, Inc.

A light snow descended onto the vast span of the Tappan Zee Bridge as we crossed the Hudson River into Westchester County on a crisp, early February morning. Darcy and I were on our way to visit the home of CEO and fashion designer, Eileen Fisher. Eileen periodically holds special meetings at her house where she brings together the leaders of each division of her company—retail, design, logistics, human resources, and so forth. What an honor, I thought to myself, to be a guest in her home and to meet the senior leaders of the Eileen Fisher empire. Despite the economic downturn, the fifty Eileen Fisher retail stores from Madison Avenue to Nob Hill continued to do a brisk business catering to fashion-conscious women in their forties, fifties, and beyond.

I turned to steal a sideways look at Darcy in the passenger seat and furrowed my brow reflexively. These days my daughter seemed increasingly wrapped up in the vicissitudes of what passes for teen style. Over the holiday break, she decided she was bored with her semiblond tresses, so she took her birthday money and dyed her hair a deep, dark chestnut. Next, she asked Santa for nothing but ear-piercings: three more holes and enough bling to trim herself like a Christmas tree. She now wore full makeup every day and dieted herself down even further to a size zero to squeeze into the skinniest of skinny jeans. All of this was carefully designed to transform her into a much cooler high schooler. I reflected back to where we were when the book project began—it was as if someone had hit the fast-forward button and aged my daughter several years over the course of eight months. I hoped that meeting women like Ms.

Fisher would be a counterweight to the intense peer pressure she was experiencing, but the scales too often seemed tilted the wrong way.

> I glanced at Mom and felt happy to be on the road with her today. Eileen Fisher interested me because, although she was a successful CEO, she seemed to run her company in a refreshingly different way. From the research we had done, she seemed to have unconventional ideas and creative ways of leading people. Her organization functioned well without the blandness and restrictions I associated with the traditional corporate world. I didn't think I would ever want to work in a place where I'd have to put on a boring suit every day and try to act just like everyone else. Although her clothes were not aimed at my demographic, I *was* curious to know more about Eileen's style…particularly her style of running a company.

I yanked my full attention back to the road as we pulled into Irvington, the eponymous town named for its most famous resident, Washington Irving, and his tales of decapitated horsemen and sleepy lawn-bowlers. Rooted in rich colonial history, this beautiful hamlet is situated a mere twenty miles north of Midtown Manhattan. The stunning riverside backdrop, charming Main Street, and dusting of white powdery snow recalled for me the Currier and Ives images I could only see on Christmas cards as a kid in San Diego.

I pointed our trusty Ford into a circular driveway at the dead end of one of Irvington's labyrinthine, colonial streets. I imagined Eileen's home would be furnished with expensive antiques, designer fabrics, imposing artwork, and the kind of odd, ridiculously expensive knickknacks that grace the pages of *Architectural Digest*. Since my only frame of reference for a chief of a fashion firm was Meryl Streep's depiction of *Vogue*'s Anna Wintour in the movie *The Devil Wears Prada*, I was a little apprehensive about how things would go. We stepped out of the car, carefully shook off the snow collected on our shoes, rang the doorbell, and braced ourselves to enter the design maven's domain.

Keri, Eileen's public relations person who coordinated our visit, opened the door and showed us down the hall to the large room where the meeting would take place.

I was shocked to see the hallway was bare as a Zen monastery, painted with neutral tones, and without a single picture on the soothing walls. My breath deepened and slowed as a sense of genuine tranquility wrapped around my shoulders and warmed my winter chill like a cashmere blanket. Even if I hadn't seen a row of shoes on the floor, I would have felt the urge to take mine off—like you know you should in a mosque or temple. This felt like a peaceful, almost sacred place. We proceeded barefoot into a wide-open meeting room.

Two of the four walls were large paned windows that revealed a breathtaking, 180-degree Hudson Valley vista just beyond the glass. The water appeared to be more like a lake than a river, expanding before our eyes to the tiny houses dotting the opposite banks miles away. A large swath of blue sky filled the upper portion of this landscape, adding its brilliant hue to the glistening scene. The whole space seemed to be one with nature.

Along the windowed walls were long, comfortable benches covered in ample bright-white cushions and punctuated with soft pillows of various sizes. Far from the intimidating seating arrangements I had envisioned, the effect was a cottony cloud that welcomed you to dive in and float away.

The opposite side of the room held a gigantic dining room table that could seat at least twenty people. It was the kind of sturdy piece you'd expect to see in an Amish farmhouse—massive enough for several generations to dine together "family style." The table rested on a plain hardwood floor; no carpet at all.

Eileen Fisher designs her clothes to make the woman the jewel, not the outfit. Every item in her stores features an uncluttered, solid color that blends with everything else in the line. The customer, then, can build interchangeable outfits that can be easily updated and enhanced. This concept flew directly in the face of almost every high-fashion clothier on the market. The whole purpose of haute couture, and those who worship it, is to create pressure to throw out last year's clothes by drawing attention to a "new" look every season. Yet, Eileen Fisher creates clothing that seems to never go out of style. A radical notion indeed.

Her house worked in the same way and expressed the same value system. Understated colors, simple furniture, and other friendly accoutrements were designed to celebrate the people inside and the nature surrounding them.

For this visit, I had chosen to wear some of my own favorite Eileen Fisher pieces—soft velvet pants, layered sweaters, and a wool scarf that gracefully looped twice around my neck. I knew my clothes wouldn't be uncomfortable during the drive or end up all wrinkled when I got out of the car like a typical business jacket and skirt would. This house was as easy to be in as my outfit.

Darcy loved the feel of the warm, friendly atmosphere. She fell into a conversation with the first person she met and disappeared around the corner with her new friend.

The enormous rectangular table would double nicely as a boardroom-type conference setting for the upcoming meeting, I imagined. Eileen would sit at the head of this great block of wood and preside with authority over each topic on the agenda. But as her staff trickled in, they immediately pulled the chairs away from the big table to form a circle in the large free space at the center of the room. Without any table in the middle, the circle felt open and casual. Wrapped in the soft sweater fabrics, chunky wool scarves, and lush leggings of their own line, everyone relaxed in the circle, some drawing over small occasional tables to hold their coffee, plates of berries, and scones from the kitchen.

I headed for the kitchen where the hot drinks and food were coming from. Focused on finding tea bags, milk, and strawberries, I didn't even notice that Eileen had come into the room until I looked up and saw her effortlessly chatting with Darcy.

> Eileen came up to me at the coffeepot and thanked me for being here! It was easy for her to guess who I was, I suppose. I looked around for my mom, nervous that I was here in Ms. Fisher's house

and I was the first one to talk to her. She wasn't putting out an energy that was domineering, though—just a strong and relaxed presence. She was cool. The small exchange of words we had intrigued me and got me excited for the rest of the meeting.

I greeted our hostess, thanked her for this wonderful opportunity, and we all three walked back to the great room together with our breakfast goodies.

Everything about this assembly was designed to refresh and reenergize the leaders of her company through a creative, free-form interchange of ideas. These quarterly sessions were organized to inspire the company's senior leaders to share, grow, and expand their thinking. Everyone was here to encourage and support each other into developing methods and strategies that would continue the trajectory of success and cooperation throughout the entire organization.

As we arrived in the main room, I noticed that people spoke to one another in the quiet, easy way old friends do when catching up. Even though the meeting was supposed to begin fifteen minutes before, there was no sense of urgency. "We don't start on time. It's not in our nature," someone leaned over to tell me.

After a bit, the room seemed to settle organically as if the universe signaled the time to begin had arrived. Everyone, including Eileen, had now gravitated to the circle. Darcy and I were seated just outside the loop, where we could see and hear everything. Even though we'd been invited to join in, I thought it better not to disturb the flow we were observing.

"Shall we?" Eileen said.

Peaceful nods and waves indicated mutual agreement.

In deference to Darcy and me, Eileen explained, "We always begin our meetings with a moment of silence." We'd read about this in articles—I couldn't wait to see it in practice.

She turned back to another woman in the circle and said, "Susan, would you lead us in a moment of silence? Do you feel like it?"

Susan nodded a peaceful assent and stepped up to a small table just inside the circle that held a Chinese brass bowl on a silk pillow. She smiled at everyone, picked up a short, thick wooden stick, and tapped once on the bowl. The vibrating-chime radiated a serene wave of sound so powerful I felt it deep in my bones. My breathing slowed once again. My nerves relaxed. I melted into the gentle stillness that seeped into the room like water flowing into every nook and cranny. I didn't want the feeling to end.

Too soon, a second tap on the gong released me from my meditation.

As my eyes opened, I felt as though we had all somehow become connected—as if we were one organism. The eleven heads, twenty-two arms, and twenty-one legs (think about it...) in the room seemed to merge together with an energy that transcended the physical nature of our beings and pervaded the proceedings with a mellifluous ease and purposefulness.

Eileen introduced Darcy and me to the group and then, to my surprise, said, "Would you say a few words about your project?"

Since I had greatly irritated Darcy many times by turning to her expectantly in situations like this, I had no intention today of tossing her unprepared into center stage. But before I could corral my wits and get a word out, my multipierced daughter rose to the occasion and wrested away the lead.

"My mom and I are writing a book together called *How Great Women Lead*," Darcy explained confidently. "Where we feature many different women like Hillary Clinton, Condoleezza Rice, an orchestra conductor, and a fighter pilot to show examples that inspire more women to see themselves as leaders. We are also weaving in our mother-daughter adventure to help get people interested in reading it like a story."

Not needing to add anything to this, I sat down at the same time she did, proud enough to pop. Darcy's ability—and desire—to take the lead was expanding each and every day.

In response, everyone introduced themselves to us and explained what they do in the organization. In their typical meeting, there is no need for this. Despite being spread across the country, they all know each other quite well. Most had been with the company for a decade or more.

By two-thirds of the way around the circle, I started to understand that the structure of their organization was like nothing I'd seen any-where in the hundreds of companies I've had a chance to visit over the course of my career. This was more like a forum for a cross-pollination of ideas than a corporate structure. Job titles included: People in Culture, Creative Liaison, Core Concept Team, and Connector.

By the time the introductions finished, I was thoroughly enamored with Eileen's leadership style—collegiality, gongs, and a hypercon-nected organizational chart. I watched for her to take charge now and run the meeting; I couldn't wait to hear what she had on the agenda.

Instead, one of the other group members leaned forward and said, "Okay, let's do the updates. What is going on for you personally and pro-fessionally? What is front burner in your area that the rest of us should know about? Who wants to start? Jackie?"

Eileen leaned over to me and whispered, "We like to keep it unstruc-tured so things just come up." This wasn't what I had expected at all.

As each person weighed in, the powerful simplicity of the meeting hit me. Every three months all the top decision makers in the company come together to increase their awareness of one another as human beings. In doing so, they all naturally touch on what their division is grappling with at this particular snapshot in time. They make interesting observations about trends in their customer base, competitors, technol-ogy, successes, failures—it all comes tumbling out.

By being aware of a recent death in the family for Murray, an upcom-ing surgery for Jane, or Beth's daughter heading to college in the fall, the whole group creates a closeness and interaction that would make it easier to pick up the phone on business issues, solve problems together, and get their people in sync once they got back to their day-to-day re-sponsibilities.

Though the meeting didn't cover pre-set topics, everyone left the room with a broad-based, truly "whole"-istic sensitivity about what was happening in other parts of the company. This senior leadership team with no conference table, meeting agenda, PowerPoint slides, flipcharts, or statistics was the most well-informed, effective group of business leaders I had ever seen!

At lunch, we collected plates and moved through the buffet line set up on the island block in the middle of the kitchen. Artistically arranged platters of mescaline greens, pasta salad with sundried tomatoes and olive oil, grilled vegetables drizzled with lemon juice, and lightly marinated sliced chicken breast offered a bountiful, healthy feast.

"What is that?" Darcy asked, pointing to something that looked like Picasso got hold of an onion ring.

"That's fried lotus root," explained Carol, who was overseeing the luncheon. "Try it."

I put several of the mangled, lightly breaded veggies on my plate and immediately took a bite. "This is good," I said as soon as I could with my mouth full.

Darcy looked skeptically at me and stuck to more familiar looking edibles.

As we sat down to eat with Eileen, we suddenly realized that she had hardly said ten words during the meeting. Now was our chance to finally get her point of view.

We had by now developed a tradition of starting off every one-on-one interview with Darcy asking the same question. We thought it was a great question, even though it tended to put people on the spot. It also gave notice to our interviewee that Darcy was not just here as window dressing. "How do you define leadership?" she asked our fashion-designer / CEO / hostess.

"Oh, goodness!" exclaimed Eileen with fervor. Then she laughed. "I don't usually define leadership, so that's a hard question. I just listen a lot." She continued, "That's really important for leadership—to watch, observe, and feel things. We can't do it all by ourselves. I'm confused by people who seem to have all the answers and direct people around. I love collaborative leadership. To me it's so interesting how many great ideas people have. I love the way people connect and the way people spark each other. So leadership is listening, caring about people, trying to help people find out what they're good at, and trying to get the right people in the right places.

"We consciously work toward creating connections, because it's through these interactions that the wonderful things happen. Like in the meeting today, we learned that the ten percent discount on our last-season basic pieces was undercutting the sales of this season's foundation pieces. If we weren't partnering across departments you wouldn't find that out. You know, there are so many examples of the critical nature of interconnectivity.

"It's the magic, letting the creative process filter in. We all think we're supposed to come to meetings with an agenda and have all the answers on PowerPoint slides. But I think it better to come, step into the conversation, and then see what magic comes out of that.

"I think women naturally lead differently because we feel the importance of harmony and connection. Women are more feelings oriented, more intuitive, and more family oriented by nature, I believe. Men are more task oriented. As someone explained it to me, men grew up playing baseball and sports much more than women, and so they are used to taking their place on the team playing their position. Women just do what has to be done.

"Men seem to feel like they're supposed to have the answers and supposed to be right all the time. It's just a thing. It must be a lot of pressure for them, too. I think my dad felt that way. He was supposed to know the answers, and he didn't always."

"So," Darcy asked, "what are your core values?"

"Oh, goodness!" said Eileen again. "Hmm. Company values? My own?"

She paused, thinking hard. We looked at her long, straight, gray-highlighted hair. We had to draw her out and be patient. She seemed to be a much more introverted person than many other women leaders we'd met.

She decided what to focus on and continued. "I'll talk about the minute of silence; that's where my thoughts went first because that's very personal for me. We do it almost everywhere in the company, at all different meetings . . . sometimes three minutes of silence, sometimes different things like breathing exercises. I'm a big believer in the energy of the group and being open to the inspiration that is coming to us.

"If we come with too much to say and too many preconceived ideas, without getting quiet, then sometimes there's so much clutter in the room we can't be open to what is happening in the moment. We miss the opportunity. It feels like things get clearer by stopping. So that's my personal value. I encourage others to make space so that we make better choices, deeper choices, right choices. Personally, I also want to make space, to be able to think, and to make conscious choices about what I'm doing with my own time."

"What shaped your leadership style?" I asked. "It's so unique . . . As you grew, did you organize the structure of the company differently from others on purpose?"

"No," she laughed. "We pretty much stumbled through it and into it. For the most part there's a sort of organic nature. Like a beehive, it has a very self-organizing concept about it. At the same time there's a guiding force.

"I just did what came naturally to me. I never really worked for other corporations, so I didn't know what it was supposed to be like. We didn't fit into any pre-prescribed idea of what a clothing company should be because we didn't know. I did it my way, which was to talk to people, explain the ideas, and try to communicate the big picture so people can think for themselves. I like it when people light up and get excited about what they're doing. I notice that."

"I felt like the language everybody was speaking during the meeting here was completely different from anything I usually see in corporate America," I told Eileen. "I wrote down certain phrases people used like: *'I want to be in on that thinking.'* Instead of a regular job description, people said things like *'I am here to hold that space or hold that value in the company.'* "

"Yeah," said Darcy. "We kept hearing that people carve their own paths, shape their jobs, and create their own goals. And they are passionate about the philosophy behind the clothing—helping women feel comfortable and beautiful at any age; creating clothes that last, complement each other, and don't go out of style."

"It's not like the old days where the leader is directing with a bunch of little doers," Eileen said. "Now we need much more creativity all the way through everything, much more leadership on many levels. In a company like ours there's room for everyone to lead from time to time, whether it's a taskforce, a solo project, the community service aspect of the company, or just within their department. People pick up and lead different things depending on who they are. As a leader, I help others find out who they are so that they can find their own leadership role. The more leaders we have in the company, the more potential the company has to grow.

"At the same time, I don't want to make it sound like everything was always smooth sailing. About ten years ago, we were growing so fast and getting so big, we reached a point where some people were feeling disconnected, like they weren't seen. A number of people were uncomfortable with how the company was being run and wanted more clarity. Susan, who you met earlier, brought in these consultants to research how we were organized and rethink it. We needed to be more conscious about our structure at that point. We've had them back from time to time to re-energize and renew the engagement of individuals by facilitating opportunities for people to contribute in creative ways. It's an ongoing process."

"What about work-life balance? Has that been a challenge for you?"

"First of all, my kids are my world. They are more important than anything else. No question," Eileen answered without hesitation. "I started the company before my son was born, so it's kind of like I have three kids: the company, a boy, and a girl. Now the company is twenty-six years old and doing well. It's the grown-up of the three. So it's easier to balance now than it was at the beginning."

"I see women all over the country," I said, "who have unconsciously absorbed the idea that if they go into leadership they will have so much more work that they can't balance their lives or have any time for the family. They don't want to take on any more responsibility."

"I didn't think of leadership as taking on more," said Eileen. "I thought of it as getting other people to help me with a project, getting my ideas out. Balance is actually easier at the leadership level—especially

having my own company. I think that's why so many women become entrepreneurs. You really can come and go as you want. And I try to model
that in the company. People feel that they can have flexibility to take care
of their family. Plenty of people don't work on Fridays or leave early
several days a week, things like that."

"Do you ever feel that people take advantage of that kind of freedom?
Go too far with it?" I asked.

"The truth is that the moms and dads are terribly responsible. People
are so appreciative that they work harder. They are the ones who will
work on the weekend if needed, take a project home, or be on the phone
for a conference call wherever they are. We want people to take care of
their private lives. Whether it's your kids, your parents, or your partner,
you have to be there for them.

"The work-life balance is also getting easier for me as I step aside
more and more. I'm starting to do more things with my personal time.
It's so great. I'm starting to cook. I feel like I'm getting my life back as
the company has gotten more independent. It's like your teenagers have
grown up and you have a lot more space."

I glanced at my own teenager and hoped that her process of leaving
the nest would provide me the kind of relaxation Eileen seemed to have.
Pretty hard to imagine, though . . .

CHAPTER 15

——— •·• ———

Cathy Sarubbi

Homemaker, Mother of Five

On this particularly chilly Saturday afternoon at the end of March, Darcy and I headed high up into the Catskill Mountains to reach a wellspring of hope, love, and laughter known as the Adaptive Sports Foundation at Windham (ASF). Tucked off in a private corner of the Windham Mountain ski area, up the hill to the left of the main lodge, this inspiring organization is one of the largest and most successful adaptive sports centers in the country.

For those of you unfamiliar with the term "adaptive sports," ASF is a place where people of all ages who live with a physical and / or mental disability—autism, amputation, CP, paralysis, visual impairments, and so forth—learn to enjoy a variety of sports using the latest techniques and technology designed to "adapt" to their particular challenge. And, if ASF doesn't have the equipment that works for a particular person's condition, they will build it right there on the spot. That means practically anyone can learn to ski.

I was first invited to speak at ASF several years ago. Darcy, Allen, and I immediately fell in love with the energy and spirit we encountered there. ASF is a kind of heaven: a place where selfishness, criticism, and prejudice just plain cease to exist. Our enthusiasm was so strong that we immediately signed up to participate. Allen became certified as an adaptive ski instructor, Darcy helped with the nursery and other tasks, and I worked with the race team and provided free inspirational and motivational presentations throughout the ski season.

After spending many days volunteering at ASF, I realized the tender, nurturing warmth that flows through every particle of this extraordinary place wasn't coming from the wood-burning fireplace, but rather from the hearts of the people who gather there. They are angels. Time and time again I've seen the most timid, tentative, or frightened people with challenges leave this magical place laughing, cheering, and pumping their fists toward the sky with the thrill of having moved their lives forward in a way they never thought possible.

We crossed the wheelchair-friendly threshold of the ASF lodge, an Alpine chalet with rough-hewn wooden gables that soften the three-story structure and blend beautifully into its snowy surroundings. Whereas ski lodges are usually vast, hectic arenas with masses of people clomping around in ski boots, fighting the lines in the cafeteria, renting skis, or browsing the latest equipment and fashions in the retail stores, the ASF lodge has an intimate, homey feel. Carpeted floors, big cushy sofas, upholstered chairs, and cozy colors welcomed us with an easy sense of calm and comfort. In the center of the ground floor great room is a huge hearth fashioned from local stone where a fire spits and crackles all day long. It felt like being invited into someone's rustic mountain home.

Darcy and I hiked up the wide staircase to a wood-paneled conference room on the top floor that fit snugly under one of the gabled rooftops. Cherisse Young, head honcho at ASF, smiled as we entered the room. Cherisse started at ASF back in the early days as an intern, working full-time right out of college, and rose to take over the helm from the group's founder in 2004. But we were not there to ask Cherisse about *her* experiences and advice on leadership, although she is a worthy role model for the book. We were here because Cherisse wanted to support another woman leader she greatly admired: the feisty, blond bundle of energy sitting beside her—Cathy Sarubbi.

At the beginning of our project, when Darcy and I asked a slew of friends to recommend women to include in our book, Cherisse was one of the first to respond by nominating Cathy, one of her volunteers at the ASF. Since we knew Cathy very well (and you can't help but know, and adore, Cathy if you ever spend any time at ASF), we absolutely agreed her story was well worth telling.

"Cherisse," I asked once the initial hugs were completed and our recorders were running, "tell us why you thought we should include Cathy among our great women leaders."

While Cherisse extolled her virtues, Cathy squirmed uncomfortably and looked down at her feet under the table.

"Well," Cherisse said, glancing with smiling eyes at her friend, "when you think of strong women, you immediately think of people like the Hillary Clintons of the world. But there are so many unsung women leaders out there like Cathy. What she does in one hour would totally exhaust me. When I nominated her, I had just given birth to my first child, Erin. I was completely overwhelmed with this one little baby—a perfectly healthy child. I compared myself to Cathy who, at age twenty-seven, gave birth to an infant with no eyelids and a host of other medical problems—requiring over fifty operations to just stay alive—and then she went on to have four more children!"

Caitlin Sarubbi, that miracle baby Cherisse described, survived her surgeries and, while legally blind, became a champion ski racer—she even qualified for the 2010 Paralympics in Vancouver, Canada, where she had represented the USA only a few weeks before this meeting. Caitie was also a student at Harvard University and had taken a year off to compete just like I did. I adore this amazing young woman and think of her a bit like my doppelganger.

"Often people are impressed by Cathy just because of the way she was able to overcome all the challenges with raising Caitie," Cherisse continued. "When you get to know her better, though, you realize Cathy's a great mom to *all* her kids, plus she does everything else for everybody else. Money is as tight as can be, but she's making food for the poor. She volunteers at four different schools. She visits elderly priests. She's constantly praying for a list of people. Here at ASF she runs the lunch program on the weekends in winter, she helps with the charity auction, and her kids volunteer all the time, too. She's always going and going.

"She leads a family, but she also leads her community just by living her life. She's not going to be the one to get up and speak in front a crowd. But she always has thirty people in tow behind her.

"We always joke about the 'Cathy Sarubbi train'—you want to be on it because you never know where it's going to take you, but you know it's going to be fun, you know it's going to be positive, and you know you just want to be a part of it. Some of the people in her wake *have* to be there because she gave birth to them, but the rest of us just *want* to be there."

Again, I agreed with Cherisse. Darcy and I had recently been on that Sarubbi train ourselves. When I was invited to go to the 2010 Paralympics Vancouver as part of President Obama's official White House delegation, I made sure to let Cathy know that Darcy and I were coming so we could see Caitie ski in the competition.

As soon as our plane landed in Vancouver, I had a dozen text messages from Cathy. Somehow, this homemaker from Brooklyn had scored a house—not a condo, mind you, a whole ski-in-ski-out *house*—right at the foot of the Whistler Mountain slopes where the slalom run was to be held. After a series of fits and starts in trying to get together, we finally decided to meet outside the BC Place Stadium and attend the opening ceremonies as part of the Sarubbi entourage.

The Paralympic Games always follow the Olympic Games and utilize the same venues. So, the skiers ski on the same slopes, the hockey players skate on the same ice, the athletes live in the same Olympic Village, and the opening ceremonies are held in the same massive arena, in this case BC Place, where the world tuned in to see the first torch blaze just weeks before.

As we looked out over the massive crowd, I was overwhelmed with how completely the Paralympic experience had changed since I competed in 1984. Back then we got a plane ticket, a hotel room shared with several other athletes, and a jacket. I remember skiing with mismatched gloves I got out of the lost and found because I didn't have the money to buy new ones. Friends and family attended the events only if they could get there on their own, and there was virtually no media coverage.

Now, sixty thousand people gathered into this enormous coliseum to cheer the crutches and wheelchairs of the finest athletes with disabilities in the world. Everywhere we turned we were imbued with all the color and pageantry of Olympic competition. The athletes were ferried around as celebrities—in full Paralympic regalia. The mascots, special events, and media coverage were top flight. This was a world-class event in every sense.

"Baaaannie! Daaaacy!" The high-pitched Brooklyn accent pierced the din. "Wee-ah ova heeah!" We looked toward the shout just in time to catch Cathy's unmistakable mane of blond hair as it rushed toward us with the rest of the Sarubbi train in tow. And this was no little commuter train. It was immediately apparent why the Sarubbi clan needed a whole house: Cathy, her husband John, the four kids who weren't competing in the games, Grandma, cousins, friends . . . I later heard there were thirty-two in all! But that number appeared tenfold as the whole gang descended upon us—like a *freight* train.

A flurry of hugs and kisses seemed to come from everywhere. Even from the people I never met before. Everybody becomes family on this railroad. But the train kept a-rollin'. Nobody stopped. The outpouring of welcoming affection came as a drive-by. In an instant, we were swept on board as the entire gang moved en masse toward the entry.

"What gate do we go into?" John yelled above the roar of the crowd.

"47A or 47B, it's not really clear from the map," came the answer from one of the older daughters, still moving forward.

This amoeba of humanity charged ahead—fast! Even Grandma, at the center of it all, was whisked along at a pace I could hardly keep up with.

As we turned a corner, Cathy suddenly started looking around with an anxious sense of urgency. "Where's Jon-Jon?" she screamed to anyone, and everyone. Her youngest son seemed to have disappeared from sight.

"What?" her husband yelled from the other end of the stampede.

"Jon-Jon," said one of the middle siblings.

"What?" Dad hollered again, still moving.

"We can't find Jon-Jon," came the clarification from another family member. It was hard to know who was who. At this volume, they all sounded the same.

"Jon-Jon's lost," echoed another.

"He better not be!"

I felt like I was caught up in a scene from one of the *Home Alone* movies.

"There he is!" another Sarubbi voice shouted.

And, there he was—all ten years of him—way ahead of us, dangling about fifteen feet off the ground. Jon-Jon decided he needed a better vantage point from which to help direct the family flow, so he had somehow scaled a light post and shimmied out to the end of one of its spars. Even at a distance, it was easy to recognize this little guy. He had dyed his hair red, white, and blue, and shaved the letters "USA" into his prickly buzz-cut. "C'mon everybody, our gate's over this way!" he screamed, and pointed from his crow's nest.

"Great! Everybody go this way!" Cathy ordered, taking Jon-Jon's directions with complete faith. The whole family ignored his acrobatics as if this sort of thing happens all the time. We plowed into the stadium and thoroughly enjoyed the rest of the evening.

That crazy day in Vancouver had been over a month ago, and I still felt the intense energy of the experience as I adjusted the position of the recorders on the ASF conference table. The pace of Cathy Sarubbi et al. is truly exhausting.

"Do you have a favorite Cathy Sarubbi quote or motto?" Darcy asked Cherisse.

"Let me say this," Cherisse answered. "Cathy is June Cleaver, St. Therese, and the girlfriend you want to be in jail next to after a night on the town . . . all rolled in one. That's my girl. She makes her kids say the Rosary in the car every day . . . and she's the last one dancing on the bar at the end of the night."

I totally agreed with her assessment, although I would add a dose of Fran Drescher's *The Nanny* to the mix. Cathy has the same in-your-face Brooklyn accent and take-no-prisoners attitude of Fran's caustic, but lovable, TV character. But none of these descriptions give you any clue that Cathy is also a beautiful, petite woman with a knockout figure— even after giving birth to five kids.

Finally turning our attention to Cathy herself, Darcy asked, "Were you always a stay-at-home mom?"

"Well, that's funny," Cathy said. "You see, I did have a big career. I had the glamorous dinners, the company parties, the jets . . . you know what

I mean. It was perfect, lots of socializing, PR, dealing with magazines, yadda, yadda, yadda. And right before Caitie was born I got a huge promotion into management.

"I might have given it all up and decided to stay at home right then, but there were so many doctor bills. I had great insurance at my job, and the specialists we needed didn't accept my husband's fire department insurance. Funny how things work out for a reason."

Cathy's husband is a firefighter in New York City. And, yes, he was there on September 11, 2001.

"Cathy, it had to be heartbreaking when you found out Caitie, your first child, was born with a severe physical disability," I asked. "Do you mind telling us about that?"

"I had three sonograms; it was a beautiful, planned pregnancy," said Cathy with a wistful look. "She was the first grandchild on my side, and the second on my husband's side. Everyone was so excited. All of a sudden Caitie comes out and the whole world changed. At first they wouldn't even let me see her, and they're rushing me to the operating room because I'm hemorrhaging all over. Poor Johnny was standing there by himself at two in the morning and the doctor told him, *'I don't know if I can save her.' 'The baby?'* asks John, distraught about his first child. *'No, your wife.'* I think the poor guy almost fainted. *'Do you have a priest? Better call a priest!'* they told him as I was pushed into the emergency room. At that time, no one really thought Caitie would live, either.

"I was so lucky that I had a woman doctor. If I had a male doctor, I think he would have done a total hysterectomy and just taken everything out to stop the bleeding. But this woman doctor, she fought for me because she didn't think Caitie was going to live. I think the reason I have four more children is because I had a female doctor with four children of her own. And of course Caitie did live.

"After all that, I had about three hours of pity for myself until this nurse who had been around the block a few times—this wise old Jamaican—came into my room. I'll never forget her. *'Okay, you finished with de cryin'?'* she said to me in that magnificent accent. *'Let's go den . . . you stop cryin' for your bebe and we move on with dis.'*

"And that was it. I haven't had a moment of pity since then. God has been good to us. For Caitie's condition, there were only nine cases in the world diagnosed. We used to go to these conferences where thirty doctors at once wanted to look at her. Other times, John and I would take whole days off work to spend in Manhattan seeing five or six doctors a day. For each of her surgeries, I would take off two or three days from work. My company was great about it. And my father-in-law became one of Caitie's major caregivers when John and I were at work. You know, you can't just leave a child with so many medical issues in a daycare center."

> I have to admit, when Mom insisted throughout the project that we include a stay-at-home mother among our great women, I was skeptical. My perception was that those moms drove their kids to lessons, tidied the house, and not much else. Interviewing Cathy was a real eye opener for me. I had no idea that she had been through so much or accomplished so much...or how much work it had taken to hold together her whole family. By this point I really was becoming convinced that she was an extraordinary woman in everything that she did. I wondered why she chose, given all her talents, to stay at home.
>
> "So when did you actually decide to be a full-time mom?" I asked.

"At child number three, my husband begged me to stay home," Cathy answered. "By that point, he was staying home with the kids and I was working. But he couldn't do it. He told me he didn't care if he had to work five jobs, he wanted me to stay home instead of him."

"And what was that transition like?" asked Darcy.

"I had Brianna six years after Caitie. I went from full-time to a part-time job in sales—which was a total disaster. You're not part-time anywhere, you're full-time everywhere. It's a trap. You get low pay, no benefits, and then end up working almost as many hours anyway. My husband was miserable, I was miserable, the kids were miserable. So that was it. Now I have a full-time job that you cannot pay anybody to do. It's the hardest job in the world with five kids!"

"What are their names, from oldest to youngest?" I asked for clarification.

"Caitie, Jamie, Bre, Jon-Jon, and then, at age forty-five, I'm thinking I have peri-menopausal symptoms—but no, it's pregnancy! So we get the princess, Casey Christine."

"And how old is she now?" I asked.

"She's three and she's the best thing that ever happened to us. Such a trooper [pronounced 'troo-pa']—and she's a real blessing. You know, I have a lot of faith . . . a lot of faith. I go to church five days a week. I only go to the gym four days, but church? Five.

"I'm not just the mother of my children. I've found that I'm their PR person, personal assistant, and agent all wrapped into one. I'm their 'Momager'—Mom plus Manager. That's what it comes down to. I know I take it way too seriously. I should chill, but I feel like this is an investment. If I do it right the first twenty years, they're not on my couch for the next thirty, you know? So this is my full-time job. The day is completely jammed up from the moment they wake up to the moment they go to bed. There's school, but then there is homework, football practice, softball clinic, etcetera. I'm their personal trainer, tutor, and driver. My husband gets done with his workday, and asks, *'Where are you?'* I tell him, *'I'm still working.'*

"Here is an idea of what our life is like: Last weekend, we were up at the mountain for the big ASF fund-raising dinner, and I didn't get out of there until 1:30 a.m. Jon-Jon got up with a fever at 4 a.m. Then we had to leave at 5 a.m. to go down the mountain 'cause Bre had to be in the pool at Lehman College by 8 a.m. for a swim meet. Bre swam two meets—8 to noon and then noon to 4—and then we came home and everybody pitched in to help Jamie finish her chemistry project that was due the next morning. That's what it's like.

"I have never regretted staying home," Cathy continued. "John's real great about it, too. Money is scarce, you know? We spend a lot of money for education—keeping the kids in a Catholic school. But we love macaroni. So there are no regrets at all."

"I'm an only child," Darcy said. "I have no idea what it's like to have so many kids around. How do you manage them as a group?"

"Even though there's tons of sibling rivalry and the usual nonsense about fighting with each other," answered Cathy, "they do pull together. This year Jamie applied to fifteen colleges, which meant she had to write about forty-five essays. On the Monday and Tuesday before Thanksgiving, we all got together to help her get them out. Jon-Jon and Bre took the baby out of the room. Caitie, Jamie, and I organized the folders and sorted out which college gets which essays. We set up a laptop for Caitie and me to proof Jaimie's writing. It was a lot of work, but we have to be a team or we can't do all the things we do."

Cathy paused for a second, musing on the structure of her family. It looked like she wanted to say something but wasn't sure how it was going to come off. "What?" I asked.

"Well, all the younger kids have a lot of pressure on them being Caitlin's siblings," Cathy said.

"You mean they have had to take care of Caitie because she's blind and they have to be more independent because you spend so much time at the doctor with her?" I asked. "That is often the case when one sibling in a family has a major disability."

"No, no, no, no." Cathy waved her arms in the air. "That's not what I mean at all. Caitlin sets the mark for the others. She's always looked after them because she was the oldest. And they look up to her because she has achieved so much in sports and now she goes to Harvard. Sympathy for her? No way! They cut her no slack. They feel pressure from her to excel because they can see and they don't have all the medical stuff she has to deal with. So, you know, what's their excuse?"

"With all the sibling dynamics," Darcy asked still curious about this world full of children, "how do manage your leadership role?"

"Well, it's hard because you want them to help each other, but you don't want to burn them out or make them resent each other. To save money on paying a guide to ski in races with Caitie, we asked Jaime to be her official guide. At first she didn't want to hear about it, but she eventually stepped up to the plate. You've got to know when to give them advice and when not to; it's a fine line."

"Most people know that you struggled with Caitie's disability," I added, "but they don't know what you went through with your family during the 9-11 crisis in New York."

"It was Jon-Jon's first day of kindergarten," Cathy explained with a sigh, "and I could finally go to church during the daytime with all the kids in school. I was just about to leave for 9 a.m. Mass at Good Shepherd when Johnny, my husband, calls me and says: *'The Twin Towers were hit by a plane and it wasn't an accident. I'm going down there. Get the kids. I'll talk to you later.'*

"At that point, the second building wasn't hit yet. But John, he just knew. You don't crash into the tallest building in New York City by accident; you know what I'm sayin'?

"I started working my way to the farthest kids, picking them up. Then the second building went down and everything just went crazy. Remember, we didn't have cell phones back then. I grabbed everybody else's kids I knew, too, because they couldn't get there. I got everybody back to our house.

"And then I was just waiting." Cathy's eyes became misty. Her rapid-fire pace slowed. Even more than ten years later, this was a moment in time that still made her hands shake and her voice choke. "It was the clearest day in history. I was watching the buildings fall on TV and I knew Johnny was down there. We didn't know if he was alive or dead until after midnight. When I picked up Jon-Jon from his brand-new teacher, she asked if my husband was okay. She said her brother was down there, too. Her brother didn't make it, though. John lost his best friend that day, too. My sister lives across the street. Her husband's also a fireman. We were all scared together. So many of them never came back.

"At 12:10 a.m., Johnny calls. *'I'm alive. I'm okay...I've got to go.'* Now we all had red, swelling eyes and lumps in our throats. Then we didn't see him for four days. He came home that fourth day, 9 at night. He hadn't shed a tear the whole time, even though he saw so much horror and death. When he came in the door covered with ash and dirt, the kids went running down the stairs to him, and that's when he lost it. He just broke down, crying and sobbing. He only stayed with us for three hours. I fed him; he took a shower; and he went back down there again for another week. He saw really graphic, horrible things. It was like a war. He was looking for his best friends, and there were bodies dropping next to him off the towers."

Right at that moment, Cathy's cell phone rang. It was her husband. "We're talking about you, handsome," she chirped, instantly switching gears from the emotional story. She put the phone on speaker so we could all hear him. It was sweet to listen to their comfortable banter. Here were two people who clearly and unequivocally value each other, their lives, their family, and their reliance on God.

"Where are you?" he asked.

"I'm sitting with Bonnie and Darcy. We're doing the book . . . the interview," Cathy explained.

"So you're with Bonnie?" repeated John. "Okay, I'll catch you later."

After hanging up the phone, Cathy told us, "From that horrific experience, though, came a real blessing. There was a program, months later, for firefighters with disabled children. They took our whole family to Colorado and that's what got Caitie started on skiing."

"Do you regret anything?" Darcy asked. "Do you feel you have made mistakes?"

"No, I don't regret anything. Doors open and I say, *'Let's give this a try.'* I'm never afraid to go out there and fail. I just listen and learn. I am always saying to Cherisse, *'It is what it is.'* You don't ever resent anybody else's life because everything comes around and goes around. You don't give up; you deal with what you have; and you give back. *'It is what it is.'* I left my fancy, high-paying job and lived through some challenges with my family. But look at the good things: I was nominated for Woman of the Year through Senator Golden. I rode in a corporate jet when Procter and Gamble sponsored Caitie in the Paralympics. Our whole family went to Canada to cheer for our daughter. People would think it's the worst thing to happen, to have a disabled child be born to you, but it is the best thing that happened to us, you know? *'It is what it is.'* "

As we left the lodge that day, Darcy said, "When I'm her age, I want to be like her. She would be great whatever she does, because of who she is. Whether she had one kid or five, it doesn't matter. If she weren't helping her blind daughter at the Olympics, she would probably be wiping out polio or Dancing with the Stars on TV. She is a force of nature, right there next to electromagnetic attraction and gravity."

Once again, I flashed back to our experience with the Sarubbi juggernaut at the Paralympics. Standing in the snow atop Whistler Mountain in Canada, Darcy and I were looking for the clan in the stands at the bottom of the slalom run. We walked around the jam-packed grandstand that had been erected for fans and supporters to cheer on their beloved athletes as they crossed the finish line.

"How will we find them?" Darcy asked. "There are thousands of people here!"

Just then, I looked up and smiled. I grabbed Darcy by the shoulders and spun her around to face the stands, and she smiled, too. There, among a dozen or so handmade posters of encouragement and pride, a huge, professionally printed banner covered an entire section of the bleachers. On the sign, a white sky rose over blue, snow-capped peaks with gigantic, red block letters: WE LOVE TEAM SARUBBI! GO CAITLIN!

And right under it was Cathy, in her boundless energy, running around making sure everybody was comfortable, sated, and having a great time. She proudly wore a stars-and-stripes wool hat with an official U.S. Ski Team jacket adorned with patches from an impressive array of all of Caitie's sponsors (Alka-Seltzer, VISA, Nature Valley, Audi, etc.).

Cathy frantically waved Darcy and me over to join the party. And it really was a party. We had a ball, even though a thick, cottony fog enveloped the entire mountain and ultimately forced the cancellation of all the ski events for that day.

At one point, Darcy asked Cathy, "How does it feel to be here, at the Paralympics, cheering for Caitie, knowing she's come this far?"

Cathy barely thought for a moment before she replied. "Pinch me. Just pinch me. Don't tell *me* miracles don't happen. Miracles happen. Miracles *happen*."

CHAPTER 16

———·••·———

Truancy

One afternoon, just before her Easter break, Darcy came home from school with an official, scary-looking document—and a face to match.

> *You are hereby notified that Darcy Deane is in violation of the Compulsory Attendance Laws of the State of New Jersey and is considered truant under its statutes. If this situation is not addressed immediately, the School Board will notify the NJ Center for Juvenile Alternatives, which will make a recommendation to the State and Juvenile Courts for prosecution. As a parent of a truant child, you can be fined and/or jailed for failure to adequately supervise school-aged children . . ."*

"I don't know what all this means," Darcy said plaintively, "but it sounds bad."

I had anticipated significant changes to my life as a result of undertaking this adventure with my daughter, but jail time wasn't one of the possibilities I considered. After planning and coordinating my speaking and lecturing dates with the incredibly complicated calendars of women like the United States Secretary of State and the President of Liberia, I never thought that my high school sophomore's schedule would be a problem!

Wherever I could, I scheduled our travels over weekends or school holidays, but pulling Darcy out of school for two or three days at a time for over fifteen interviews had added up to a lot of school days missed. As the absences mounted, I curried favor with her teachers and met with her school guidance counselor to mitigate the disruption to her formal education. Still, the rules and regulations governing public school attendance marched on, oblivious to the particular circumstances that may or may not make these absences legitimately excused. Reports are filed. Notices are sent. Parents end up in the slammer.

Since I've never looked very good in stripes, I met with the principal of Darcy's school ASAP. Thankfully, the warden presiding over Darcy's education was open minded, magnanimous, and delighted with our project. He gave it his full support. "This is what education is all about," he said emphatically. "If we can't make something like this work, what are we doing here?"

I was extremely relieved to have his backing. Darcy's absences were now officially blessed as educationally valid activities.

But just having the law off our tails didn't eliminate the entire problem. Missed classes meant Darcy had to work double time to make up assignments upon her return. A full load of honors level subjects like hers seldom allows enough time to do the current work—never mind doubling up with previously due tests, homework, and other projects.

When we returned home from our leadership adventures, Darcy would sometimes wake up at 4:30 a.m. to do makeup work after slogging through her regular homework the night before. On top of all that, she frequently rode the roller coaster of teen angst as she tried to balance friends and popularity with life goals and ambitions. Despite all these challenges, she was working incredibly hard and maintaining excellent grades overall.

No matter how hard she studied, though, she would be tripped up at times when she'd miss a concept or two from a skipped class that would appear on a test later. One day she came to me holding a bright red B on a math exam she'd killed herself to study for.

"There were two problems on the test that they went over in class when I was gone on one of our trips," she said in a level voice. "One I figured out—even though I had never seen it before. The other one, I just couldn't do." Tears fell as she worked through the ramifications. "I want to go to a good college, so I need to get A's." The sobbing choked her words. "If I had gotten that one problem right, I would have gotten an A instead of a B. I am already working as hard as I can to keep my average up in that class, and we don't have many exams or quizzes left in the semester. Now I'm going to need to get A's on everything—every quiz, every homework, every test—just to offset that B!" Her face was now puffy, red, and swollen. "I just don't know if I can do it."

The reality of her situation smacked me in the face. I never meant to put all this pressure on her. I never once said that I expected her to go to an Ivy League school, but here I was flying her all around to meet with the likes of Condi Rice at Stanford, Wendy Kopp from Princeton, and Ellen Johnson Sirleaf from Harvard. Not to mention the fact that her parents both graduated from Oxford! Darcy felt like her whole life would be ruined if she didn't get into the "right" college. It didn't matter what I said to the contrary, I had put her in the position of being surrounded by driven, successful graduates of the upper echelons of academic achievement. At the same time, by yanking her out of school repeatedly and dragging her all around the world, I made it twice as hard to live up to the very pressures I created in her life.

There I was watching those salty droplets skid over my daughter's cheeks. I wondered if I was unintentionally orchestrating the very kind of circumstances that drive some teen girls to bulimia, drug use, and even thoughts of suicide. In that moment, I angrily thought, I wished I'd never started this project at all! I should not have worried about the Ophelia syndrome. I should have ignored all the evidence I'd seen that women often don't feel that the leadership track is for them. Maybe I should not have even tried to show my daughter that she is and can be a leader. Would she be better off if I had just let her be a normal teen and enjoy life?

Then I remembered that Darcy loved every moment of our adventure. She often told me so. But even if she hadn't told me, I saw it on her face, time after time. I could already tell that Darcy would never be the same after she'd come face to face with real poverty in Central America and held her own, toe-to-toe, with not just one but *two* U.S. Secretaries of State. I was personally moved knowing that Cathy

Sarubbi had expanded Darcy's appreciation for what stay-at-home moms do; a brand of women's leadership with too little respect in many places. More than anything else, I believe that Darcy was surprised and impacted by the depth of the bonds of mutual respect and understanding she built with these great women. Once she'd laughed, eaten pizza, or sat in their kitchen with them, they didn't seem so distant or different. She could picture herself as a leader. No matter how much she struggled with grades, excessive pressure to succeed, or finding time to write for the book, I knew I couldn't take it all away from her. She wouldn't view my letting her off the hook as a kindness. She'd see it as a humiliation. The message she would hear would be, *"You aren't good enough; you've failed."* Plus, all that time, effort, and sacrifice she'd put in up 'til this point would have been wasted.

Darcy stoically wiped away her tears and redoubled her efforts on the math homework in front of her. I would have gone over to hug her, but I know how much she hates being touched when upset. There would be no sitcom ending to this half hour of the show. I quietly left the room but kept a watchful eye on her as I baked some homemade mac and cheese— her favorite—for dinner.

CHAPTER 17

Lisa P. Jackson

Administrator, the United States
Environmental Protection Agency

Running in the rain with two people under one umbrella is not easy, especially when one of those people has a prosthetic leg. My intrepid daughter and I were hoofing it down a treacherous strip of Manhattan sidewalk, trying to stay dry in this early April shower without knocking each other into a filthy splashdown on West 51st Street. The address I had neatly typed on a sheet of white paper was clear enough, but the corresponding numerals on the buildings around us were not. And we were getting really wet.

"This sucks," the ever eloquent Darcy pointed out.

Down the block in front of us, I noticed a couple of big burly guys in black suits huddling uncomfortably close to each other under a pathetic little awning. "Let's ask those bouncers if they know where this address is," I said, pointing to the well-dressed hulks. It's not unusual in New York City to see bouncers standing outside a dark unmarked door. Behind that bleak slab of metal could lurk the latest noisy hip-hop mecca for models and young money, with these two linebackers acting as a human barricade between chic and bleak. But it was three o'clock in the afternoon—hardly party time—and we saw no velvet rope draped between shiny aluminum poles. No crowds, no fuss impeded our progress as we squished up to the suspicious behemoths. "Excuse me, we're looking for the stage door to *The Daily Show with Jon Stewart*. You wouldn't happen to know where that is, would you?"

Without a sound, a beefy hand grabbed the rusted door handle and tugged it open.

"This is it?" Darcy asked, surprised by the plain brown wrapper.

Inside the doorway, dozens of harried folks zipped back and forth mumbling and/or receiving instructions through headsets attached to small walkie-talkie transmitters clipped to their belts. This was definitely backstage at a TV show. I've been on live television many times, and I'm always amazed at the level of manic frenzy that surrounds every production. I don't know how people do this for a living every day. I'd collapse after one afternoon.

I tried to grab a red-faced woman as she scooted by us. She didn't quite stop, but she did give me a moment's attention while she managed to shift her unruly pile of multicolored paperwork away from contact with our moisture. "We're looking for . . ."

"One of the guests?" she snapped. "Green Room, down this hall on the left." She pointed. And disappeared.

We followed her directions and trotted toward the "Green Room" as directed, dodging her colleagues as they bustled up and down the narrow corridor.

I've often wondered why they always call these places where you wait before an appearance on stage the Green Room. They are invariably comfortable, usually well stocked with all sorts of goodies to eat and drink, but rarely, if ever, *green*. The term can be found as far back as the early seventeenth century in English theatre, but no one seems to know its exact origin. True to form, this one was beige.

We were here to shadow Lisa P. Jackson, Administrator of the Environmental Protection Agency. As the highest-ranking environmental czar in the Obama administration, Lisa was about to sit in the hot seat across from Jon Stewart in honor of the fortieth anniversary of Earth Day. But, as we settled into the comfy, sand-colored sofa, Madam Administrator was nowhere to be seen. I noisily crunched a celery stalk while I looked around for someone else to direct us. Darcy settled for a much quieter, soft baked chocolate chip cookie.

We had first met Lisa a few months earlier, in Canada, during the 2010 Winter Paralympics. When we weren't chugging along on the Sarubbi train with the whole clan in tow, Darcy and I were enveloped in

a completely different entourage: The Official White House Delegation
to the Paralympic Games. I was thrilled to represent my country and our
government in this way. As the first African American to win Olympic
medals in ski racing, I have been afforded many great honors, but this
was certainly one of the most fun. Darcy and I traveled in full VIP mode,
along with Secret Service agents, State Department officials, and several
high-ranking government appointees including Gen. Eric Shinseki, the
Secretary of the Veterans Affairs; Kareem Dale, the President's Special
Assistant for Disability Policy; other Paralympians including Mike May,
Jim Martinson, and disabled veteran Melissa Stockwell; and . . . EPA Administrator Lisa P. Jackson.

Lisa had brought along her teenage son, Brian, so Darcy and I naturally seemed to gravitate to them over the course of the vast number of
official dinners, tours, and sporting events as we represented the White
House. We immediately hit it off. I felt like I had found a long lost
friend. Darcy and I were enchanted by this down-to-earth scientist—
the first African American to hold this Cabinet-level post and lead the
American charge in protecting the environment. We begged her to participate in our book on women leaders.

I didn't see my new bestie anywhere around the not-green room,
and as far as I knew no one had told her we arrived. A group of well-
dressed men were huddled in a corner, engaged in a constant flow of
information—cell phones buzzing, laptops strewn about, digits flying
with dazzling speed over tiny, handheld keyboards. Definitely Washington
types. "Excuse me, are you guys with Administrator Jackson?" I asked.

"Yes . . ." said the one who seemed most in charge. He looked up from
his furious thumbing, distracted at first, but after a moment of recognition said, "Oh, my, you must be Bonnie!"

I nodded.

"I'm Seth, the Administrator's Associate and Chief Communications
Officer. Welcome! We're so happy you're here!"

We exchanged warm smiles. I introduced him to Darcy, and he rat-
tled off the names of his colleagues who looked up, smiled politely, but
quickly returned to their newsgathering.

"I'm so sorry for not seeing you come in. We're all a little distracted at the moment. There's this 'thing' going on. It's probably nothing, but we're just monitoring the situation. Let me take you to the Administrator. She's just down the hall."

I followed Seth's lead back out into the narrow hallway. I was curious what the "thing" was. I could have asked, but my years in Washington taught me not to bother. He'd never tell me.

I could hear Lisa's sharp, powerful voice exhale through a doorway on the right. We rounded the corner and there she sat in one of those salon-type swivel chairs. A gaggle of hair and makeup artists fussed over her head so completely that she couldn't move, so she spoke to us via the reflection in the huge mirror in front of her. Even as the experts continued to poke, prod, and paint, I thought she looked beautiful.

"Hello, you two!" Lisa said. Her face was framed in the fringe of naked lightbulbs that inevitably surround a dressing room mirror.

We crowded into the impossibly small room. "Is this a little too intimate for job shadowing you, Lisa?"

"Oh, listen," she said in her easygoing way, waving her hand toward the fashionably slim fellow wielding a curling iron, "Ask Jody. When I came here for my first time on the show, we had five more people in here, right?"

Jody nodded affably and shook our hands as we introduced ourselves, careful not to interrupt the flow of his work.

"Well," Seth chimed in, "I'm going to slip out. You okay?" he said with a glance toward the boss. When their eyes met, an interesting, silent interchange occurred between them. It was subtle, but serious.

"So, Darcy, I'm going to give you a little background about what's going on here today."

"Okay, great." I answered. I had watched one or two episodes of the show, so I was excited to be here. But I really didn't know much about how it all worked or what she was planning to say. I leaned in even closer to get the scoop.

The stylist smoothed and pulled on Lisa's trendy, highlighted locks as she continued. "With this show, just like other news shows, Jon doesn't tell you what he's going to ask. There's no script."

"Does he give you any clues at all about what he's going to ask?" I wondered aloud.

"Not entirely. Both this show and the Letterman show do a pre-interview where one of their producers asks me a few questions ahead of time. That gives me an idea of what they are thinking about, but you really never know. Anything can happen.

"The political context is that we thought a new climate change bill would be introduced today in Congress for Earth Day, which would have been a big deal. It didn't transpire because, as can happen in government, one of the senators who has been very involved in it became upset when people were shifting attention to immigration instead of climate change. Tensions rose in Arizona over a controversial new law there, and the whole environmental dynamic went sideways. It is just one more bump in a road that looks a lot like this." With her hand Lisa made a motion that traced the curves of imaginary hills. "Jon is likely to ask some questions about that bill." She paused to consider other possibilities. "Let's see, what else? There's an offshore drilling platform that exploded down home in Louisiana, but I don't think he's going to mention it unless he wants to bring up the whole drilling issue." Lisa ran her fingers through her hair and said, "That's nice and soft . . ."

Suddenly the energy in the room shifted. Someone had surreptitiously come up behind me—practically putting his head on my shoulder.

"Is there *Administrating* going on in here?" The familiar, high-octane voice of Jon Stewart himself just about knocked me over. "Are you *administrating* right now?" he said to Lisa. "Don't let me interrupt— *administrate. Administrate!*"

We all laughed as the TV legend quickly exchanged pleasantries with Lisa before swooping out again after barely a minute. It felt like we'd been hit by a tornado. A really handsome tornado.

"You must be pretty comfortable with Jon Stewart by now," I said

more as an observation than a question. "You've been on the show before
and he seems to like you."

"Well . . . I think you should never get *too* comfortable," answered the
media-savvy government official in a tone that made us laugh, just as we
had with Jon. "This is a big deal, so I will be a little nervous out there
even though I have been on the show a couple of times."

The stylist stopped to consult Lisa on two options for parting her hair.
"I like that, to the side," she responded. "Yeah, that's great."

Turning back to us she continued, "We also ask the White House for
one page of talking points about where we are on the energy bill and immigration. That way you sync up the message. If it were just Lisa Jackson
talking, no one would care what I have to say. They're interviewing me
because I express the positions of the Obama administration. Although I
have very strong personal views, I'm here to represent the president."

An assistant producer poked her head in the door. "Two minutes to
start. Administrator Jackson, you're on in the last segment, so I'll need
you in about fifteen." The makeup artist stepped up her pace; she only
had time for a last touch-up before Lisa would be on camera.

"Did you ever get any formal media training for this?" I asked Lisa.

"Years ago in senior executive training I did a little bit, but now I practice occasionally with a teleprompter, with coaches . . ."

"What are the most helpful things you've learned?" Darcy asked.

"Smile no matter what the question is," she said firmly. "When I first
started, if you asked me a hard question, I would think about the answer. And when I think, my face does this—" Lisa furrowed her brow
in concentration. "It's totally natural, but it looks like a frown, and that
comes off very mean to some people who are watching." She waited a
beat while a flourish of mascara was applied. "I've also learned not to
shake my head. It's easy to nod as someone is talking to you, to show
you are listening and that you understand the question. But if the interviewer is asking a question and insulting the president at the same time,
you don't want to be seen nodding up and down while they say it."

A brief conference on the colors for her eyes and cheeks broke her
flow for a second.

"That looks gorgeous," enthused Darcy. "She was so pretty when we first came in that I didn't think you guys could make her look better, but you have!"

"I am still not as good as I'd like to be," Lisa continued, "at the whole *'Don't answer the question just say what you want to say'* thing. On a show like this it's almost impossible—"

Jody was almost done. He scrutinized every detail.

"Here's the necklace I was thinking about wearing." Lisa handed it to Jody. "Do you think it's too fly?"

As Jody fastened it behind Lisa's perfectly coiffed hair he asked, "What do you mean, 'too fly'?"

"You know—like going to a party. Not serious enough."

"It looks great!" Darcy lobbied.

"I'm fine with it as long as it doesn't make too much noise for the mics," Jody said, and stepped back to look her over. "Collar up or collar down?"

"Up," we all answered in unison.

"Some women aspiring to be leaders are scared of being on the hot seat and getting asked tough questions. What advice would you give them?" I asked, anxious to squeeze in a final question before she hit the stage.

"You mean they don't want to be in the spotlight because they think they might mess up?" Lisa asked.

> "People are terrified of that." I nodded to Lisa, thinking about how hard it would be to have to represent the whole government while people watched you who are paid to criticize everything you say! Given my ambitions to work with global cultures, I could see myself in that hot seat one day, too. That thought petrified me.

"Well, first thing I would say is: *'Why are you doing this?'* For me, what overcomes the fear is that I care about the environment and making a difference for people. At the federal level there's nobody else who can stand up and speak out on these issues. It's part of the job. You can't be a doctor and say I don't like giving injections. If you want to lead in certain arenas, you have to get yourself comfortable with being in the spotlight. Get training. Prepare yourself. It's part of the job."

She stood up from her chair, straightened her jacket, and gave herself the once-over in the mirror.

"One more thing," she said straight into Darcy's eyes, "an important part of what got me here is realizing that it's not about me. Caring about the environment trumps everything else. Even the fear of being in the hot seat."

"I think the environment is lucky to have such a hottie in the hot seat!" Darcy said with a big smile as we all kissed the air and wished her well.

We watched the show back in the Beige Room. On the hi-def monitor in front of us, Jon Stewart jumped in immediately with informed, erudite comments about the stymied climate bill. Then he went in for the joke:

"Lisa, do you want to tell that senator he is a *Big, Fat Baby?*" Jon asked with mock seriousness. "Go ahead, say to him on the air: waah, waah, waah!"

We watched Lisa, true to her training, laugh easily at his joke, relax, and then make substantive comments that skillfully brought the conversation back around. She made it look easy. They lobbed the ball back and forth a few more times, each scoring points in this lively, amicable game. And the explosion on the Deep Horizon oil rig six days prior, which killed eleven men and injured seventeen others, didn't come up at all. BP still maintained that no oil was leaking and there was no environmental problem in the Gulf of Mexico.

We did not know the "thing" Seth was monitoring earlier would erupt into the largest, most devastating environmental disaster in the history of our country. And our friend, Lisa, was about to be thrust into the forefront to deal with it. Her ability to communicate with the public through mass media would soon be tested more than ever before.

Darcy and I had planned to do a follow-up interview after the show where we could ask Lisa about her leadership style and insights, but with the Gulf crisis in the headlines every day, we knew we had to wait. Several months later, once the well was finally capped and the oil stopped gushing, Lisa made time for us to interview her informally at her home in the suburbs just north of Washington, D.C.

Lisa's "home-girl" style instantly made us feel comfortable. It was a warm, breezy summer afternoon, so she served us iced tea alfresco on the lovely patio overlooking her backyard. We talked while nibbling exotic cheeses and fancy crackers she'd spread across the redwood picnic table. I particularly liked the truffle-infused honey spread that added an exquisite sweetness to the sharp cheese.

Munching my delightful morsel, I began: "The BP oil spill put you in the limelight in a much more demanding way than usual."

"Yes and no," Lisa answered. "The hardest part was that it wasn't really the EPA's responsibility to manage. My phone was ringing off the hook with people asking what I was going to do about this environmental catastrophe happening in my own stomping grounds where I grew up. But my hands were tied. If something happens in water that's inland— like rivers or lakes—then the EPA would be in the lead. But since the spill was in coastal waters, the Coast Guard takes charge. That's how we split up the work. Here's an environmental disaster, but the actual operations are under control of another branch of government. You absolutely have to work as a team, though . . . and we did.

"I decided one thing I could do personally was to be a voice for people down there and at the same time be a conduit for them to the administration. They needed to have their concerns taken seriously by BP and everyone else. I went down about sixteen times and always held public meetings, talked on drive-time radio, and appeared on morning TV."

"You suddenly went from doing a few TV shows a year to being on camera all the time. Was that a big challenge?" I asked.

"I think a lot of it came naturally because I really care about the people living in the Gulf. It was unusual, though. Things came up like: *'What do you wear to an oil spill?'* Since I've been a field engineer I showed up wearing a hat, a blue shirt with rolled-up sleeves, and a vest with gear in the pockets. That's just standard operating procedure for me. Other people came in suits, city shoes, and high heels to walk around on the beach and look for tar balls. That didn't look good on TV. So the next time, everyone dressed in working clothes like me. It's important to look like you are there to get something done."

"Did you ever get any really negative coverage?" I followed up.

"A major blogging site in D.C. ran a story saying that the head of the EPA was going to a political fund-raiser in the middle of this horrible oil spill. I heard about it right when my plane landed in D.C. after a trip to New Orleans. They called my office, but since I was in an airplane they ran the story without my comment. They didn't wait. The real story, however, was that the fund-raiser was ten days out. Every two days we would look at the schedule and cancel everything to focus on the oil spill. We weren't going a week out, because the well could have been capped by then. Something new was being tried every day. The fund-raiser was still on the calendar only because we hadn't canceled it yet. So it became a story that absorbed a whole morning news cycle with: *How could the EPA administrator go to a political fund-raiser?* Nobody covered that it was ten days away. Nobody reported that I planned to cancel."

"That is so unfair!" Darcy said incredulously.

"Yeah, well, that's the kind of thing you just can't fight," Lisa said, shaking her head.

"So what do you do about that?" I queried. "What advice do you have for other people about how to deal with that kind of trickery?"

"First, you just need to be thick skinned. We had a conference call with editors who ran the story and I said: *'Listen, I want to make myself available. I want you to know how hard I'm working, and what you're saying doesn't help me. It's personally damaging. I don't care, because there is nothing you can do about it at this point, but it would have been nice if you picked up the phone.'*"

"Were they more willing to work with you after that?"

"It did get better, somewhat. It's a leadership strategy I use a lot. Do you guys watch football? In football they say 'run in the crease.' It's one of my favorite tactics when everything is coming at you and there is this seemingly impenetrable wall. You only have a few options. You can try to run around it, or you can go backward and throw a pass over it. But a lot of times the best plays—the ones that are the most fun to watch—

are when the running back just goes right into it and finds the crease in the defense. You find the one place where there is a tiny little opening and you can make progress amidst the very people who were trying to stop you. I love the looks of that play. I think it's a great way to go as a leader. We have a tendency when under attack, especially in politics, to see people as your enemy. You think you cannot work with them, that you shouldn't deal with them at all. I'm just the opposite. The person who is criticizing me the loudest, I'm going to ask to sit down for a meeting. And they might not come. And sometimes when they do come—this has backfired on me—they say horrible things about you afterward. I am sure this happens in the business world, too.

"But even though it can go wrong, I really believe that it's mostly in our interest—especially as women—to physically confront people who are trying to attack you in the abstract, or from a distance. It's much harder for them to be a jerk to you in person. *Much* harder. And I also think it is harder to attack a woman you know personally. Maybe that's sexism, but it works in our favor."

A summer zephyr suddenly whipped across the deck and threatened to upset our snacks. We all dove for our favorite foods. I vaulted across the table to snag the truffle honey just before it took flight. In case I wasn't so lucky next time, I built myself another sample and took my time savoring the exquisite blend of flavors.

"We've noticed that an interesting part of your leadership style is to engage many different groups of people who aren't typically 'environmentalists.'" Darcy took the lead as I enjoyed my treat.

"Oh, yes," Lisa answered. "Most people think of environmentalism as only concerning wide-open vistas and beautiful places to be. They don't think about a city block or a school where the kids are affected by lead paint and diesel pollution. They don't think of a business owner who is dealing with high absenteeism because the workforce has chronic asthma. They don't think about the devastating impact on an urban community when there is a large brownfield site no one wants to pay to clean up. It could be a job generator or a place for kids to play, but instead it's a haven for crime and drugs. And then you start adding in one of the bigger problems we have, which is goods movement, and all the communities that are around ports. L.A. and Long Beach have lower to middle class, mostly Hispanic communities fighting to clean up the pollution from the heavy traffic of trucks and trains. If you breathe, the environment affects you. If you drink water, the environment affects you."

"There will be people reading this book who are in their twenties or thirties and they want to lead, but they want to have a family, too. What perspective would you give them from your experience as a mother of two teen boys?" I asked.

"First, I don't think you can plan it all out. I thought I had planned it out, but when the 9-11 crisis hit I took the 'mommy track.' I gave up my high-flying EPA job in New York City and moved to New Jersey, which I thought would be better for my family. As it turned out, that experience and that set of relationships are probably most responsible for giving me the chance to have this job. Sometimes you make a mommy track decision that turns out to be the best decision of all.

"I am a huge fan of leaving as many avenues open for as long as you humanly can. I am very suspicious, if not outright antagonistic, of people who try to get you to close off avenues really early. That's such an unfair thing to ask people to do. I'm always mad when I hear women who feel any amount of pressure to decide while they're pregnant when they're coming back to work. How the heck do you know? I mean how do you know how you're going to feel the first time you hold your baby? Or how do you know how you're going to feel the first time you have to interview someone to take care of them? Or how do you know whether you're going to be comfortable with family doing it? Tell your boss: *'I intend to come back to work as soon as I possibly can, but I'm hoping for a healthy baby, I'm hoping for an easy delivery, I'm hoping for an easy road to finding the perfect caregiver. I'll keep you posted.'* By law you should get that courtesy. But, of course, what's legal and what's done are sometimes two different things."

"But how does it actually work for you?" Darcy asked.

"Well I have a good husband. That helps tremendously, it really does," said Lisa.

"My mom helped a lot when the boys were young, for a long, long time. Then we had au pairs who made our lives easier. For every mom it's different and I got lucky. It helped, too, that I grew up with a mother who worked. It must be hard to have a stay-at-home mom and then choose to go to work. It's important for my boys to see a mother who is a professional in her own right and chooses to work. That is now embedded in them."

The biggest gust of the day whistled through the patio, and Lisa's glass went flying—spilling tea all over her sweatshirt!

After the laughter subsided, Darcy nudged me with her elbow and pointed at the top of our list of notes. We became so carried away with our conversation, we'd forgotten to ask our number one question.

"Go ahead," I said. "You ask it."

"How do you define leadership?" Darcy asked.

"Hmmm. That's a good one," Lisa replied, still dabbing at the sticky stains on her clothes. "It keeps changing. If you asked me a year ago, it would be a different answer. But my current working definition—and it's partly influenced by the BP spill—is that it's all about the table you set and then how you conduct the meal.

"Leadership is about putting in place a team of people who represent all the sides that need to work on the issue, big or small. You can have leadership of a team of eight; you can have leadership as the head of the EPA; or leadership in the form of our president.

"It's also about defining a common vision. People come to the table and they want to be heard, but at the end of the day you have to pull it together. Then there is leadership inside the agency to implement that vision. Outside the agency, the leadership is about speaking and communicating the same big vision."

"You said your definition has changed a lot over time. What has been a major evolution in your thinking about leadership?" I asked.

"The evolution has happened on what I would call that humanist scale, the realization that the very best leaders are people who resonate with other people. When I was younger and less experienced, I would have thought that leadership was always about having the best plan and being the smartest one. I was always a smart kid."

"You started with a chemical engineering mind-set focused on problem solving, but you learned to also focus on the people?" I asked.

"Yeah. I have grown that way. Coming to Washington, however, was yet another evolution. Sadly, how you look still counts a lot more for women than it does for men. What you wear says a lot about what people will think of you as a woman. I'm kind of a city girl. I like suits, but I don't necessarily like suits that match. I like separates and coordinates. I realized I have to think about how I look a lot more. I also used to just give speeches without writing them ahead of time. I am very comfortable with speaking. But here in Washington, one silly word can give ten thousand people the wrong impression about what it is you're trying to do. It can derail the president's agenda.

"My latest evolution is coming to realize that there is a portion of my job that is about how I look and how I convey my messages. I still don't always stick to a speech, but I think a lot more about the importance of my words. One thing that hasn't changed over the years in how I see leadership is the importance of investing time growing your skills in the art of leadership. I have had many mentors and coaches—and they aren't the same thing. I have taken classes, gone through training. It all helps me to do the job I have today. I make sure my people can invest in themselves and get training, too."

This seemed to be a good place to end the interview. We turned off the recorders and let the conversation drift to more casual topics while we nibbled and soaked up the sun.

I looked across at my new friend. Strong, smart, confident, and gorgeous, yet still finding her way day by day by adapting to the situations presented before her. Sometimes we look up at the person at the podium and see a vision of someone we think is way beyond ourselves. But what we see isn't that person at all—it's an image they've created to do a job or convey a message in a way that will seem polished, thoughtful, careful, and correct.

But, get them down off the podium, put them in a sweatshirt, and they'll still spill their iced tea all over themselves just like the rest of us.

CHAPTER 18

—— • • • ——

Rishika Daryanani

High School Junior

Rishika Daryanani's school would be on hiatus during the only time we could come out to California to interview her. It was Darcy's spring break, too, so she was already scheduled to visit her father in San Diego.

"No problem," Rishika told us. "I can arrange to video one of our meetings before the break." Within a week she had captured a meeting of one of the community service groups she leads, posted it on the Internet for us to watch, and sent us a DVD as backup. Organized, responsive, and proactive at solving problems, this dynamic high school junior didn't just agree to participate in our project—she was way ahead of us.

Then, she went even farther. Rishika convinced ten members of her school's global awareness and social change organization, The Cambio Club, to convene, over their vacation (!), and hold another brainstorming session just for us on the dates we were in town. She also persuaded the school to open the building, provide the meeting space, and authorize her club adviser to be present. There seemed to be nothing the seventeen-year-old couldn't get done.

We arrived on the largely deserted high school campus and found our way to the main entrance. The ever-efficient Rishika was already waiting to greet us, dressed casually in jeans, ballet flats, and a gray sweater with a lilac pashmina wrapped loosely around her neck. Vibrant pastels of student-painted murals decorated the walls—depicting scenes of dancing animals, castles, and a smiling "man-in-the-moon" watching over them. This display reminded me of Darcy's school, where similar splashes of artwork brighten up the otherwise Band-Aid bland cinder block hallways.

Rishika ushered us into a clean, well-designed seminar room, with tables and chairs arranged in tiered arches that faced the central staging area in the middle. Easels adorned with colorful charts and notes displayed the agenda for the meeting and outlined the group's progress to date. Many executive sessions at Fortune 500 companies aren't as neatly planned as this gathering!

> I was surprised at how organized, creative, and inclusive Rishika's leadership style was. She and her co-president stood at the whiteboard in front of the room and took suggestions for next year's fund-raising events, writing each one in an alternate color to make them stand out. They led a discussion of each idea's practicality, value, and "fun-ness" and then used a bright green marker to assess priorities with a tally of votes. It went way beyond what most kids would do, and there wasn't a hint of the leaders trying to tell others what to think. By the end, everyone was excited and committed to the plan for senior year.

After the meeting, we sat down to talk with Rishika and her activities adviser, Melissa. As they sat close together, this Hispanic faculty member and the Indian student looked at each other with obvious affection and respect. We started by asking Melissa to give us some background perspective on Rishika as a leader.

"Initiative," Melissa replied without hesitation. "I would say first and foremost. It's very common to find high school students who want to lead, but they fear decision making. That is not something that Rishika fears. She is willing to take the initiative to make a decision when one needs to be made, but also has the work ethic to do the research to come up with ideas.

"Rishika is good, also, at fostering a decision-making culture. Our principal says that the best leaders make the fewest decisions possible. It's easy for students to feel empowered and to feel comfortable with

Rishika because she is so positive and people trust her. Even the most sarcastic of voices or the most glass-half-empty students, Rishika can get them going forward. She gets them making decisions for themselves."

Darcy turned to Rishika and asked our lead question: "How do you define leadership?"

"The first image that comes to mind is someone standing in front of a group of people talking, but then, there's so much more to it. What goes into planning that meeting? How is that person interacting with everyone? How are they managing each and every one of their group members? So, for me, that image translates into how a person can empower a group to complete the task at hand."

"Has your understanding of leadership evolved over time?" Darcy asked, peer to peer.

"In every recommendation letter anyone's ever written about me, they always called me a natural leader. I used to think that meant I was bossy and told other people what to do. Over time I have learned that isn't the kind of leader I want to be. If I tell people what to do and they do it, what did they learn from it? What have I learned from it? Absolutely nothing. What did they gain from it? What did I gain from it? Absolutely nothing. My real passion is around international relations and making a difference for humanity. Real leadership isn't about getting people to do things. It's getting people to buy into what I'm talking about or what I'm trying to convey."

"Have you had any formal leadership training?" asked Darcy while I sat there in shock that a girl so young had discovered the essential difference between management and leadership that many adults never, ever identify.

"I went through a weeklong program with the California Association of Student Councils in a group of about three hundred people at UC Santa Barbara over the summer a couple of years ago. We learned the systems you saw in the meeting—using alternating colors to make things easier to see while brainstorming, the tally system for prioritizing, and communicating the agenda ahead of time. You got my agenda for this meeting, right?"

"Yep," I said. "We got it day before yesterday."

"I stayed on after the leadership program and attended their staff development program for camp counselors. That way I could go back the following summer and teach—all the teachers are fifteen to eighteen years old, just like the participants. I learned so much more on the staff side: speaking skills, the art of leading a team, and the phases of leadership. I have books this thick from them," she said, spreading her thumb and index fingers about two and half inches apart.

"I picked up on a lot more effective leadership skills like how to bring a meeting back to focus. I've gone back to teach it to others now twice. My favorite workshop to teach is the art of leading a team because it goes through the phases of team growth and how to react to them as a leader. I hope I get to teach it again this September."

"How did you hear about the training program?" Darcy asked. "What made you want to go and do that?"

"A lot of the stuff that I've ever heard about is through blast e-mails through the school. They send out a lot of amazing, amazing opportunities. I'm apparently one of the very few students who actually read them. For one competition I wrote an essay on how cross-cultural interaction affects my daily life and why it's so important in a global age. Only fifteen people from our school applied and I won the competition, which meant I was able to go on a special trip to China. There were people from across the United States and people from India as well who met up in Chicago and left for Shanghai. It was unbelievable. I just got back on Sunday."

"Any 'aha' moments you want to share with us?" I asked, leaning forward, eager to hear what she had to say.

"I've always heard about global competition, but it was never tangible to me before. Seeing the resources and intelligence of the Chinese people and meeting the Indian participants on the tour—it really hit me. Global competition is *real*—and we all need to be prepared. Our normal high school life makes us so American centric."

"Right, right," said Darcy, nodding. She was probably imagining a trip to China herself so she could practice the Mandarin she'd been studying.

"What is your family like?" Darcy decided to ask next.

"My family here in San Diego is pretty big. My grandmother lives with us, and my two aunts come over for dinner almost every night. In our house, on any given day, we can easily have ten people at dinner. I have two younger brothers and their friends come over; my friends come over. It's not a big deal. Before I left for China we had seventeen people for dinner—that meant a lot of lasagna!

"My mom always says it takes a village to raise a child, and that's exactly what we have. We wouldn't want it any other way now. I've been brought up by a lot of strong women; my dad's sisters, my grandmother, my mother, and my mom's mom. My mom only has sisters, and there are three of them. That upbringing has made me a stronger woman because I see them being strong all the time."

"When you say strong, what do you think of them doing?" asked Darcy.

"They never let men dictate their lives. I picked that up at an early age. It didn't matter if you were a boy or a girl, you did what you wanted and you did it because you wanted to do it. My aunt just moved here from London after a bad divorce, and I see her happy and recovered. When I say strong, I mean independent."

"It looks like you're incredible with time management and staying focused, but how does that translate into balancing all the different clubs you are in, socializing, family, and school?" asked Darcy. I knew this was a tough issue for her personally.

"I truly believe this—it's one of my core values—there is time in the day for everything you want to get done," said Rishika in such a passionate way that she made me believe it. I felt like I should go back, reexamine my life, and stop making excuses about being busy. If she could do it . . .

"If it means sleeping a little less sometimes, so be it," she continued. "I like to say: 'It is the way it is.' I should show you my planner. It's right over there. I'll grab it." She kept talking as she got her calendar and brought it over for us to see. "It's hectic—a lot of people get scared when they see it. But it is what it is. Everything goes down in my planner because otherwise I'll forget to do it."

There were colors, lines, words, information, and times covering every millimeter of space on every page. Where my planner would have had two or three things on a day, hers was filled to the brim with events, projects, and stuff to do.

It scared the pants off me because she had so much to do *and* she was so organized about it. I felt worried that I was behind, disorganized, and didn't have enough to do. At the same time I wondered, does my life really need to be that overwhelmingly busy? "Do you ever get to be a regular teenager? Are you a workaholic?" I asked her.

"I've always been older than my age. I love my friends and I see them whenever I have time, but they understand, too, that I am doing things I love. They care about me and will tell me: *'You're exhausted, you should go to bed—it's time.'* But I definitely, definitely make time for my friends. I hang out with my friends all the time. I'm going to a concert tomorrow."

"Would you say relationship building and trust is a number one skill for leadership?" I asked.

"Absolutely," answered Rishika. "If I didn't have the trust from my team members, we wouldn't get anything done. All the people in this room were my friends. I felt really close to them, really comfortable with them. I trust them completely and that's from getting to know each other. We work so cohesively because of the closeness of the group. The other four members you didn't see are just as close. If we didn't know each other, I would find time to go to lunch or do a team-building activity or something that allows us to have conversations that are authentic."

"I feel like we've touched on this a little, but what would you say are your core values and how do they influence the way you lead?" Darcy asked.

"There are certain things I really care about. Freshman year I attended a conference called the Youth Town Summit where eight hundred kids from all over the country came together to discuss global issues. I came back crying my eyes out. I was just bawling because of all the things going wrong in the world. I heard about rape in Africa and homelessness in

Mexico City. I felt so empathetic. I'm one of those people who puts my-self in everyone else's shoes. My family had to calm me down and affirm that I would be able to make a difference. They kept me grounded by reminding me that there are bad things going on in the world, but you can still be a force of good. That, I would say, is one of my core values.

"I feel like we're put on this earth for a specific reason. If I can help build a school or encourage more recycling, then I've done my part con-tributing to the global community. It's easy to get a little sidetracked with worrying about getting A's or B's, did I get on the sports team, or do my friends think I'm weird, you know? There's so much going on in life. Sometimes I feel that way, too, but for me, above everything else, is how can I contribute to my world and how can I leave a mark that's important and helpful?"

"It sounds like you are that natural leader and then you've studied the tools to make it easier for you. A lot of people, though, wouldn't take leadership training because they don't see themselves in that position. They don't think that they can do it. What advice would you offer to people who feel like they aren't natural leaders at all?" Darcy asked. I thought it was a great question, since at this point most people listening to Rishika would be feeling inferior as a leader.

"My advice would be to keep trying. Find your passions first. Find your fight, you know? Figure out what you want to do; figure out what presses your buttons and then go with that. If you're not passionate about something, then there's no point in pursuing it. If you're doing it for a college application, I would say give up right now . . ."

We started laughing because we know so many people who do things just to look good on their résumé.

" . . . I'm just being frank! Honestly, if you're not passionate about it, if you don't absolutely love and breathe what you do, then there's no point." Rishika spoke with an authority far beyond her years. "The first step, I would say, is find out what you want to lead, figure out what you want to do, figure out what you like, figure out what you dislike, and then from there, leadership comes naturally. If you're passionate about something and you love it enough, then things will naturally fall into place. I would say also to develop your leadership skills, go to camps, and emulate things that you appreciate in other leaders around you. But the very first thing before any of that is to find what you love and what you want to do. Unfortunately I think a lot of schools stress conformity so it's hard to find yourself. If you can't find the opportunities to figure out what you are passionate about in school, go outside of school. Do something in the community. Really explore your passions and what they might be."

"How do you envision the leader of the future versus leaders who were trained in the past?" asked Darcy.

"Communication is evolving wildly. I was obstinate about not getting a Facebook page and not getting into social networking—but I finally gave in. In fact, I organized this meeting today using Facebook. Communication is evolving so rapidly that if you don't embrace it, you'll fall behind. Whether it's getting the message out online or graphically designing a poster or whatever it is, media and technology are going to be more integral parts of leadership.

"Team building has also become even more prevalent. From my understanding, it used to be just about getting the work done. Now since global competitiveness means we have to draw on higher caliber, more intelligent workers, you need to be able to get their buy-in. Those kinds of people have choices; they want to care about their work. The leader of the future has to get them to pull together cohesively to achieve a goal."

"What scares you most about being a leader and how do you deal with it?" I asked.

"What scares me most is whether or not everyone's opinion is being heard and they feel respected. I'm so cognizant about making sure that I'm getting a consensus from the group. I don't know if you heard me in the meeting, but I'm always asking: *'Is anyone not okay with this?'* That's my phrase: *'Is anyone not okay with this?'* People quote it. I end every e-mail with: *'Please, if you have any comments, suggestions, questions, anything, let me know.'* So my biggest fear is that I'm not respecting everyone's opinion."

Darcy turned to Melissa, Rishika's club adviser, who had been listening quietly the whole time.

"What is *your* definition of leadership?" she asked.

"I learned pretty quickly that leadership is absolutely never top down, and if it is, then it's not really leadership; it's actually control. The definition of leadership, to me, is the structures that allow people, groups, and ideas to flourish. It's the stem of the flower; it's the balloon that creates the papier mâché; it's the foundation under the building."

"Which is exactly what we see in Rishika," I concluded.

As we drove back to her dad's house, I prodded Darcy about what she thought of Rishika.

"She's very different from me," Darcy started.

"In what way?" I wanted to know.

Darcy took a long breath and measured her response, as she often does when she has something important to say.

"She's not like the kind of kids I hang out with. She doesn't wear much makeup. Her clothing is very nice, but not really hip. She's kind of a nerd, but she's so likable. She has a lot of friends. Heck, I'd hang out with her in a second! And that's what's weird."

"Why is it weird?"

"'Cause I never thought I'd like being friends with someone like her. It's really interesting."

A sadness began to well up in her teenage eyes. I could tell she was rolling her entire value system around in her head, and she was confused. "What about Rishika appeals to you?" I posed, hoping to shift her thinking in a more positive direction.

"Well, she's clearly amazing. Just the volume of everything she's doing is staggering—she's really making a difference in the world! It makes me feel like I'm not accomplishing anything in my life. It's humbling, but inspiring at the same time, you know? It's like, no one is telling her to go do this stuff. She's grabbing life by the lapels all by herself!"

"So, what are you going to take away from this?" I asked, hoping for the answer I got.

"Well, first of all, maybe I shouldn't be so judgmental of people who look or act differently from what I think is cool. Maybe I shouldn't feel so much pressure to put on makeup and wear the right clothes. And..." Her voice trailed off. She was doing her deep thinking again.

"And what?" I prodded.

"And...that life is full of opportunities—all you have to do is pay attention and focus on what really makes you happy and you can lead a really satisfying, really interesting life."

CHAPTER 19

Dr. Condoleezza Rice

Former United States Secretary of State
Professor at Stanford University

An azure-blue, cloudless dome stretched above our heads from horizon to horizon. It was a perfect early summer day in California—seventy degrees, just the hint of a cool ocean breeze tickling the treetops—and once again Darcy and I drove around the green, grassy knolls of Stanford University. After our previous voyage manqué ten months before, I found it much easier to navigate the expansive campus. As we pulled up to the grand Mediterranean archways of the Hoover Institution, I knew exactly where to find the closest blue, disability parking spot before we hopped on the trail to Dr. Rice's office.

We arrived twenty minutes ahead, had a quick snack, checked our pens and recorders, and at about T-minus ten minutes, announced our arrival to Marilyn, Condoleezza's charming assistant. As soon as I saw Marilyn's face, though, I realized I had forgotten the gift copies of my latest book I had brought for her and Condoleezza. I silently weighed the option of sending them later by mail, but decided I would rather give them as a "thank-you" on the spot. They had performed a logistical miracle to make this moment happen, and I wanted to show my appreciation.

"Marilyn, we're a bit early. Would it be all right if we waited in the anteroom out there?" I said, trying to buy myself a little time without making us late.

"Sure, no problem," replied the always cheerful Marilyn, "I'll just come out and get you when Dr. Rice is ready."

I grabbed my slightly perplexed daughter and ushered her to the tasteful grouping of sofas and chairs just outside the office door. "Listen, honey," I whispered to Darcy, "I left the books in the car, so I have to run back to get them. I'll just be a second."

It took a moment for the implications to set in. *"What!?!!"* she whisper/screeched. "You're going to leave me here? *Alone?*"

"Sure, why not?" I thought playing it cool would calm her down.

"What if they come out to get us? What if she's ready to start?"

"Well, then," I mustered my best reassuring-mother voice, "you go in, introduce yourself, turn on the recorder, and start asking questions. We've done it so many times. We've planned the questions for her. You're good at this. I know you can do it."

Every muscle in her face tightened like a drum. Even her hair looked clenched. "Can I go to the car instead of you?" my petrified teen sputtered. "I don't mind getting the books . . . And I walk faster . . ."

"No, you might get lost. It is a twisty path." Darcy is one of the smartest people I know, but directional orientation isn't one of her strong suits. She gets lost going to the bathroom.

"Please, Mom . . . don't leave me here without you!"

"C'mon. You'll be fine. I should make it back in six, seven minutes tops. Let me go, so I can get back." I headed for the car at a brisk walk.

As I dashed off, I thought back to when we first embarked on this journey. I would have never considered letting Darcy go it alone with one of the world's most important diplomats. But after proudly watching the exquisite arc she had taken in terms of her poise and confidence, I now had no doubt she'd do a perfect job.

My pearl of a parking spot now felt like a real trek. Down stairs, across a courtyard, under archways—the car was much farther away than I thought! Unlike its city-based counterparts back east in New Haven or Cambridge, Stanford's campus has a lot of wide-open spaces. The long, low buildings are spread across acres of well-manicured greenscape. It's a lovely, parklike feeling, but time consuming to get around on foot. Especially when you have only one. Part of me hoped Darcy would get a chance to prove to herself she had the moxie to pull off the interview with Dr. Rice alone, yet I didn't really want to miss any of our precious time with this great woman!

When I finally returned, Darcy was sitting exactly where I left her. But the scared, abandoned young girl, who moments ago had begged her mom not to leave, was transformed into a young woman who looked up at me with an edge of toughness in her eyes I had never seen before. "I can do it, Mom," she said with her newfound confidence, "I know I can! When you left, I felt panicked. I have never been more scared in my life. After about two minutes, though, I reckoned I better figure it out before they came for me. So I ran through everything in my mind: what I would say when I first saw her, how I would start the interview, all of it. Over and over I practiced until I felt really ready."

"You want me to leave again?" I teased.

"*No!*" she punched me in the arm lightly. "But I know I could do it without you."

At that very moment, Marilyn came out and said those sweet words we had waited so many months to hear. "Dr. Rice is ready for you!"

Darcy led us in.

Every corner of Condoleezza Rice's office paints a vivid portrait of this deep, complicated international diplomat. Framed pictures of the secretary smiling with every major world leader line the wood-paneled walls. Interesting souvenirs from the myriad places she's visited seem to dot every horizontal surface of the light, elegant décor. Football memorabilia reminds visitors of the passion for the game she inherited from her beloved father. Pictures of a young, ponytailed, southern black girl remind us of her roots. Off to one side, I notice a model of a huge oil tanker perched on the shelf of an antique credenza. "What's this?" I asked as we collected around a polished oval conference table.

"Oh." She chuckled with a friendly, simple grace. "It's a tradition at Chevron to name their ships after board members. So, when I was appointed to the board, I got my own tanker! That's the *Condoleezza Rice!*" Describing a 500,000-ton merchant ship with her name painted on the side seemed as humble and natural for her as if she were showing us a set of monogrammed dishtowels.

We settled around the table, and with all the poise and confidence of a seasoned journalist, Darcy turned on her recorder and started the interview.

"Typically," Super-teen began, "we like to start by asking how you define leadership, because we have seen how it comes in so many different shapes and forms."

"Principally, it's inspiring people to work toward a common goal," Condoleezza answered without hesitation. "I use the word 'inspiring' because I think it's no longer possible to think of leaders who simply command people to do things. We're long past that as a culture, as a society. People just don't respond very well any longer to command leadership. Even in the most command-like orientation, for instance, the military, you'll find that the leaders who are best can command, but they're also leaders who inspire."

"I'm sure your definition of leadership has changed over time," I said. "What have been some of the big evolutions in how you think of what it means to lead?"

"For me there have been two big turning points. The first is when I was Provost here at Stanford, because I was extremely inexperienced to take on that job. I was only thirty-eight years old and I'd never even been a department chair. The President of Stanford at the time wanted to, as he put it, 'skip a generation of leaders.' The college had been through some very difficult times, and he wanted to get someone who would not have been thought of as having checked all the boxes along the way and having been part of the cause of our problems. It was 1992, and I had just come out of Washington where I'd been President Bush's Soviet and East European Affairs person at the end of the Cold War. I wasn't without experience that was relevant, but I had not been a university administrator before.

"In my first year I would characterize my own leadership style as being a bit rough and not particularly capable of delegating. I was somebody who, if things weren't getting done, I'd just try to do them myself. After about a year, I finally figured out that if you do that, you're not going to have very good people working with you for very long. One of the elements of leadership and management—and I consider them two halves of the same walnut—is that you are really supposed to help people do their jobs. So, if you have someone who's having trouble getting something done, it's better to figure out why that's happening and to help them get it done, rather than trying to do it yourself. That was my epiphany about leading better at that time: you'll drive yourself crazy trying to do everything and you'll drive talented people away.

"My second major turning point came while I was Secretary of State. The State Department was such a huge organization with fifty-five thousand people worldwide, and more than thirty thousand of them are foreigners who are locally engaged staff. You're dealing with fourteen or so different time zones. By the time I got up in the morning, my organization had already been working a full day...and some of them had already gone back to bed!

"Learning to lead, to inspire, and to keep people on the same page over great expanses and different cultures was the challenge in front of me at that time. It was a period when things were not always going so well, so I had to find a way to inspire people to get up the next day and be positive even if it's been a bad day the day before. Those are some of the elements that I learned the second time around."

"One of the things that we read about you," I said, "is the value you put on face-to-face relationships. We heard that you logged more miles than any previous Secretary of State. What was it that brought you to making that a real anchor in your approach? Was there a mentor who instilled that belief in you?"

"Well, it was really my good friend George Shultz who warned me about that. He'd been secretary from 1982 to1988; and he talked about 'gardening,' the importance of keeping relationships fresh and working with them, even when you didn't need something from somebody. Talk to people regularly, was his advice. There's a sense now that you can do this via technology. You can talk on the phone, you can be across a television screen, or you can just send an e-mail."

"It's the social media generation," I quipped.

"That's right," said Condoleezza, turning to Darcy. "With your generation, I watch people texting each other when they are in the same room! I think, hmm . . . How about looking up and talking to that person? Nothing can replace the face-to-face connection. We had to use video conferencing a lot, for instance, when I was meeting with my ambassador to Iraq two or three times a week. The technology itself for video conferencing is now fantastic, so you don't get those funny movements on screen anymore. But you still can't read body language or truly sense how the other person is reacting. I felt that it was both a sign of respect and that it was much more effective to try to see people in person.

"Maybe your generation will be different," she said to Darcy, "but people still freeze up around technology. You can just feel that the interactions are not very smooth."

"There's something missing," said Darcy in agreement.

I was proud that she sidestepped what might have been a temptation to defend her generation's proclivity for technology.

"Yeah, there's something missing," Condi continued. "Particularly, because we had problems with some of our allies and we'd been through a really difficult period in 2003 and 2004, I felt that getting on a plane and going to see them would make a difference. And it *did* make a difference."

Darcy adeptly steered us in a new direction: "With this mother-daughter theme we have going here, we often ask people about the inspiration from their mothers. But we were reading about your relationship with your father and wondered whether having your father as a key role model made it easier to have other male mentors later on in your career?"

"It's a good point," she answered with enthusiasm, "but I thought of my parents very much as a package. I had the great fortune to have a mother and father who interacted very well. I never saw my mother treated as the subordinate figure by my father—in fact, quite the opposite. She was a very strong personality. I remember one particular moment when I was about ten or eleven years old and I learned for the first time that my mother and father had taught at the same place— they met when they were teaching at the same school. Since Birmingham had a nepotism rule that meant one of them had to leave when they got married...and it was my father who moved on, not my mother. At that time the women's movement was starting to get a little bit of momentum and I asked my father, *'How did you make that decision?' 'Well,'* he said, *'Your mother had been teaching at Fairfield first, so of course she would stay, and I would leave.'* That was a very strong message to me that they considered themselves as equals and their careers were equally important. My parents were important role models because their behavior patterned equality for me. My father never seemed to suggest that there were things that I should do—or shouldn't do—because I was a girl. Since I believe that fathers are probably the most important signal to girls about how they're supposed to be treated, he was very important to me in that way. He was also a very strong presence in our community so he shaped the world I grew up in.

"My parents also, very early on, tried to give me leadership opportunities. I was 'president' of the family by the time I was about four. It was my responsibility to call family meetings when we had important things to do like managing the move from the back of the church to a new little house they built for us. I remained president of the family because we didn't have any term limits...and I think my mother voted for me every year. I'm not so sure about my father," Condoleezza said in a mischievous tone. "It was a secret ballot."

> She was much warmer than I had expected her to be. When we started the interview with the more political and technical leadership questions, I mainly noticed her strength and discerning air. But, as we slipped into talking about more personal subjects, her natural personality came out and she seemed more real. I hadn't imagined we would ever get to this point with her.

"Building on the theme of male role models," I asked, "do you want to give some advice about reaching out and connecting with male mentors, with white mentors, and generally with people who are different from you?"

"Sure," she said easily. "I've always said your role models don't need to look like you. I think one of the most destructive notions that we've absorbed is the idea that you can't do something until you see somebody who looks like you do it. There wouldn't be any firsts if that were the case. If my good friend Sally Ride had waited for a female astronaut role model, she wouldn't have gone into space. If Colin Powell had been waiting for a role model who looked like him to be Chairman of the Joint Chiefs of Staff, he wouldn't have been one. And so, I don't know where this concept comes from that you can't do something until you see somebody who looks like you do it. It's great to have role models who look like you, don't get me wrong. But people shouldn't wait around for someone else to blaze the trail. Besides, if you confine your pool of role models to people who look like you, then you may miss out. First of all, you can't assume that people who look like you are good role models; they may or may not be. Second, there may be a lot of really good role models who don't look like you at all and have a lot to teach you. Look for your role models among people who give indications that they're going to care about you, be available to you, push you, and challenge you. That's how you choose role models."

"Let's ask about the decision simulation class that she teaches," Darcy said as much to me as to Condoleezza.

"I've been teaching with decision simulation for a really long time—" she started to answer before I interrupted, "Oh, it's not new?"

"Oh, no, no, no," she said. "I started using decision simulation by my third or fourth year of teaching because, when you read about decisions, you find that we have a tendency in retrospect to create a sort of order to the way those decisions were taken. That post-facto sense of order is not really indicative of how the decision-making environment actually looks.

"People are operating with imperfect information. They're operating under stress. Things come up from nowhere that you suddenly have to take into account in the decision. Yet, historians tend to go back and create a very orderly story about how a decision was made. I had been a part of a couple of game simulations myself, and I realized how much it expanded my thinking. I wanted to import the simulation concept into the classroom because it puts students into the role of a decision maker.

They have to cope with uncertainties, lack of information, and the stress of time pressure. You never have as much time as you want to make a decision."

"So what is the advice can you share with us about the nitty-gritty of real decision making?" I asked. "What are the headlines?"

"First of all, you have to learn to ask the essential questions of people you trust because you're not always going to have all of the expertise and data yourself. That's one of the things you have to get over when you go into decision-making roles in government. As an academic in particular, my tendency was to want to know things in depth. Earlier in my career, I once knew more about the Soviet general staff than they knew about themselves. But I couldn't know that much about everything as I went up the ladder. In the first Bush administration, I was the Soviet Specialist for the President. In that world, I was the expert. But all of a sudden we got to German unification and I also had to be the Soviet expert who knew how to unify Germany. Already my world was a little broader. When I was Provost at Stanford, I couldn't possibly know everything about the telescope that was going to cost the university $7 million, nor could I argue science with the three Nobel laureate physicists who came to convince me we needed it. But I had to be able to make a judgment about whether or not it was really necessary because the music department needed something and the physical campus needed to be rebuilt. Part of decision making is learning to ask tough questions, to keep your priorities and values in mind, and then make a decision in a timely fashion."

"Well," I interjected, "I was thinking about you in the National Security Advisor role. There, you were on the other side of the table, distilling vast amounts of information and providing options to the president so he can make the decisions. It's like you are the lens through which he sees an issue." I was acutely aware of this process since I had served as part of the National Economic Council, the team that presented options to President Clinton for major economic decisions.

"Part of the role of the National Security Advisor is to make sure that the president is getting a full picture," she answered. "So sometimes you distill it down for him, but at other times I felt he needed to see the raw data rather than just the presentation from the Joint Chiefs of Staff. Sometimes I thought he actually needed to hear an alternative view or to hear what was really underneath the summary. The higher you go up the ladder, the more people filter and condense what you get. Pretty soon, you're operating on almost no information at all. When I was secretary, I would very often ask for the desk officer to brief me."

To clarify for Darcy, and to make sure I understood what she meant, I said, "The 'desk officer' is the specialist in a certain region. You're going down several levels of the chain of command to people who would normally never talk to you."

"Exactly!" said Condoleezza. "It means you can hear straight from someone who is talking directly to people on the ground. Your information isn't being filtered through three or four people. Of course you can't do that for every single decision. You have to know when to get more detail—and when not to. It's back to that lesson about trusting the talented people around you or losing them."

"We have talked to a number of women," I began, shifting directions again, "about the importance of being a better public speaker in order to lead people. But you, as an academic, have influenced people more by writing papers and books. You are an expert. Can you tell us more about influencing through writing?"

"Oh, I wouldn't say that at all. I had much more influence through speaking than writing. My academic papers were mainly read by specialists; not the largest audience, really. I made the most impact at the State Department by getting out and talking to groups of staff, large and small, all over the world. I had to inspire them to redefine and update their roles to be effective in our globally interdependent era. Historically, the State Department staff observes and reports back from their postings across the globe. But now we need more than that. We need people to reach out and build bridges across cultures. To make the connections and cultivate the relationships that will help us to understand each other and lay the groundwork for true collaboration. With State Department employees everywhere, I held town meetings, led discussions, and made numerous speeches to begin shifting the behavior of thousands and thousands of people. Writing papers would not have moved the needle. I had to reach out to people—live and in person."

"That leads us to another key question," said Darcy. "What do you think are the skills that the leader of the future needs? What is needed now more than it was in the past?"

"In today's world you can travel among the elites of almost every nation and never speak anything but English. But we can't settle for that. It is important that we speak other languages to gain a deeper understanding and insight into foreign cultures. Nations have become increasingly interdependent with one another and therefore must communicate better and better. The leader of the future must be better at understanding languages and cultures than ever before."

> I was stunned by her answer to my question. The words "linguistic anthropology" are a real mouthful for most people. When I explain that's what I plan to study in college, people often asked: *"How does that translate into any occupation other than ivory tower professor?"* I, too, didn't really know what to do with my own passions. With a few simple words, Dr. Rice suddenly gave me a new direction for my dreams and showed me that there is a real connection between what I most want to learn and the skill set of a leader. Prior to this conversation, I had no idea that "world leader" was a career path for me to consider.
>
> "I love languages!" I said, the words finally bursting out, "and I love studying other cultures. It's all I have ever wanted to do."

"Then you are on the right track," Condoleezza said. The feeling in the room was as if she had touched each of Darcy's shoulders with a ceremonial sword and bestowed on her knighthood and a mission to find the Holy Grail.

"She's studying Mandarin," I bragged.

"Really?" Condoleezza said to Darcy. "I have always had a passion for languages, too. My Russian is pretty rusty now, though."

The more she talked about languages, the more I could feel excitement building up inside me. I wanted to shout out: I love this! I love you! What you are talking about is amazing and I am fascinated! To share that with her was really, really cool!

"Are you an only child, too?" she asked Darcy.

"Yeah, I am." Darcy answered.

"It tends to make you grow up faster and be a high achiever. Did you play an instrument?"

"Cello. But not at the level you play piano!"

In addition to her extraordinary accomplishments on the world's stage, Dr. Rice is also a highly gifted musician. At age fifteen, she played Mozart with the Denver Symphony. As Secretary of State, she performed in public with Yo-Yo Ma and once even gave a concert for Her Majesty, Queen Elizabeth II. But when she played on tour with Aretha Franklin . . . that put her over the top for me!

Their love fest continued on for a while longer, but soon it was time for us to gather up the memories of one of the most exciting few hours of our lives and bid our leave to Dr. Condoleezza Rice.

In the quiet of the gray-and-yellow-tiled bathroom of the Hertz rental car return building at SFO, Darcy and I changed out of our business suits into more comfortable clothes for the red-eye flight home to Princeton.

"You know," Darcy said, "when you start a journey like this, you hope that it will be life changing . . . but you really don't know for sure." A big grin broke out across her face. "Today, Mom, *this* was life changing."

CHAPTER 20

————•••————

Sheryl Sandberg
Chief Operating Officer, Facebook

The flight from Newark to San Francisco had a distinctly familiar feel. Perhaps this was because Darcy and I had bounced across our country from sea to shining sea so often in the past year we felt like we knew the flight attendants by name. We'd been to California for Amy Pascal, Wendy Kopp, Rishika Daryanani, Geena Davis, and Condi Rice . . . *twice*. We'd frugally managed to use frequent flyer miles and/or combine trips with Darcy's visits to her father and with my job as a speaker. Once again we landed at SFO, grabbed our rental car, and in no time found ourselves amidst the highways and byways along the southern reaches of the Frisco Bay. This time, though, the journey had an extra electric spark to it. Our destination was the headquarters of the biggest cultural phenomenon of the 21st century: *Facebook*.

"Look, there's *Google*!" Darcy shouted as she spied the familiar, multicolored letters dangling from a huge sign that marked the entrance to a beautiful campus. The 101 Freeway heading south from the airport cuts right through the heart of the famous Silicon Valley, home to the largest concentration of high-tech think tanks anywhere on the planet. Logo after iconic logo that surrounded Darcy's life from the moment she was first able to crawl over to a computer and bang her tiny fingers on the keyboard passed by as we zipped along the freeway. "I had no idea these guys were all so close together! There's *Yahoo*! There's *eBay*!" she gushed, with increasing enthusiasm. "OMG. There's *APPLE*!"

That last one was uttered with an almost holy reverence. I half expected her to force me to pull off the freeway and drive up the "infinite loop" so we could bow down and worship the massive glass-encased shrine of the bitten fruit. We had no time for detours, however, no matter how sacrosanct. As enticing as a visit to these famous companies might be, Darcy was happy to forgo a pilgrimage to any of these legendary locales as we were heading to the very center of teenage social networking zeitgeist.

Founded on a lark by a group of super smart, hormonally ravaged undergraduate guys at Harvard as a way to meet girls, Facebook has spawned a revolution in the way people, particularly young people, communicate with each other. Since its inception in 2004, this seductively addictive website has amassed an international following of almost twice the population of the United States, and made a billionaire out of its principal founder, Mark Zuckerberg, before his twenty-fifth birthday.

"I think we just missed it!" Darcy exclaimed, counting the numbers on the buildings as we passed by them.

"Okay, I'll turn around." I made a U-turn as soon as I could, and we doubled back down the street toward the address we'd been given. I was surprised we had gone by it. The unique blue-and-white logo should have been easy to spot. Also, since I knew Facebook employed over 850 people, I figured the building had to be one of the larger ones on the block.

"Wait a second," Darcy said, perplexed. "We passed it again!"

Was it hiding? Did we have the wrong address? We refined our scrutiny with the next pass and identified a low, nondescript concrete building that displayed the correct digits by the curb. Could this be it? We drove into the small parking lot and found our way to the front door. As we got closer, I was pretty sure this couldn't possibly be the place. Where were the fountains? Where was the big, fancy sign? Where was the spectacularly cutting-edge architectural design like the ones we saw from the freeway?

Now it made sense. Less than seven years ago, this entire company was just a couple of guys in a Cambridge dorm room. They've grown so fast, they haven't had time to build themselves a mother ship. They rent space where they can find it. And they probably got a good deal by picking up the lease from some defunct, overspent victim of the burst dot-com bubble.

"What does that say?" Darcy asked, pointing to the etching on the glass of the front door.

I squinted to make out the lettering as we continued our approach. Finally we got close enough to focus.

"I think it says . . . *Hack?*" I said, more than a little confused.

Yes, it's true. The first image visible on the approach to the Facebook headquarters is the word "Hack."

"Wow," Darcy immediately got it. "These guys are the ultimate hackers! I never really thought about that before."

We pulled open the four-lettered door and immediately knew we were in the right place. Everything about the interior, in stark contrast to its dull exterior, screamed *"Young, fun people work here."* Bright colors dazzled the senses from every surface. Huge bowls of assorted candies flanked each end of the long receptionist's desk. Even the carpeting jumped off the floor with vibrant brilliance. The famous logo was now conspicuously displayed, framed behind glass and hanging on a stone wall just inside the doorway. This version, though, was a reverse of the usual white lettering over a blue background. Here there were blue letters over white, with the entire white background covered in scrawled signatures.

"May I help you?" the friendly receptionist chirped.

"Yes," I replied, "Bonnie St. John and Darcy Deane to see Sheryl Sandberg."

Once she dialed the appropriate extension and announced our arrival, I indulged my curiosity while Darcy dug into an orange Starburst. "Whose signatures are those?" I asked, pointing to the wall hanging.

"Oh," she happily replied, "those are all the original employees."

"Really? All of them?"

She immediately knew where I was going with this.

"Yes," she smiled wisely. This wasn't the first time she had an interchange like this.

"Mark's signature is the one just above the C."

I unabashedly strolled over to get a closer look at the personal mark of the world's youngest billionaire.

The receptionist's multibuttoned phone emitted a cute electronic jingle. I turned my attention toward the sound just in time to catch the Reese's Peanut Butter Cup Darcy tossed my way. She knows those are my favorite.

"Okay," the receptionist said after receiving her message. "Stephanie from our public relations office will be here for you in a minute. In the meantime, would you mind filling this out? Everyone who enters the facility has to sign this agreement." She handed us each a clipboard with a very legal looking form on it. This was the first time, in all our travels, that we were presented with such a document. The people who work inside these doors are on the bleeding edge of technological advances and are rightly concerned their intellectual property might be stolen. We scrawled our "John Hancocks" on the appropriate lines.

"Hi, I'm Stephanie," said the fresh-faced young woman who arrived to be our escort. "Welcome to Facebook!" She beckoned us to follow her into the secure area behind the reception lounge. Once inside the doors, we were stunned by what we saw first. "We start all our tours here . . ." said Stephanie, grinning at our reaction.

There in front of us was the one and only, original Facebook Wall— a floor-to-ceiling whitewashed background with the Facebook logo stretched across the top. Just below the familiar blue-and-white rectangle was the simple invitation: *'Write Something.'* And it appeared everyone who entered this portal was happy to oblige. Almost every inch of available space was covered by thousands of multicolored signatures, notes, drawings, pictures—it was the literal manifestation of the cyber-based splash page that anchors all the website's interactions.

"Go ahead," Stephanie offered, handing us each bright, red and blue markers.

As Mom and I scrawled our names alongside all the messages already posted, I thought about all of the people entering this building—some famous, most not—and adding to the total creative spark that is Facebook. It hit me that, at this moment, I was really inside the place that created and runs about 60 percent of my whole social interaction with a really large community. I was about to go behind the curtain of a tool I use constantly and find out about the Facebook culture that permeates every aspect of my life.

Stephanie proceeded to give us the VIP tour all around the facility. The environment was that of an open, roughed-out industrial space that had splashes of warmth and color tossed into it. Clever seating areas with potted foliage sprang up from the unfinished cement floors in random patterns—like little parks with benches where people could gather around brightly painted sofas and chairs to share ideas and inspiration. In the tradition of young, hip work arenas, there were practically no four-walled rooms anywhere. No one has an office; instead, every Facebook denizen plugs into an open-air workstation, in close proximity to his or her coworkers. Departments have delineated areas, but the entire operation is designed to foster a free-flowing interchange of thoughts and interactions without barriers—real or implied.

For those times where a moment of isolation is necessary, conference rooms can be reserved for meetings. They line, and in some cases delineate, the corridors throughout the building. Each conference room is adorned with a plaque outside its glass door proudly identifying it by name. "ITALY, SPAIN, CANADA . . ." Darcy read the nameplates. "How come you named these after countries?"

"Well," Stephanie replied, smiling at Darcy's perceptive nature, "each of these rooms was christened with the name of a country as the total number of Facebook members exceeded their populations."

It was also clear that this was a place where people work around the clock. We passed a dozen snack areas well stocked with all sorts of choices—healthy and otherwise (one even featured fresh-baked goods)—for sustenance any time of the day or night. The gorgeous cafeteria serves a deliciously elaborate menu for breakfast, lunch, and dinner seven days a week. There's even a place to have laundry and dry cleaning done. And all this is completely free for every employee and their families.

Our heels clicked loudly on the unfinished concrete floor as we passed a line of the game rooms filled with the latest noisy electronic challenges, quiet rooms for peaceful meditation where you can snuggle up onto big, comfy pillows in soft pastel colors, even a life-size chess board (the king was taller than Darcy)—all designed to keep whizzing hot minds from burning out.

"What's that?" I asked, pointing to a large hole cut into one of the walls that provided a counter behind which there seemed to be a plethora of computer systems all pulled apart in various stage of disrepair.

"Oh, that's the 24 hour help desk," Stephanie told us. "We don't want anyone slowed down by a hardware problem, so these guys are available to fix your Mac or PC any time of the day or night. It's kind of like the 'Genius Bar' at an Apple store."

I chuckled to myself at the use of the word "genius." You couldn't swing a cat around here without hitting a genius. The telltale signs of young, raucous, overactive cerebral cortexes were everywhere. We spied a constant barrage of sayings and slogans randomly littered about the walls and ceilings that reinforced the guerrilla-style intellectual culture. On one room divider, a poster read: *"What would you do if you weren't afraid?"* On another: *"Done is better than perfect." "The job is only 1% finished"* screamed down from a huge banner, and *"Fortune favors the bold"* was scrawled (was that crayon?) along one of the staircases. My personal favorite was painted across the doorway that framed a prominent walkway—one that almost everyone working there would have to pass by at least once a day:

"Move fast and break things."

If there were ever a corporate ideology to sum up Facebook, this was it.

We rounded another corner, and I was surprised to notice there was, in fact, one area right smack in the middle of the floor that seemed to be self-contained. Surrounded by glass on three sides to be consistent with the open concept yet still retain a modicum of privacy, this was the sanctum sanctorum of Facebook—the founder's office. We walked past trying hard not to gawk at the tall, not-as-geeky-as-we-thought young man rocking back and forth on a classic, lime-green Eames chair. The legend himself, Mark Zuckerberg, held court in a meeting with about half a dozen very intense-looking Asian twenty-somethings. I noticed Darcy's stunned face as she quickly and discreetly tapped out a message on her phone. She obviously couldn't wait to share this moment with her friends.

"Is he here every day?" I asked, wondering why someone with all his money wouldn't be off enjoying it.

"Oh, yes," Stephanie answered. "Mark is very hands-on. He spends a lot of time just meandering around the floor looking into what people are working on—offering advice and encouragement. Once a week, he and several other senior executives have an open Q-and-A session where they answer questions any of the employees may have. It's amazing. Nobody misses those meetings!"

Stephanie's cell phone rang, and she took what seemed to be an urgent message. "Oh, I have some bad news," Stephanie said to us. "Sheryl was tied up and won't be able to be here in person for your meeting. But don't worry; we'll set you up with her over the phone. Please follow me." Stephanie escorted us to another cluster of conference rooms. These, I noticed, were *not* titled after countries.

"What's the story with these names?" I asked.

Stephanie smiled. "These rooms were named after famously bad ideas. People nominate names for conference rooms, and then we all take a vote." We walked past *"Mounting a Land War in Asia," "Glass Hammer,"* and *"Inflatable Cellar,"* finally settling into *"Fighting with Chuck Norris."* One of those fancy speakerphones that looks like a three-pointed alien spaceship was already lit up on the simple, round conference table. As soon as we walked in, Stephanie punched a flashing red button. I grabbed a yellow plastic chair. Darcy's was bright red.

"Hi, guys." Sheryl was instantly "live" on the device.

"Thanks for taking the time to connect with us," I said into the UFO.

"I'm so sorry I couldn't be there in person, but I'm really glad you had a chance to visit Facebook," Sheryl answered in a very friendly tone.

"This sounds like a really great project. I hope I do something this cool with my daughter one day. You two are an inspiration to me!"

Wow, I thought to myself, can you believe that she thinks we are cool? "I can't wait to tell my friends at home about seeing Facebook on the inside," I told Sheryl. "I already posted that I am here." I knew my friends would think it was cool, because Facebook is the epitome of cool. When I told them I saw Zuckerberg, I knew everyone would go "ooh!" and "ah!"

"Tell us more, from your perspective, about what we've just seen here on the tour," I prodded.

"Everything about the way we structure our company is like our product," Sheryl said, immediately warming to the subject, "ensuring maximum openness and access for everyone. As you saw, there are no offices, no closed doors, not even cubes—just open desks in big open rooms. Mark and I, as well as our other leaders and everyone else, have open desks. We hold a company-wide open Q-and-A every Friday where anyone can ask a question or comment. When people disagree with the decisions we make, they post public notes to each other. Where? On Facebook, of course."

"I'd like to know more about the culture of working here," Darcy, the future anthropologist, asked.

"We give our employees an enormous sense of ownership," Sheryl answered. "Let me give you an example. When I first joined the company, Michael Phelps won his eighth gold medal, setting the world's record. And whenever he was interviewed, he kept thanking Facebook for enabling him to keep in touch with his friends during the Olympics. Facebook had long had a policy of not using 'editorial voice'; each user's page was theirs and the company view was that we should intrude as little as possible on that space. But it was pretty cool that Phelps kept thanking us, and I thought we should thank him, too.

"Over a weekend, Mark and I decided to put a small note on the top of the pages of U.S. users, which said, 'Facebook congratulates Michael

Phelps and the U.S. Olympic team.' Pretty uncontroversial stuff. The company went *crazy*. Not just because we used 'editorial voice,' but because Mark and I made a decision without them. This built over the course of the week to the point where Mark and I used the Friday Q-and-A to apologize to the company and say we would never make a decision like this without them again."

"It's more like being the mayor of a city than the head of a traditional business," observed Darcy. "Just like the relationship Facebook has with all the users. They revolt if they aren't included in certain policy decisions. We've seen it."

"What do you look for in the people you bring on board?" I asked.

"We reward taking risk," said Sheryl. "That's part of it. A few years ago, we had a summer intern who thought he had a great idea. He built it and then tested it during peak traffic time . . . and took down the Facebook site."

We gasped at the horror of it. "What did you do?" I asked, expecting to hear about some sort of seppuku, the traditional Japanese suicide ritual.

"We hired him!" Sheryl laughed. "We hired him because he thought big and believed in his ideas. Also, apparently we like people who crash computer systems." She was making an oblique reference to the fact that Mark had crashed the Harvard University computer systems with the first iteration of his "Face Book." It was also true, but not widely known, that Sheryl had crashed the same system about fifteen years earlier while running regressions for her senior thesis. Back then computers were much smaller and easier to crash. But no one bothered to make a movie out of Sheryl's transgression.

Sheryl continued, "It strikes me that the openness and, well, insubordination that we relish at Facebook wouldn't work everywhere. If you had signs on the walls of a hospital that said, *'Move fast and break things,'* I'd be afraid to enter the building. The flexibility and fluidity of our culture is right for us and for our mission—but it's not for everyone."

"What is it like working in a very young and male environment?" I asked. "When I told my friends online that I was going to get to talk with you, that's what a lot of people wanted to know. After the film *The So-*

cial Network, I think people imagine you're like Wendy brought to Never Never Land to sort out the Lost Boys."

"Working here is not like the movie—that's a Hollywood story. It's actually a very mixed-gender atmosphere here. We have a ton of female leaders across the company. There's a woman head of sales; there's a woman leading public policy. We also have a woman engineering director, and so on. It is, however, a very young workforce. Sometimes I feel old, and I just have to deal with that. But in most ways, it's pretty fantastic. I feel like I'm in touch with what's really happening at the forefront of information—and it's mostly the product that matters. The product keeps us all in touch with each other."

"What would you say are your core values?" Darcy asked next. "For you personally, not Facebook as a whole."

"It's really important to do things you believe in," she said unequivocally. "People talk all the time about what makes a good manager, what makes good leader. And fundamentally, what makes a good leader is someone who inspires you. The only way to inspire anyone or inspire yourself is if you care about what you're doing. You have to actually care about what you're doing. I've only ever worked on things I care about. I started my career right out of college working on leprosy in India for the World Bank. I went on to work at the Treasury Department during the Asian financial crisis, and then moved to Google where, I really believed, they were also shaping the world we live in. Now, I'm here at Facebook where I believe in the mission. I'm passionate about it."

We heard paper rustling and some chewing sounds. "—sorry, I'm eating as I speak to you. I apologize for being rude!"

"In your role as COO," I continued, "you are not only dealing with people inside Facebook, but also so many different cultures, different countries, and different governments around the world. It must help that you have a background in international relations. Can you talk about that?"

"When I first joined Facebook early in 2008, there were seventy million active users. Today, there are over half a billion. If Facebook were a single community, its population would make it the third most populous country in the world. But it's not a single community. It is millions of overlapping communities, held together by common concerns, interests, and experiences. We offer seventy translations of Facebook, making us available in almost every major language around the world. I absolutely think the government background I have has made me cut out to do my job well."

"In a lot of our interviews we've asked: what do you think about the leader of the future? What do people who aspire to be leaders need to be good at?" asked Darcy.

"The world is changing so quickly. Actually I am giving a speech on leadership in a few weeks and it's for young people at the beginning of their careers. I can tell you what I am planning to say to them. Does that sound good?"

"That sounds great," Darcy answered.

"Hang on, my notes are right here . . ." We could hear her rummaging around for the draft of the speech.

"There are four main points," Sheryl began. "First of all, a good leader doesn't just command, they inspire. This is perhaps the most important, universal principle of leadership: it is better to inspire than to direct. Sure, authority generates compliance. People will do what you tell them to do in most organizations. Even at Facebook . . . well, sometimes." She laughed.

"But great leaders don't just want compliance. They want to elicit genuine enthusiasm, complete trust, and real dedication. If people understand and believe in the mission, they will figure out how to do the daily tasks that support it. A great leader's most important role is not to direct the details, but to clearly articulate the goal and keep everyone focused on it.

"The second point about leadership I am going to make in my speech springs naturally from the first point: great leaders don't just talk, they listen. All of us—and especially leaders—need to hear the truth. Yet, as a leader, setting yourself up to hear the truth is a real challenge. It's hard to encourage people to tell you things you might not want to hear. And it's hard for them to believe they can do so without repercussions. One trick I've discovered is to speak openly about what you are bad at. This gives people permission to agree with you about your weaknesses. For example, one of my weaknesses is that in meetings, I sometimes speak too much. Okay, I *often* speak too much! And I talk about it openly because by saying it in advance and asking people to point it out to me in the moment, they do. But if I never said this, would anyone who works for me ever walk up and say, *'Hey, Sheryl, I think you talked too much today'* . . . ? I doubt it.

"Hearing the truth is also better served by using simple and clear language. Here's an example: along with running Facebook, Mark has been studying Chinese this past year. To practice, he spends two hours each week with a group of Facebook employees who are native Chinese speakers, many of whom are quite junior."

As soon as Sheryl said that, I realized that Mark was probably practicing his Chinese when we saw him in the conference room earlier.

"He tries to have work conversations with them, but because he is learning the language, he often finds himself asking people to use more basic language. They say something—and he says, *'more basic Chinese please.'* They try again and he says, *'simpler please.'* By the end of the back and forth, they say something very clear and simple—something like, *'my manager is bad.'* Much of the truth is lost in the nuances of adult language. This is especially true in hierarchical organizations. No one tells anyone *'my manager is bad.'* By the time we might try to divulge that a colleague is underperforming, we have buried it in so many preambles and caveats and parentheticals that the message gets lost. A leader has to solicit the truth and get people to use simple and clear language when possible.

"To get the truth, you also have to reward it. Last summer, we held a barbecue for our summer interns at Mark's house. One of them said to him in front of all of the others that he needed to improve his public speaking skills. After the barbecue, Mark and I tracked down who that guy was . . . to make sure we hired him. That's the kind of person we want in our company.

"When anyone tells me that I did something badly, I thank them publicly. If they tell me privately, I share their thoughts with others so they still get public credit. And when I am wrong—as I so often am—I say so publicly and thank the people that helped me see it. Also, leaders don't just have great ideas, they recognize them," Sheryl said. "Not every idea has to come from the top, and often the best ideas don't. The best leaders for the future will have the confidence to acknowledge that the people on the front line know more about their specific job—because they do it all day. This was always true, but today's world of access to information and easy ability to share and collaborate makes this even more important. Being willing to accept and say publicly that others know more—and that great ideas can and should come from everyone—is the ultimate sign of strength.

"The third point in the speech I'm giving is about valuing diversity, but I'm not going to focus on diversity in general. Because of my unique vantage point, I am going to talk more about the importance of leaders—male and female—getting good at developing women as leaders all around them.

"We have a real problem in the world," Sheryl continued. "Women are not making it to the top of any profession anywhere. Out of one hundred and ninety heads of state, only nine are women. Of all the people in Parliaments in the world, thirteen percent are women. In the corporate sector, women in C-level jobs and board seats top out at fifteen to sixteen percent. These numbers have not moved up since 2002 and are currently going in the wrong direction. It starts by acknowledging that in some important ways, women are different. Women often don't negotiate for themselves. A study in the last two years of people entering the workforce out of college showed that fifty-seven percent of men negotiate their first salary while only seven percent of women do. Women also tend to underestimate their own abilities compared to men. Studies show that when surveyed on quantifiable performance criteria like GPAs, men overestimate their performance and women underestimate. And men attribute success to themselves while women attribute it to external factors. When men are asked why they succeeded at something, they'll basically say, *'I'm awesome!'* "

We all laughed.

"It's almost as if they think it's obvious, so why would you even ask? When women are asked why they did something well, they attribute it to luck, help from others, or working hard. This matters because no one gets to the corner office if they don't believe in themselves or understand what makes them successful. I wish the answer was easy. Flextime, mentoring, and other programs that companies create to develop women are important, but not enough. I wish I could just tell all the fabulous women I work with: Believe in yourself! Negotiate for yourself! Own your success! I really wish I could tell that to my daughter, but it isn't that simple. Studies have shown that for men, success and likability are positively correlated while for women, they are negatively correlated. So, as a man gets more successful, he is liked more. As a woman gets more successful, she is liked less. A powerful man is 'exacting,' while a woman 'nitpicks.' That same man is a 'consensus-builder' while a woman is 'political.' It's a societal problem, and change is happening slowly.

"As the fourth point in the speech I am going to give, I will tell the young men and women, these future leaders, that they can move this change along faster. When you hear that a woman leader is not well liked by her peers, take a moment to consider if this might be based on the knee-jerk reaction people have to successful women. Challenge your assumptions."

"So, how would you teach your daughter versus your son differently about leadership . . . or would you?" asked Darcy.

"On leadership, I would teach them the same things. Better to inspire than command, get your hands dirty, and do real work with your team. As you become more of a leader, you actually become more dependent on other people, not less dependent. I will also say to both my son and daughter that their careers will be more determined by whom they partner with in life than by any other decision they make. I want my son to have a choice to be a full partner at home and a full success in the workforce, and I want my daughter to have that choice, too. And I understand that if my son doesn't have that choice, my daughter won't, either. I said that in my TED talk, too. Did you know that in families with two full-time parents and at least one child, women do twice as much housework and three times the childcare? In those households the woman has two or three jobs whereas the husband only has one."

"Yes, I loved what you said about the struggles with work-life balance for women as opposed to men," Darcy said. "But how do you address that challenge in your own personal life?"

"I have a fifty-fifty marriage. I have a husband who's a CEO of a company, and we each do half—well, I don't mean fifty percent every day. It ebbs and flows. We work our travel around each other's schedule and try not to be gone at the same time. When I signed up to be a volunteer in my kid's school one morning, and then I couldn't go, he went in my place. I don't think most women have that. There are not a lot of fifty-fifty marriages. If you want to understand more about how to do it and what it looks like, check out the book, *The Fifty-fifty Partnership*, by Sharon Meers. I think every person who wants to have a career and a marriage should read it. Did you know that fifty-fifty marriages have half the divorce rate?

"Oh, we've arrived at our next meeting. My time is running out." Sheryl needed to wrap it up.

"What is the most rewarding thing about the work you do?" I asked as a coda to our discussion. "What gets you up in the morning? What makes you excited when you go to bed at night?"

"It's what people do with the technology. People find organ donors for their ten-year-old children on Facebook. People organize political criticism on Facebook. A friend of mine from college just told me that his wife was missing and they found her because of Facebook. I know I am in the middle of what is amazing in the world right now."

———·•·———

CHAPTER 21

Dr. Susan E. Rice

United States Ambassador to the United Nations

Since the inception of the United Nations immediately after WWII, the United States Ambassador to the UN has been one of the most powerful and influential government officials engaged in international diplomatic relations for our country. From this office, U.S. foreign policy initiatives are administered and implemented on the world's stage at the highest levels. And, in 2009, when President Barack Obama announced his cabinet, he appointed Dr. Susan E. Rice to this illustrious post—the first African-American woman to hold the office.

I first met Susan Rice twenty-five years ago when we were Rhodes Scholars together at Oxford. We were both short, black, American women and thus became fast friends. Later, during the Clinton administration, we worked one floor apart in the Old Executive Office Building next to the White House. Susan worked upstairs at the National Security Council, and I was downstairs at the National Economic Council. When Darcy was born, I left politics and returned to the private sector work I loved while Susan stuck with the battles of the Beltway; but we've always remained close. Ours is one of those friendships where, even if we haven't seen each other for months at a time, we always pick up right where we left off as if we had been together yesterday.

From the moment I met her, it was clear my pal had a one-in-a-million mind. Her brilliant grasp of the nuances of international diplomacy is, and always has been, astounding. I sleep better at night knowing she's there doing this job for my country.

We set up a meeting with Susan at her office in the brand-new U.S. Mission building on the corner of 45th Street and First Avenue—right across the street from the UN headquarters. Opened just a few months earlier, this spectacularly designed structure replaced the storied honeycombed façade of the original mission built in 1961 where former UN Ambassadors such as George H.W. Bush, Madeleine Albright, and Henry Cabot Lodge staged many important diplomatic initiatives— including the strategy for staring down the Soviets during the Cuban Missile Crisis when Ambassador Adlai Stevenson made his famous, "I'll wait for my answer until hell freezes over" speech on the floor of the UN Security Council.

The new building is a stunning architectural achievement. Twice the size of the previous structure, a twenty-three-story concrete tower sits elegantly atop a flowing façade that forms a clean, graceful wave of glistening steel to frame the elegant entryway. Its beautifully designed offices, meeting rooms, and presentation areas include a state-of-the-art press briefing room as well as secure, electronically sterilized, soundproof locations for sending and receiving classified communications from all over the world.

Darcy and I cleared security, walked into the gray-blocked lobby facing First Avenue, and immediately smelled that "new building" scent of fresh paint and well-scrubbed surfaces. The first thing we saw was a gallery of four large portraits: President Barack Obama, Vice President Joe Biden, Secretary of State Hillary Clinton, and Darcy's "Auntie Susan," aka Ambassador Susan Rice.

I smiled. It will be fun for Darcy to see Susan in this milieu, surrounded by her security detail and presiding over a dedicated staff of smart, motivated intellectuals. Darcy knew her auntie Susan had an important job, but her previous interactions with "Mom's friend" were raucous overnights at her house in Washington where Darcy riled up Susan's kids, Jake and Maris, and helped her whip up a batch of delicious waffles in the morning.

A charming young man named Alex from Susan's public relations department ushered us into a small office upstairs to wait for our allotted time. As that day's UN Security Council meeting stretched longer and longer, Susan's friendly and efficient staff was apologetic but kept us well aware of her demanding schedule. We were supposed to meet with her at 1 p.m., and at 2 p.m. she was slated to give a speech at the Young Woman's Leadership School of East Harlem—easily a thirty- to forty-minute drive. I became concerned that our interview slot was rapidly disappearing. At 1:30, I really started to worry. At 1:45, I was anxiously checking my watch when Priva, Susan's special assistant, quickly breezed into the room. Priva was one of those young, super-bright, energetic people who was grateful for this opportunity and worked hard at it. The daughter of immigrants from India, she had long dark hair, penetrating eyes, and cappuccino skin, making her tiny, elegant nose piercing seem more cultural than rebellious.

That knot started in my gut. Here we go again . . . cancellation purgatory . . .

"Okay, here's the situation." Priva got right to the point. "As you know, the ambassador is running behind schedule and we're due up in Harlem at the school in a few minutes. I'm really, really sorry about this, but would you mind doing your meeting in the car as we travel?"

"Sure, that would be fine," I enthusiastically replied, feeling my muscles unlock. This wasn't bad at all. It might be fun to be part of Susan's entourage.

"Great! Thanks for being so patient and understanding." Priva bolted from the room as quickly as she came.

We sat back down on the colorful, modern furniture and waited. And waited some more. Suddenly, a burst of adrenaline seemed to shoot through everyone around us, and things started moving really fast. Cell phones rang, muffled conversations rippled back and forth.

"Council meeting's over."

"She's in transit."

"The ambassador's in the building."

"Car's pulling up . . . meet in the lobby . . . go, go, *GO!*"

Darcy and I were rushed into an elevator and whisked to the ground floor of the building. Just as we landed, Madam Ambassador swooped around a corner with a stream of aides and advisers flowing behind, as if attracted by her gravitational pull.

"Hi guys!" She rushed over to us and gave us big hugs and kisses. The reunion lasted only seconds, as we were briskly shepherded out onto the sidewalk toward the enormous, black SUV waiting at the curb.

Susan and I sat next to each other on the black leather captain's chairs in the back, with Darcy and Priva on jump seats that folded down across from us. We turned on our recorder right away and started talking as soon as the heavy vehicle rocketed away from the curb.

"How would you describe your personal leadership style?" Darcy asked as we bounced along the Upper East Side of Manhattan.

There was a pause as Susan thought for a moment. "I can't wait to hear this one," I said with a chuckle. I was aware of her tough-as-nails, you-do-not-want-to-cross-her style.

She responded with laughter in her voice, too, "Then you should let Priva answer that!" We all laughed, then Susan continued. "Okay, I'll tell you how I perceive it," she said, still carrying a humorous note, "and Priva can give you a validation or a contradiction." Becoming more serious, Susan said, "I'm straightforward. People know when they talk to me that what they see is what they get—that I'm not playing games. I think that's very important. They see me as pretty open and collaborative, tough when I need to be, but not confrontational for its own sake. I think people know not to mess with me. And if they haven't learned," she continued, smiling, "and they try, then they will learn."

We turned to Priva, who happily weighed in on her boss's leadership style. "She's very honest, she's very straightforward, and she's very tough," Priva said with obvious affection for her boss. "She expects a lot from everyone around her, but I think that's because she expects a lot from herself. She's giving 110 percent, so everyone else should be, too. That's a fair demand."

"Where do you think the sense of toughness comes from?" Darcy asked.

"I'm no tougher than your mom," Susan said, looking at me.

"No," I disagreed. "You're *much* tougher than I am!" I would crumble in the face of pressure from international leaders, but, when I think about it, I suppose skiing at seventy miles per hour on one leg might mess with Susan!

Turning back to Darcy, Susan answered her question. "I think it comes from a certain amount of self-confidence and a certain amount of belief in the righteousness of what we're trying to do. I'm not out for my own interests. I'm not trying to hurt anybody else. Everything that we're doing and that I've done, all my professional life, has been, at least in my view, for a larger and better end. There's nothing to be ashamed of or any reason to back down on substance or principle. Another part of it is just character and how I was raised. I was raised to do my best and to give my 100 percent to whatever it was I was doing. And I think generally that that approach has served me well. So, it's not about being aggressive or being difficult. It's just about not backing down when I think I'm doing the right thing for the right reasons."

"Talk about your development as a leader." I switched directions. "Can you think of a time when you learned something that changed the way you lead?"

"I learned a lot from my time as Assistant Secretary for African Affairs. As you know I started that when I was thirty-two and just had my first child, Jake. One of the things I learned at that time was patience . . . well, at least I ended up with more than when I started. Patience still isn't my strong suit. I began recognizing that the best way to get from A to Z was not always in a straight line . . . sometimes you need to tack and adjust. Sometimes you have to slow down to bring as many people along as possible. Priva saw two examples of strategic patience today in the Security Council. My gut was telling me to jump in right at the beginning, pile on the table, and say what I'm going to say. Instead, I decided to let everybody else speak, hang back in conscious restraint, and then very calmly and almost gingerly try to kill the proposal.

"One of the most important ways I make a difference is being part of making the decisions that determine how we approach key issues or challenges in the world, getting to execute them, and doing it in a way that tries to build support and consensus rather than creating confrontation. Here at the UN I have some freedom to figure out how I'm going to do things, not just take orders. I participate in the decisions about what we're going to do. That's one of the really gratifying things about the job.

"Today was a good example. We normally get our instructions on various issues from the State Department or the White House. It was a situation where it wasn't a big issue that we had to litigate at the highest levels. In that instance, I would be at the table in Washington and argue my point of view. The president or somebody else would make a decision and we'd have to implement it. This was not of that degree of profile, but it had the potential to poison the atmosphere here at the UN and create some resentment toward us that I figured we didn't need to create.

"The original instruction was to go kill this proposal outright with blunt force. My team in Washington got me a modified instruction that didn't soften it as much as I wanted. It basically said, kill it with a bunch of questions. But these are questions that I had already delayed it with six weeks ago, so to come back with that tactic wasn't going to work, either. I decided to do it a different way, toward the same end. My view is that, if we can kill it without a lot of cost, that's fine.

"I created an environment in which we may not have to kill the proposal overtly ourselves, and the thing can collapse of its own weight. It's not all done, by the way, but I think it's going to die a slow death now. It's fun to figure out not just what it is we have to do, but also to have some opportunity to carry out how we do it."

"You come off as being fearless," Darcy asked. "Is there anything that scares you about leadership?"

"About leadership?" Susan thought for no more than a split second and said, "No."

"Is there anything that you're afraid of?" I asked.

"Yeah. I fear for the well-being of my kids. I worry about losing my parents. But there's nothing about my work or my job that I inherently fear. I never have. I worry about some of the issues we're dealing with, which are really challenging, but I'm not afraid."

If you have to get through midtown Manhattan traffic in a hurry, an official diplomatic motorcade is *the* way to go. We arrived at our destination much faster than I ever thought possible. The school's administrators were waiting out front to greet Susan. "Can we continue the interview on the way back?" Susan said.

"Sure!" I said as I reached over to open the door. One of the large, muscles-in-a-suit guards was quickly on his way, but I thought I'd be helpful and open up before he got there. Priva stopped me gently but urgently.

"Oh, no," she said. "Let him get the door. It's bulletproof and weighs a ton. It could pull you out onto the sidewalk."

As we spilled out of the SUV, I heard Susan tell the security detail that she was going to give the school the full thirty minutes they were promised, even though we had arrived so late. Another reason to admire my friend.

Following in the wake of the school officials, security, Susan, Priva, and other staffers who arrived in separate cars, we snaked through hallways, up an elevator, and into an auditorium full of girls who were already waiting for Susan's arrival. She mounted the stage and stood behind the podium with the comfort and ease that comes from having done this so many times.

"I want you to know how much you inspire me," Susan said, surveying the young women in front of her.

> I watched the girls looking back in rapt attention at Madam Ambassador. Their uniforms limited their clothing to grays, blues, and whites. Yet the skin colors in the room represented an infinite range of shades from dark to light, embracing black, white, Indian, Hispanic, and every possible mixture between. Beautiful! Some of the girls covered their hair with scarves for religious or cultural reasons, while others sported henna tattoos and multiple ear piercings for their own enjoyment. I felt like I could relate to them even though their lives were probably much harder than mine had ever been. I knew I was privileged to be on a journey to meet women

leaders; I was glad that Ambassador Rice had come to join their journey.

"When I heard about how extraordinarily successful you are as individuals and as a school," Susan continued, "I really wanted to come to visit. You all are part of a tradition in which one hundred percent are graduating from high school and getting into college—and some excellent colleges, too. It makes me enormously proud of you and what you have achieved."

A rustle of joyful sounds rippled through this ocean of teen estrogen. I heard a girl behind me whisper to her friend, *"She looks just like my aunt Ruby."*

"You all are the next generation," said Susan. "When I am sitting downtown from here at the United Nations, negotiating on behalf of President Obama and the United States for what is best for the safety and prosperity of our country, I do so first and foremost as a mother— the mother of a thirteen-year-old son and an eight-year-old daughter.

"When those negotiations sometimes get so tough and frustrating that I want to scream and run out of the room, I think about all of you in the next generation. You depend on strong leadership and effective policies that will make you safer and your futures brighter. So if I feel a little bit down or demoralized, seeing the image of wonderful, beautiful, talented young women like you helps turn my attitude around. Knowing that your future is why I fight every day gets me excited and feeling empowered.

"In the time that we've got this afternoon, I am looking forward to having a conversation. I want to hear your questions, your thoughts, and your comments. But before I get there, let me just say one thing. The education that you are getting here at this great school—and the knowledge you will continue to build afterward—is your most important asset.

"There is no greater source of empowerment than to strive for getting the best education. And you all have the privilege of doing it in a context of an all girls' school, as I did, where there's no question—ever—about what it is you can do and what your hopes and expectations can be. I hope every one of you knows that you can do whatever you set out to do—absolutely anything you set out to do.

"You may not have much money. You may not have all of the family support that you might want or need. You may not be able to see how you're going to get from here to your dreams. But my advice is that you figure out what it is you are passionate about, consider how you want to contribute, and just go in that direction.

"Don't let anyone ever tell you that you can't do something. Please. Just do it. And then stretch yourself every day to do a little more and do it a little better. Be who you want to be . . . and do your best at it."

The girls rose to their feet clapping for this pint-size leader with a warm, tender heart and nerves of icy steel.

"Thank you for welcoming me into your school," Susan said in conclusion. "Now, I'd like to begin that conversation with you all. Do you have questions?"

One by one they came up to the microphone:

"Hello, Ambassador Rice. My name is Giselle, and my question for you is, how do you go about fighting for women's rights in countries where there is oppressive poverty?"

"Hello, Ambassador Rice. My name is Adrianna and my question for you is, how much progress have you personally witnessed in women's rights and what, in your opinion, is the most vital area that needs the most improvement?"

> Their questions were well thought out, well spoken, and really polished. For the next twenty-five minutes they peppered Susan with questions and sat mesmerized listening to her answers. Like Mom and me, they relished the opportunity to interact live with a great woman leader.

It seemed as though it ended all too soon when Priva gave the signal that we had to move on. We were hustled through the narrow school hallways back to our dark, armor-plated chariot. Once we were settled again, I asked Susan, "How does it feel to inspire all these young girls in

Harlem who look at you in all your glory and can see themselves running the world?"

"I don't know . . . is that what we did?" Susan asked with an uncharacteristic hesitation.

I was surprised by her response. She wasn't being humble. She didn't seem to properly estimate the value of her brief appearance. I give many such speeches and afterward talk with the kids. I often receive letters, indeed whole essays about what meeting a role model means to them. I said, "Susan, they got to look on stage and see someone with this monumentally important job, integral to running U.S. foreign policy, *but who looks like them*! They obviously researched you. They know who you are. There's been no African-American woman in your job before."

"But there's been an African-American woman Secretary of State," said Susan playfully, "with the same last name!"

Not wanting Susan to minimize the importance of her time with the girls, Darcy said, "But it's special for them to have you right there, talking to them, answering their questions . . ."

"I'm not arguing with you," Susan said earnestly, "but I find it hard to judge whether they're just being polite because they're told to pay attention or if they actually get something out of it. I hope they do."

"We asked several girls as we were leaving what they were going to remember most about what you said," Darcy continued, "and they agreed: 'It was the first thing she said, that we can really do anything. We really can go out and try . . . even if we can't see any possible way to get there. Try.'"

"That's the most important thing I said," the ambassador nodded. "Our generation of African Americans had a completely different experience psychologically than what your parents and my parents lived through."

"Do you feel an obligation to live up to those opportunities that our parents didn't have?" I asked, knowing that Susan's father, the elder Dr. Rice, was a Cornell University economics professor, an expert on the monetary systems of developing countries, and a former governor of the U.S. Federal Reserve. He was a great man who enjoyed the blessed good fortune to witness the accomplishments of both Susan and her brother, John, who founded Management Leadership for Tomorrow, a premier career development institution for minorities in this country.

"I look at my mom and dad, but especially my dad. He was born into the segregated South, around the end of World War I. He fought in a segregated army in World War II. He broke through all the ceilings and went on to be a governor of the Federal Reserve Board. He got to the top of his career, and my mom did, too, but he never to this day has lost the psychological scars of growing up in a segregated country and fighting in a segregated army. Our generation, including President Obama, was the first to have a lesser psychological burden. There was nothing stopping us from dreaming that we could get there. I think that's the biggest gift. I want those girls at that school to know that. They have even more freedom, and more opportunity than we had—and hopefully each successive generation will have more."

"When you think about those girls you were just talking to, are there things they need to do to prepare differently to lead in the future than you did? Are there going to be different demands on the leader of the future?" Darcy asked.

"That's interesting," Susan responded. "Some things are the same: the importance of an education, feeling grounded in family and community, and feeling not just an obligation, but a desire to give back. What's different? Maybe it's the world I live in, but I think we're in a much more global environment than when you and I were growing up. It is more important now to have competence in various languages and to experience living and traveling abroad. That's so much more important than it was thirty or forty years ago. A lot of people speak English, which is why I can get away with being an ambassador who only poorly understands Spanish. But it's not right. We're missing a lot as a result. We're missing a real in-depth insight into important societies that we need to better understand. We don't understand enough about the Middle East or South Asia. We don't understand enough about different religions like Islam and Hindu. I'm trying to convince my kids that they need to study not just the Spanish and French that might be offered at school, but Arabic or Chinese."

"Darcy is studying Mandarin and Spanish," I boasted. "She's told me, *'I have two-thirds of the globe covered!'*"

"I've been thinking about taking Arabic, too," Darcy added.

"Darcy, if you can do Chinese and Spanish, that'll be hell on wheels," Auntie Susan said affectionately. "If you want to add anything to it, that's just icing on the cake. It's not good enough for the Chinese to speak our language, when we don't know theirs. They know us better than we know them. When I sit in a meeting and negotiate with the Chinese, if I turn to my colleague and say something in English they know what I'm saying. If they turn to a colleague and say something in Chinese, I have no idea what the heck they're talking about."

> Having been in my high school Model United Nations club and ex-perienced the value of overhearing other people's conversations, I knew it would be critical to understand something when they think you can't speak their language. Fluency helps you get an edge over other people, but it also buys you deeper relationships. If you really want to get inside someone's head, the way they think is embed-ded in their syntax, grammar, and colloquialisms. In politics, if you want to bring morality into the discussion and create policy around it, you need that deeper level of connection between delegates.
>
> "I've been participating in Model UN," I shared with Susan, hop-ing it didn't sound silly. "I love this stuff."

"I think it's really important," Susan continued. "It's not just the lan-guage . . . it's the culture, it's the history . . . it's understanding how other people think and what motivates them."

"When did you first get a taste of making a difference . . . feeling like the things you do make a difference internationally?" I asked.

"From the day I started working in government actually," she an-swered. "Or maybe even the first campaign I worked on: for Mike Dukakis, when I was twenty-three. Of course, with more responsibility you feel like you have more opportunity for more impact."

"Another line of questioning we want to go down is work-life balance," I said. "You mentioned when you were talking to the girls that colleagues can help cover for you at work, but no one can be there for you at your mother's bedside in the hospital. Right now both of your parents are ill; you are commuting to work in New York while your husband and your kids live in D.C. What advice do you have for women about work-life balance?"

"Marry a good man!" she said, getting us all to laugh again. "I'm serious!" she insisted. "Where would I be without Ian? I wouldn't be able to sleep at night without worrying about whether my kids were in good hands; I wouldn't feel supported in what I do up here . . . a partner who is really an equal partner and who's accepting of you doing what you do is crucial."

"The other observation I would make," I said, "because I know you, is that you've had some ebb and flow. You haven't been going at this pace all the time you've been raising children."

"No one can go at this pace forever anyway," she said.

"So you may not have work-life balance at one point in time, but you can have it over a decade. How do you make those choices?" I asked.

"Well, the minute I think what I'm doing is not worth doing, that it can be done just as well by somebody else, or that it's not appreciated . . . I'm done. Because it is too much to give up in terms of family, kids, your own health. One is healthier when they're not living like this."

The car had stopped at the curb in front of the U.S. Mission once again. Outside the window behind Susan I could see the curved row of 193 member nations' flags waving in front of the iconic UN Tower. I asked one last question before the burly protection guy opened the steel-reinforced door to let us out. "What is the most rewarding thing about what you do? What makes it worth it?"

"It's different at different times. I'm very, very proud to serve this president. It's not just him, the individual." Susan's voice gained a quiet intensity that conveyed the weightiness of her words. "It is what he stands for, his policies, his vision, and what he's trying to get done, which I completely embrace and believe in. I think it's a huge privilege to serve our country. I don't think it gets better than that. One of the things I like about this job is that I actually get to be the face and the interface with every other country in the world all the time simultaneously. And that's fun. Sure, it's crazy frustrating sometimes, but most days what we're doing makes a difference—changes the dynamic in some fashion. That's what makes it worth the sacrifice."

Just days after this interview, Susan's father passed away at age ninety-one. I'd like to dedicate this chapter to the memory of Dr. Emmett J. Rice.

CHAPTER 22

Dr. Denise Dresser

Human Rights Activist
Professor, Instituto Tecnológico Autónomo de México

From the moment Denise Dresser began to speak, it was as if the clanking noise of silverware, busing dishes, and layer upon layer of others' conversations faded into the background. The dark wood paneling of Anisette Brasserie, a swank restaurant in Santa Monica, California, seemed to disappear. Dr. Denise Dresser took us away with her to experience the México she cares about so passionately.

We had to dive right in since our time with Denise was limited to this lunch meeting while she was briefly in the United States. In addition to her work as an activist, lobbyist, journalist, filmmaker, video blogger, and many other things, Denise's primary function is as a professor of political science at the Instituto Tecnológico Autónomo de México (ITAM), widely considered to be the best private university in Mexico, and she was due to lead a seminar there the next day.

"How do you define leadership?" Darcy began the interview with strength and confidence.

"In my case," Denise answered, "leadership is the capacity to speak for those who don't have a voice. Given that I am from an extremely dysfunctional country where people's rights are trampled on all the time— a democracy under construction—it means giving a public hearing to the dispossessed, to the poor, and to those who don't have access or representation.

"What moves me the most is when I travel and people come up to me, people who are complete strangers to me, and they stop me on the street and they say, *'Gracias. Thank you.'* Last week, for example, I was leaving a public parking lot and I had to drive my car over the sidewalk to get to the street. Given that people are mistreated generally in Mexico, I make it a point to be very nice to pedestrians. So when I saw a man on the sidewalk, I stopped and signaled with my hand, *'Go ahead,'* in front of my car. He signaled back: *'No, usted.'*

"*'No, you go ahead.'* I waved again. *'No, continua,'* he signaled again. After a few minutes of this back and forth I thought: What is wrong with this man? I rolled down my window and he yelled to me vehemently, *'¡à Doña Denise siempre pasar primero!'* which means: *Lady Denise always goes first!*"

This woman with the Chanel purse, Vidal Sassoon–style asymmetrical haircut, and Prada shoes clearly feels a connection with those less fortunate—and they have a reciprocal bond with her. Her detractors have labeled her as a *"gringa"* and a troublemaker, but the people of Mexico idolize her as their powerful advocate—an unstoppable crusader for the rights and honor of a society that has had their civil liberties so thoroughly trampled as to render them almost hopelessly moot.

"Leadership," Denise continued, "is being a standard-bearer for the causes that don't matter to the establishment. It's being a thorn in the side of those in Mexico who have it too good. Like Carlos Slim."

"Who is Carlos Slim?" asked Darcy.

"He's one of the richest men in the world because he bought a state-owned monopoly, which has now become a private monopoly. Mexican consumers are routinely fleeced. But many Mexicans admire him and his wealth because they don't understand their rights as consumers. I wrote an article called *Yo Naranja*, which means 'Me—The Orange.' It was about being squeezed every day by Carlos Slim. I wanted to raise awareness, get people talking."

I could hear Denise's lyrical Spanish syntax even when she spoke English. I loved the way she used language.

"Since I have made it a personal cause to take on Carlos Slim, he once invited me for coffee. I think he was curious to see who I was—what I was made of. At one point he became quite arrogant. He shoved some papers across the table and said, *'You keep saying that my phone rates are not competitive, well, here are the charts that prove that they are competitive.'* Telmex had put together its charts in a very arbitrary fashion to make a case for the owner. I knew the figures were not fair or reasonable. But it was his high-handed tone that really made me angry. *'Don't speak to me that way,'* I told him very directly in his face. *'I am a Mexican citizen with rights. I have a Ph.D. from Princeton. I'm not your wife. I'm not your secretary. I'm not your employee.'*

"He was stunned. No one had ever spoken to him that way. He immediately backed down. After that, we engaged in a sort of fencing match. I wouldn't say it was the greatest parry of my life because he's not very intellectually sophisticated. He has one singular talent, which is, of course, buying distressed assets, investing in them, and then selling them off again. But I could certainly out-debate Carlos Slim. When our conversation finished, he accompanied me out to my car, looked at me, and said, *'I respect you.'* "

This petite, well-mannered, highly manicured lady had no fear of going toe to toe with the richest man in the world...not only with the power of her pen, but also face to face with her passion.

Darcy then asked Denise, "Who are some of the people you admire?"

"Definitely Martin Luther King. Our struggle is also for civil rights. It's not an issue of the color of your skin, but it's an issue of full rights as a Mexican citizen." She stopped to think for a moment and then continued. "Oh, and you know who else?" Denise warmed to the subject. "You're going to laugh: Ida Tarbell. Ida was the muckraking journalist who took on John D. Rockefeller. Her seminal work is considered one of the top fifty pieces of journalism that have made a difference in the United States in the past one hundred years. Her writings became a book about Standard Oil, led to the beginning of the progressive movement, and ultimately resulted in Theodore Roosevelt cracking down on the robber barons. In many ways, Mexico is like the United States at the beginning of the twentieth century when rapacious capitalism did not allow for fully representative democracy or anything close to a level playing field."

"I can see why," Darcy enthused, "despite different countries and different eras, Ida Tarbell would be a powerful role model for you. Can you tell us about anyone you look up to in Mexico?"

"Another of my favorite heroes is 'La Corregidora,' Josefa Ortiz de Domínguez who was the wife of a criollo magistrate during the Mexican War of Independence in the early nineteenth century. She went behind her husband's back to help the revolutionaries, actually saving the life of Hidalgo who ignited the Indians and Mestizos to take up arms. I happen to like the fact that she always looked impeccable—she was viewed as part of the establishment—and yet she organized a group of intellectual rebels right under her husband's nose and helped the downtrodden in Mexico to free their country from Spanish colonial rule."

"She was a well-dressed revolutionary—just like you!" I chimed in.

"Some of my friends actually call me the Chanel opposition in Mexico." Denise was amused at her own shtick. "I'm a well brought up Mexican. I was raised up to be a princess; my mother wouldn't even let me go out of the house unless I wore stockings. But the princess that I try to embody is not the one who's sitting around in the castle waiting for someone to come and save her. Before my father died, when I was seven." Denise paused, and her voice faltered for the first time in our interview. "On Sunday mornings, he used to bring this giant globe and spin it around for me. I would choose a country, and he'd invent a story for me. The protagonist was always *La Princessa Denise*. His narratives about a fearless, bold princess who slayed her own dragons instilled in me a sense of what I could become.

"I interviewed a female Minister of the Supreme Court in Mexico for my book, *Gritos y Susurros*. She said women become what their parents whisper in their ear at night. No one whispered into my ear, *'Be a great mother,'* or *'Find yourself a husband.'* What my father whispered into my ear was, *'You have the capacity to fight the great battles against the villains in the world.'* "

"It seems that you still feel so intensely the pain of losing your father at such a young age," I observed.

"It does shape you forever," she confessed, "in some profound ways.

It's almost as if I have to introduce myself to you and say: *'Hello, I'm Denise Dresser, my father died when I was seven.'* I'm frequently asked about my fearlessness in Mexico: *'How can you take on Carlos Slim? Aren't you scared?'* And in my heart I say to myself, why would I be scared if I already survived this? Life took away what I loved the most and I lived through it. Carlos Slim doesn't scare me."

> Thinking about Denise's grief for her dad made me glad I was once again spending the summer with mine in San Diego. You really never know how much time you have.
>
> "What do you advise," I asked, "for women and girls who want to take on these kinds of roles but have not been through experiences like that? How can we be brave, too?"

"My advice? Always think of things that are beyond yourself, beyond your life. I've always felt that I'm part of some cause. It can be the cause of the week, the cause of the month, the cause of the year . . . or the cause of México. *Soy un mujer de causas*—I am a woman of causes—and whenever there is a good fight to be had, I'm the first one to stand in line. I'm known in Mexico for being extremely combative, and it's strange because I was very shy as a child. In college I didn't speak out at all for four years."

"How did that turn around?" asked Darcy.

"I trained myself to do the things that scared me the most. I trained myself to speak in public by practicing in front of a mirror in the bathroom. I had to do it when I got to Princeton for my Ph.D. studies because I was suddenly put in a seminar room with ten people where you couldn't hide; you had to express an opinion. Then, when I got back to Mexico, people started asking me to give conferences to convey my thoughts to a broader audience. First it was fifty; then it was one hundred. Now, I speak in front of two thousand people or more."

"We saw your famous speech on YouTube with over a hundred thousand views!" I told her.

My aunt April, who is fluent in Spanish, and I had spent several hours translating this really moving and impassioned speech. Dr. Dresser used this great metaphor of a young woman who arrived in Mexico and was confronted with injustice and monopolistic manipulation from the moment she got off the plane in the airport and was unjustly taxed. She tried to get a phone, and the service was limited and ridiculously expensive. The story built and built, illuminating the problems that permeated almost every public and private service in the country. By the end, she had painted this portrait of a nation whose citizens were stymied at every turn, with little chance for fairness or redemption. It was amazing.

"That was in front of Congress. I was the only woman asked to speak and got a standing ovation from the people whom I had just chastised for their lack of leadership! I was thinking, Why are they applauding? Who do they think I'm talking about? The person next to them?

"I'm not a relativist. I do believe that there is right and there is wrong; there's justice and injustice. There is a correct side of history, and I want to be firmly standing on that side. I love that Martin Luther King phrase: *'The arc of the moral universe is long, but it ultimately bends towards justice.'* I have to believe the arc I'm mounted on is going to end in justice sometime, somewhere, even if it's not in my lifetime."

"What do you hope for?" I asked next. "If all your work goes well and people pull together, what would you expect to see in five to ten years?"

"Unfortunately the structural trends are not good in Mexico. The United States spent billions of dollars getting the drug lords out of Colombia, and now they've moved to Mexico, bringing horrible violence and unrest to the country.* So many young people are leaving. I frequently say that the only thing that has happened since I first started writing about Carlos Slim—and I just won the National Journalism

---

*Source: *New York Times* "War Without Borders" series, 10/25/11. *Mexico Drug Cartels Battle Government.* http://topics.nytimes.com/top/news/international/countriesandterritories/mexico/drug_trafficking/index.html?emc=eta2

Award for writing about him—the only thing that has changed has been his position on the Forbes list. The regulatory environment has not changed, the fleecing of consumers has not changed, and the government's position has not changed." After a pause Denise continued, "What do I hope for, you ask? That someday we manage to change those trends."

"You mentioned the importation of drugs and crime. Don't you worry about your own safety when you stand up to these people of power and wealth?"

Denise shook her head slowly and threw up her hands. "It's true. In Mexico, you can hire someone to kill someone else for $5,000. Less than that even. And it would be just one more unexplained crime in the context of violence."

"What is it that keeps you safe, then?" I asked.

"When they picked me up at the airport the last time I went to speak in Ciudad Juarez, there was a police car in front, a police car behind, and a helicopter above. They probably thought, If anything happens to this woman in Ciudad Juarez, this is going to be terrible. Ciudad Juarez is the place where so much of the violence has occurred, where the councilor officials were killed. The fact that it would be major news is my protection right now. I try to keep a transnational profile. I'm an associate writer for the *LA Times*. I come to the United States once a month. I'm on the board of Human Rights Watch for Latin America and I've received research grants from places like the Ford Foundation and the Rockefeller Foundation. The fact that I'm married to a foreigner also matters, because it would entail the involvement of another government."

When Denise began talking about cheap assassins and police helicopter escorts, she amazingly was matter of fact in her description of the terrifying realities. But as she continued she seemed increasingly agitated. "That's all I can say. I don't like to talk about this issue because I don't want to reflect too deeply on it. If I put the pros and the cons on a list, the only pro is my love for Mexico. I frequently say that I'm Mexican by birth *and* by choice. My father was American and my husband is Canadian, so we could live elsewhere. We choose to stay in Mexico. But there is such a long list of cons: the violence, the insecurity, and the fact that my children cannot lead normal lives. They don't ever play outside. They don't ever go anywhere alone. They lead a very protected life. They are my hostages to fortune."

At this point her eyes misted with unshed tears. She looked up into the far corner of the ceiling as if searching for answers there. "I sometimes think that it's all right to make my own sacrifices—no public safety, no secure public spaces. But am I imposing too high of a cost on my children? As much as I hate to say it, I will sleep more soundly and be more at ease when they are no longer in Mexico."

"You sound more concerned about the safety of your children than yourself," I commented.

She lost her composure. Suppressed anxiety boiled over. "But see . . . this is what I don't want. I don't want to have this conversation! I don't, I don't, I don't! I don't want to have this conversation!" Her hands were shaking. "Those are not the things I think about," Denise said, redirecting our conversation in the same ways she must habitually redirect her internal dialogue every day. "I'm constantly thinking about things like: *'Who do I call? How do I change this? How do I lobby this opinion? How do I get these people together? How do we overturn this law? How do we protest? How do we mobilize? How do we celebrate what we've gained?'* That is what I think about." This pillar of fortitude sighed heavily, revealing without words that the shift from cons back to pros in Mexico took a great deal of effort. She leaned forward, eager to make us understand why she would risk everything to stay in Mexico. "There's something about being in a country that is still under construction and believing—and perhaps it's completely false, but I need to believe this—that what you do has an impact."

"Mexico needs you." I nodded, leaning toward her.

"Exactly, yes!" Denise sat up straighter in her chair. "In Mexico I'm leaving *una buena huella* . . . you know, when you put your foot down and you leave an impression; a good imprint—that's what it means."

"What is the most influential form of protest? Is it writing?" Darcy asked. I could have hugged my daughter in that moment for pulling us back to a line of questioning where Denise would be more comfortable.

"Well, what I've discovered is I have to have multiple audiences," responded Denise, brightening noticeably. "One audience is the television audience. However, because of my opposition to certain monopolies, I was kicked off television for a number of years. When that happened, in a country where ninety-eight percent of people receive their political information from television, it was almost like being nonexistent.

"Now, what helps me—and people like me—is the Internet, because it becomes an equalizer, becomes an alternative route for information. I do two video commentaries a week for *Reporte Indigo* on YouTube. You should check it out. It's the only Internet magazine in Mexico and it's viewed like *Rolling Stone*. Another audience is the people who are more sophisticated, who read columns. The *Reforma*, which publishes one of my columns, probably has a circulation of one hundred and twenty thousand in Mexico City, and they're also syndicated in about fifty newspapers across the country. It's paradoxical because you don't reach a lot of people, but you reach the elites, the decision makers. And the other thing that I do, I'd say a fundamental thing, is teach. Some people deride teaching. Most academics would prefer to do research. I love to teach!"

"And are you teaching undergrads?" I asked.

"I teach undergrads in their last year—one course on contemporary Mexican politics and another course in comparative political economy. I think it is one of the most important things I do because I teach people more than the specifics of my discipline. I teach them how to question, how to not take things for granted, and how to feel invested in their own country. Larry Summers had this great quote about how people sometimes view their countries as a rented car . . . and no one has ever washed a rented car. So that's what I say in Mexico: *'Everybody treats this country as if it were a rented car. Nobody cleans it up. Nobody takes it to the service station!'* I frequently say to my students at the beginning of the term: *'Yes, I want you to read the readings, fulfill your obligations, and do the exams . . . but the most important thing I want you to learn in this class is that you're a stakeholder.*

The future of this country is something that you have to care for; otherwise, I'm wasting my time in this classroom.'

"I got an e-mail from one of my former students today, who is gay and leads the movement for gay rights in Mexico. The Supreme Court is currently reviewing the constitutionality of gay marriage, which is allowed in Mexico City. At the end of the e-mail he wrote, *'I've never said it to you so clearly, but I want you to know that it was your class that led me to lose my apathy.'* That's ultimately what it's about. And now he's gone on to carry his own banner. People say that I live in the state of permanent indignation, which I believe is an essential part of participatory citizenship. Leadership to me is having those who listen to me begin to share that indignation and put it to good use."

Darcy chose this moment to jump in again with one of her favorite questions, "Would you give different advice to your daughter and son about how to become a leader?"

"I think life is harder for women. This generalization perhaps doesn't apply to the United States; or perhaps it does. But in Mexico, life is harder. That's why I tell all of my women students to get a doctorate degree. I think there's just more to overcome and there's less acceptance. You still have to fight for your place in the world. Women need to know that they have a right to occupy that space. So many women in my country are taught to be an appendix, to accept inferior treatment, and to be viewed as lesser in some fundamental way.

"The reason that I felt I could have that conversation with Carlos Slim and not feel undermined or diminished was because I have this Ph.D. John, my husband, still makes fun of the fact that when people ask me, *'What has been the most important day of your life?'* I never say when my children were born. I say, *'The day I finished my doctorate.'* Earning my Ph.D. is something that I did absolutely by myself and in very tough circumstances. After my father died, we had no money, no money whatsoever. My mother was a bilingual secretary, so I was always the child on scholarship. I got a Fulbright to go to Princeton. Had I not won that grant, I would not have been able to go there. I was so poor that when my stockings would get holes, I'd darn them up. I barely ate—I couldn't afford it."

"You have so much courage and strength. You're taking on huge issues," said Darcy to this petite, powerful, impressive woman. "Are there certain points when you feel like you just don't have the spiritual or emotional energy to tackle it all? What advice do you have for girls and women of all ages to restore themselves so they can keep going as leaders?"

"It's important not to take yourself too seriously. When I finish my column and come home in the evenings, I'm not Dr. Denise Dresser to my children; I'm just their mother. They don't really care at this point in their lives if Carlos Slim is going to reduce his rates or not. I come home and shed my armor. John is also crucial for my sanity. My husband is indeed my best friend. He is the person whom I discuss all of my work with, all the time. Bless him! He must be so tired of Mexican politics. It is important to have someone dear to you, who you trust; someone with whom you can share the weariness of the day. I think that's fundamental. Until I met John, I recurrently fell in love with the wrong men. I suffered a great deal and lost a lot of time in relationships that covered me with scars and distracted me from what was truly important. For too long, I stayed with people who wanted me to be different. They wanted someone who was more serene, who was less antagonistic, and who was less out there in the world. I tried to do it. I tried very hard, until I met someone who was completely comfortable with me as I am. The gods sent him to me to save me from myself!

"One more thing, perhaps the most essential. In one of these recent books on happiness I read that being part of a group that meets twice a month generates more happiness for people than a raise does. It's very important for women to have their group. I am part of several groups. In one, we meet for lunch every two weeks on Tuesdays. We come from different walks of life. It's a lunch where we can discuss the recent Supreme Court ruling in one minute and then in the next minute, what the best color of foundation is after you've gotten sunburn. It ranges from the truly fundamental to the most trivial. It's important to have those groups. I always go into battles thinking, *'I'm going to win.'* That comes from the confidence and the security that other women give to you. How do you say it? *Las porristas?* We're like this collective group of cheerleaders for ourselves. They may be in some completely different area from me, but they've seen my speech or they've read my column and they have a comment that gives me optimism. It feeds my attitude and arms me with the fearlessness and commitment to go back out there. Find a group of like-minded women who share what they're doing; that's my best advice."

"Denise, I read somewhere that you said, *'I am crazy in love with Mexico!'* and I thought immediately how much I would like to hear that in Spanish. How do you say it?"

"Amo México con un amor perro..." she said for me with the rolled rr's and romantic expression native to her mother tongue.

As she left the restaurant, I noticed that her shoes looked like the simple Mary Janes we all wore in grade school with white stockings, except for the fact that they had the large square heels of a grown woman's elegant designer pumps.

It was as if the child princess had grown up. Nothing had changed about her pure spirit and penchant for adventure. The heels were just a little higher.

CHAPTER 23

—•—

Dr. Fay Deane

*First Woman Dairy Company Chairman
in New Zealand*

Our journey was coming to an end. Mom and I had crisscrossed the country to the forests of Maine, the U.S. State Department, the United Nations, Hollywood Boulevard, and Silicon Valley; we'd ventured to London and Nicaragua. We'd taken a Verizon journey to the capital of Liberia and Skyped into North Carolina. After researching and discovering all these incredible women with backgrounds and experiences so far from my own, it suddenly dawned on me that one of the most interesting people I could talk with about leadership was someone I'd known my whole life: my grandmother in New Zealand, Dr. Fay Deane.

Over the years my father made a significant commitment to be sure I stayed connected with my family on the other side of the world. Ever since I can remember, we take a yearly vacation in Aotearoa, "The Land of the Long White Cloud," where he grew up and where his family still lives. I have always felt close to my Kiwi cousins, aunts, and uncles, Granddad, and my grandmother, "Mema." One look at Mema and you can see where I get the blue eyes, petite stature, and the bit of blond I have. Though my most vivid visions of her are as she putters around her rose gardens, cooks my dad's favorite foods, or whips up her delicious plum sauce, I had heard bits and pieces over the years about her amazing story in business.

As was the custom in that time and place, Mema married Granddad while still in her teens, had three babies about as fast as humanly possible, and did even more hard labor outdoors as a farmer's wife. On a dairy farm there is always work to do—cows need to be milked, hay needs to be made, fences need repair, calves insist on being born, and a million other chores from dawn to dusk. As first-generation farmers, they didn't have armies of workers like a big business, but rather a true family farm aided only occasionally by temporary helpers. It is hard for me to imagine, but in those days men rarely even picked up a diaper, never mind doing any work inside the house. Yet Mema drove tractors, mended fences, and did whatever she could to help outside *in addition* to washing, cooking, and making sure my dad and his siblings got all their homework done. Like me, she's small—but no pushover.

Mema went back to school when her kids were able to fend for themselves and not only finished her undergraduate degree, but also powered through her master's and Ph.D. with a plan to teach at university. But before the ink was dry on her diplomas, the business world began to demand her leadership skills. Trouble was brewing in rural Dargaville, where they lived. The local farmers' dairy co-operative manufacturing plant was about to be bought out by a larger, mega-company and closed down due to poor profitability.

The Northern Wairoa Dairy Company had been founded in the late 1890s when a group of individual farmers organized themselves together to have their milk combined and processed in bulk. The company grew from those small beginnings, and over the later twentieth century was able to establish itself throughout the world as a significant producer of very high-quality milk powder.

Mema and Granddad—whose name is David Deane by the way—helped organize a group that would fire the company's current management, reorganize the company, and try to avoid the devastating takeover in order to keep jobs in the area and boost the incomes of farmers across the Wairoa Valley. No one was as surprised as the young Dr. Fay Deane when she was drafted by her confederates to take the lead…and run for chairman of this $50 million company!

The election was a biblical, David-and-Goliath-style confrontation as our newly minted Ph.D. in *child development* attempted to win the votes of 450 old-fashioned, male farmers by convincing them that she could manage the company better than the experienced businessmen and influential members of their small community who had led it for years. Although she'd been a director for two terms, she had never run a manufacturing business before, and no woman had been elected to the top position at a dairy manufacturer in the entire country—ever! But after as nasty a political campaign as you have seen anywhere, Dr. Fay Deane triumphed and took the helm as the first woman chairman of a dairy company in the history of New Zealand.

Now that I had learned so much about the challenges of leadership from other women, I had a new thirst to find out what Mema could teach me. Fortunately, it wasn't a hard sell to convince my mom to include her in the book. While married to my dad, Mom traveled to Dargaville many times, worked on the farm, and developed the same respect for the local Dr. Deane that I had.

Mom was only sad, she told me, that we couldn't also interview her mother on whom not one, but two Ph.D. theses had been written to analyze her leadership style. Ruby, whom I called Grandma, had also earned her own Ph.D. and used her knowledge as a high school principal to transform underfunded, inner city schools filled with minority kids—much like the segregated schools she was forced to attend as a child. When she passed away several years ago, three hundred people showed up at her funeral and sang her praises at length, including the Gospel Choir from Lincoln High School, the place she'd raised to prominence from the ashes of neglect. Sadly, there were so many questions I would never have a chance to ask Grandma. However, one thing is sure—I can claim a legacy of great women leaders on both sides of my genealogy.

Since Dad and I would head without Mom to New Zealand over the summer (well, it's their winter), I knew I was going to take the lead on this particular great woman profile. I had to research her the way I did Condi Rice or Eileen Fisher, but the traditional sources such as Wikipedia, online news articles, and reference books were in short supply. Instead, I spent hours sifting through the large cache of newspaper clippings Mema had saved over the years on episodes of the Dairy Company drama. I also tackled my dad and other members of the Deane clan to wrestle out tidbits of useful information. It was in the pre-interview I did with Granddad, though, where I really struck gold.

"There was a group of people still supporting the chairman who was unseated in the election," Granddad explained while we sipped a batch of strong NZ coffee in their cozy living room one evening. "That gang went to great lengths to try to rally the troops and obtain the numbers to get rid of Fay as chairman."

"How did you fight back?" I asked, amazed at the story.

With a sneaky, conspiratorial grin, he answered, "First of all, we had a grapevine of Fay's supporters who gave us reports about what was going on in the other faction, what their next effort would be, and how they would attempt to carry all this out. We found out that one person was ringing up the other farmers and saying, *'We've simply got to get rid of this woman, but we need all the help we can get—she's a very hard nut to crack.'* "

Granddad paused and gave me a wink. "Only they didn't really say 'a hard nut to crack,' they used much stronger language. The supporters and opponents alike had all sorts of nicknames for our Fay!"

"Oooh! What did they call her?" I felt heat rising in my body as if it was all happening right now. I wanted to go out and use some of my jujitsu moves on anyone who was sullying my Mema's honor and reputation.

Granddad admitted cheekily, "One person was known to say, *'That's the first woman I've ever met with cajones.'* Another one said, *'We've got a new name for her, we're gonna call her the Great White Shark!'* I even heard a guy say, *'Well, there are two camps really. One would like to have a knife in their hand and find her in a dark alley in the dead of night. The other thinks she can walk across the Wairoa River without using the bridge.'* It all might've been amusing without the death threats. For a wee while there, I stashed the shotgun under our bed at night."

"Wait a minute, she was risking her life?" I asked. Suddenly I felt small and terrified for Mema's very existence. "Why didn't she stop?"

"Your Mema has a real determination," he said affectionately about his wife of fifty-four years. "Once she's started out on a course of action, she will carry it through. There were many, many times, where in fact she didn't even want to do the job of Chairman of the Dairy Company. But having started on it, she just wouldn't give up. In a way, one of her most constant battles was with herself. I never doubted, though, that she would carry on with the job, even though it wasn't really what she wanted in the first place."

"What do you think is unique about Mema's leadership style?" I asked my father's father.

"She has this special skill of bringing people together with one purpose," he replied. "She provides them with the ideas and they accept them—or they don't—and they become a team. She does that."

The next day, I finally felt ready. I had done my research, prepared my list of questions, and knew that I could follow my nose to discover new information. I had brought a notepad, my mini-recorders, and a folder full of clippings in case I needed to reference them. Though it was early winter, it was mild enough in this part of New Zealand to sit out on my uncle John's back porch, where we could see my cousin Connor practicing for a dressage competition in the nearby riding ring. Mema, still blond and elegant in her early seventies, wore a cream-colored sweater set with cotton pants and turquoise earrings that matched her blue eyes. She had laid out a plate of homemade Anzac biscuits (cookies to us Yanks) with a lovely porcelain teapot and steaming mugs of milky tea to ward off the damp winter chill in the air. It was time to begin.

"So, Mema, what's your definition of leadership?"

My grandmother thought carefully, then replied, "Bringing a team together and taking them forward to success with an agreed agenda, having recognized the talents of others and the contribution they will make to a positive outcome. Bringing people with you is paramount in a leadership role."

"What was the biggest challenge you had as the Chairman of Northern Wairoa?" I probed further.

Mema seemed mostly happy about my eagerness to investigate her achievements. Given how nasty some of the situations were, though, recalling these scenes in her life was a difficult, painful process. She had told me earlier that she probably wouldn't be willing to sit down and rehash the old memories for anyone except her one and only granddaughter.

"When I was the Chair," Mema slowly explained, "there was always the threat of being pushed into an unwanted amalgamation because of the poor payout to the shareholders—the farmers *are* the shareholders, remember, since it's a co-operative. To offset the threat, we developed a very strong strategic plan with the main thrust being that of establishing a close relationship with an overseas company who wanted our product, the milk powder, exclusively.

"We achieved this aim by improving the processing quality of the milk powder and building a close relationship with a company in Malaysia. Becoming the preferred supplier for an overseas and desirable market gave Northern

Wairoa a strong position from which to establish a sound financial base. Eventually we were able to pay more money to our shareholders than the company that tried to take us over—we were more profitable per kilo of milk fat than an operation ten times our size! It was truly amazing."

In simple words, that meant that farmers like David Deane who sent a thousand liters of milk to be processed at Fay's factory were getting paid more than farmers who sent a thousand liters to the bigger factory, which should have had the "economy of scale" advantage.

"So insisting on quality, like you did everywhere, even when you were growing and selling strawberries from your backyard, was that what raised the profits and saved the company?" I queried, referencing one of the many background stories I had accumulated.

"Not only did we have to have quality for its own sake, but we had to have consistent quality. Every time you put the product through the milk dryer it had to come out as near as possible to how the last product came out. The specifications of the product were tremendously important, and that was very technical. We had great staff that could manage the dryers and get all that aspect of it right, but in order to get their best effort you had to build up the morale of the company.

"When we were down in the bottom of the payout structure, everyone was saying we were going to the dogs anyway, so it didn't matter. They wouldn't push to adhere to the tight standards required. So we built up the staff morale and they got rewarded when the payout was better. We created a more harmonious company."

"Didn't the other leaders before you push for higher quality, too?" I wondered aloud.

"The men before me just took a broad-brush stroke and relied a lot on the staff to make it work. I attended to detail. Detail mattered. I wanted to know everything: *How's this happening in minute detail? What's the research that needs to be done to make sure it happens?*"

"Do you think that is a difference in how men and women lead?"

"Oh, yes! Yes, I do. I think the sense of responsibility women get in raising children, running the home, and being forced to attend to detail comes through in a leadership role in a way that I don't see with men."

Mema leaned forward and rifled through the clippings I had in my folder to show me a quote from one of the *Northern Advocate* articles:

Dr. Deane has often been the only woman surrounded by male colleagues, but says she has regarded herself as a person with skills to offer from her own perspective which happens to be female: She spends considerable time attending to detail.

"I also saw that many men were capable of having two personas," Mema continued. "Certain of these guys were being deceitful and taking advantage of the shareholders concerning the volumes of milk received and the subsequent payout, but their wives knew nothing about it. In their private life they went home to really nice wives and children."

I could hear Mema's voice begin to tighten up a little with emotion as she dug into some of the more hurtful memories.

"In fact, I can remember when I was in the dairy company one day doing research to find out about some reports I suspected were inaccurate. One of those directors from the faction that opposed me stood in the doorway and said: *'Look, why don't you give that up? Why don't you just join the winning side?'*

"What that really meant was: *'Honesty doesn't matter. We're the big guys, and you're just being stupid.'* "

I silently wondered whether Mema's degree in child development helped her to deal with the immature attitudes around her at that time.

"Well, in the end they all left and I stayed. I think women take who they are into the job much more so than men. I'm not saying *all* women do that, but I really didn't see many men who did that."

"How did you get so much strength and conviction," I truly wanted to know, "to be able to stand up to so much sexism in the agricultural industry which is so male dominated?"

"I think the biggest impact on my ability to cope with all this antagonism from men was that my father went to the war when I was two years old and didn't come back until I was eight," said Mema, explaining to me some of the harsh realities of her childhood. "It meant that I grew up in an all-female household during a really critical period of my life in terms of bonding with males."

Nodding, I acknowledged that this simple remark arose from Mema's extensive training in the way children think and grow.

"My mother, my two sisters, and I were together for six years without a man in the house. After that, male authority really meant very little to me. You challenged it in the same way you'd challenge anything! I never learned to be subjugated by gender roles. I was able to put up with all the flack I received because I never doubted that I was just as good as they were."

"Do you feel like there were ways in which your mother or your grand-mother imparted certain leadership skills to you at a young age?" I inquired.

"I was very young when both my grandparents died. With my mother, it was sort of an anti-model. My mother was a very intelligent, very determined lady, but she never had opportunity to realize her potential, because she put up with so much rubbish to keep her family together. I can recall very often in my life, particularly in my twenties, thinking, *I am not going to end up in the same situation as my mother, so what are the things I need to do to ensure that doesn't happen?'*

"One of the main ones was having a sense of purpose and a real goal after my children had grown up, particularly since I had my children when I was very young. I knew there was going to come a time in my life when they'd be gone and I was only going to be forty! That's when I started in on the academic work. There were other reasons, too, but that was part of it."

"It was fortunate that you did the academic work. The doctorate ended up making a big difference in making men treat you with more respect, didn't it?" I conjectured, remembering some of the earlier conversations with Mema as well as some of what Denise Dresser had shared in this regard.

"Many of my detractors would call me 'Mrs. Deane' as a way to undermine my authority. They didn't want to give me any credit."

Mema stopped to refill our tea mugs, adding the milk first in proper British style.

"The man who was in charge in Malaysia, who eventually became our big-gest customer, valued hierarchy. It was very important to him that I had a doctorate and that I was Dr. Deane. He gave me the basic level of respect because of the title, and I was able to build on that and create a solid relationship."

"You mentioned earlier that relationship building, in addition to quality, was what saved Northern Wairoa," I observed. "Do you think the face-to-face connection is important?"

"Personal contact is very important. You have to get the feel of the place, the atmosphere. We visited their sites and viewed where the product was going, what the consumer wanted, what the air conditions were over there, which were so different from what we had in New Zealand.

"And that particular group from Malaysia came to our company, too, and inspected it from top to bottom. Is this where we want the whole milk powder for our young families coming from? Is it clean enough? Is there quality control? Is it consistently good product?

"But before we could ever get to that point we had to research their customs and culture. You had to take just the right kind of gifts, which had to be wrapped carefully and presented in certain ways. It showed that you respected them."

"So you did a lot of cultural research?" I asked, even more excited now that we were getting into my anthropological sweet spot.

"I set up the strategy for how our team would approach this visit because it was very, very important to the company that we land this particular client. We produced our own little booklet on their customs, what would be expected, and how we were going to approach it. We also set up another document that outlined our company, our vision, our mission, our goals, and our strategies to give to the customer. On top of that we did a big, quite professional, video presentation of our company—that was a big deal twenty years ago. The New Zealand Dairy Board thought we couldn't accomplish all this given our competition from other, larger companies, but we won that market. Since all exports go through the Dairy Board, the Malaysian company went to them and specified that they wanted milk powder from Northern Wairoa exclusively. It was a real coup."

"So, what ever happened to the Northern Wairoa Dairy Company?"

"Looking into the future at that time, the indicators were that there would eventually be just one combined dairy company in all of New Zealand. Fonterra, the largest combined dairy company in NZ today, is also the largest exporter of dairy produce in the world.

"So, in 1989 I led our company into amalgamation with the same big company that had tried to buy us out earlier. However, because our financial position was so much healthier when we merged, we could demand a premium payment to our shareholders. It was a well-founded strategic move that brought financial gain to our farmers. Not well received by everyone, but by a majority of some 90 percent."

"Wow, that's amazing." I was very proud of Mema's accomplishments and so glad I had the chance to sit down with her like this. Hearing about what she'd lived through retold by Dad or Mom just wouldn't have been the same. "So, I just have one more question: What advice do you have for the next generation of women leaders?"

"Three things really. First, attend to the detail. We talked about that already." She brushed the bickie crumbs from the table.

"Second, never underestimate the issues and difficulties inherent in a task undertaken, especially when the result or outcomes mean change for people, organizations, or communities. People become afraid of change and may not do the logical thing you would expect.

"Third and finally, in undertaking a leadership role it is critical to weigh one's motives against the spiritual and philosophical values held up in public—is there congruence between these aspects—do they support each other and uphold your sense of integrity? If you get involved in power for its own sake, you've got problems. When I have had power over other people, it was a responsibility, not a right."

I sat back, enveloped by the comfy cushions of the wicker chairs on Uncle John's breezy back porch. The sun was setting to the west, providing an orange and pink glow on Connor and his horse as they continued drilling their complex choreography.

Once I finished the interview, Mema put down her mug and seemed to get a little larger as she turned the full focus of her attention on me. I sensed that I was no longer driving this conversation. It was her turn now to step out of the process and say her piece.

"Darcy, what I most want you to remember is this: I see strong character and leadership capacity in you. You must nurture your abundant talents and focus your attention toward achieving better lives for women and children—and men, too, by the way—around the world, who do not have the same opportunities as we have. Other people's negative attitudes toward strong women should never be a deterrent to realizing your potential so long as there is a sense of 'rightness' and peace about what you undertake. Do you understand what I'm saying to you?"

I nodded my assent.

As always, Dr. Fay Deane had the last word. I sat still savoring everything: the New Zealand air, the sound of hoofbeats, the warmth of the mug in my hands. Here I sat with another Great Woman. But she wasn't in a portrait, or on television, or up on a pedestal; she was my own flesh and blood.

CHAPTER 24

The Road Home

Panels of angled metal clicked and clacked while yet another baggage carousel made its monotonous circular cruise in front of us. As we patiently waited for the giant machine to deposit Darcy's Samsonite from the belly of American Airlines flight 7315 from Auckland, New Zealand, I couldn't wait to pepper my daughter with questions about her trip to visit her family "down under." My particular interest was the interview she had done with her grandmother. I felt a bit left out from this, the final episode of our entire expedition, and wanted to know about every last detail. "What was it like? How did it feel?" I asked.

"Well, you know I had heard a little about Mema's story here and there, so I knew it would be cool," Darcy told me, "but sitting with her and feeling her emotions, her ferocity, as she described what happened was more intense than I could ever have imagined. I looked in her eyes. I felt her pain. I will never forget that."

"What did you learn from Mema's life?" I persisted.

"It was incredible," Darcy answered. "To hear her speak about all the drama and intrigue of her experience in the dairy business, I could see the elements of her character projected on a much bigger screen. I knew she could be strong willed, tough minded, and even cantankerous, but I got to see how she channeled all that into something positive. She's a wild spirit!" the proud granddaughter added with a grin.

"They told her she couldn't do it—couldn't get a Ph.D. while raising kids, couldn't turn around a nearly bankrupt $50 million company—and she was defiant, but in a way that was constructive," Darcy continued. "I'm sure they underestimated her and were convinced she would fail. She walked up to that glass cliff Deborah Tom talked about in London, stared into the abyss, mustered all her strength and courage, and succeeded against impossible odds.

"The most profound thing was that I actually felt more compassion for *myself* as a strong woman, which was a bit of a relief. Women who are confident, smart, and stand their ground when they are right, like Mema—and you, too, Mom—will often be labeled stubborn, opinionated, and forceful in a really negative way. I see those same 'difficult woman' traits in me, but now I know I can do something good with it. I feel proud to have these great genes and confident they'll serve me well."

I scanned my only child from head to toe. In many ways, I hardly recognized her. The gawky, gangly girl who blindly agreed to devote almost two precious years of her adolescence to join me on a crazy, half-baked journey into the unknown world of woman's leadership had somehow morphed into this lovely young woman staring back at me. Still a teenager, to be sure, but so much more polished. So much more sophisticated. So much taller! From now on, the only way we'll ever see eye to eye is if I look up to her.

Finally Darcy's distinctive black-and-yellow "bumble bee" ID tag turned the corner on the conveyor and ever so slowly arrived within reach. We grabbed her hefty luggage and trudged out to the blue Ford Escape—our loyal and trusty companion on so many adventures along this yellow-bricked odyssey to Oz.

"Is this really the end?" Darcy asked once we were settled in our familiar front seats and headed toward home. "Did we do it, Mom? Will our stories really give women a roadmap to seeing themselves as leaders? Will they really get it?"

"Did it help you to see yourself as more of a leader?" I turned the question back on her.

"Uh, *yeah*! When we started, I had no idea how many stereotypes and assumptions about leaders were swimming around in my brain. Yet, from the moment we found ourselves in that dark, Maine forest in the middle of the night bouncing around on a golf cart with Leslie Lewin, my preconceived notions were shattered. Remember how she stopped to deliver some sleeping bags, to radio in the repair request for a broken screen door, and then to answer questions from staffers? Even though she's the executive director of Seeds of Peace, there was no authoritative tone that said *'I'm the boss here.'* She rolled up her sleeves, did whatever needed to be done—and people followed her! As the days went by, I really saw how her love and affection for every bunk and camper infected her whole team with the same caring attitudes. She didn't have to direct them to do every specific thing, she *inspired* them to work hard and attend to the details. She also, by her example, instilled in them the importance of their overall mission: to bring teens from war-torn countries together in meaningful dialogue with their enemies. It actually surprised me how well her style of leadership worked."

I caught Darcy's eye briefly as I navigated the elliptical JFK Airport roadways. "Condoleezza Rice mentioned that same idea when we asked her to define leadership," I reminded her. "She said that people don't generally respond well to command and control styles of leadership anymore. Even in the military, the best leaders can command but they also inspire."

"That was really interesting," Darcy replied. "I couldn't believe that even the army has shifted away from command and control. It makes me wonder, though: do men have a choice between an inspirational style versus a command style, whereas women are more limited? If a woman does decide to command, is she dismissed as 'bossy'? Remember how Marin Alsop said she can't make some of the same gestures that male orchestra conductors make because she can look domineering or angry?"

"That was one of my favorite moments of our whole trip!" I replied, "when we were sitting in her office after the rehearsal and she picked up her baton to show us how big pounding movements or a scrunched-up face would be acceptable for a man, but not for her. She had to create a whole new language in order to communicate effectively. That's what women do in this day and age, don't they? Do you remember what Sharon Allen at Deloitte said about it?"

"Hmmm. It was something about the future of leadership..."

"Exactly." I felt so emphatic about this, I subconsciously squeezed the steering wheel until my knuckles turned white. "She basically said that the historically traditional methods often don't work for women—partly because people don't want to accept a command attitude from us, and partly because it's just not the way we tick.

"The good news is the future of leadership lies in a different direction anyway," I continued. "Flatter organizations, more complex problems, global interdependencies . . . all these changes demand a more collaborative brand of leadership from men and women. We're just better suited to get there."

"Speaking of the future," Darcy chimed in, "didn't Sheryl Sandberg at Facebook also talk about great leaders wanting genuine enthusiasm, trust, and real dedication instead of just compliance? You feel like you can really see the future walking around their headquarters in Silicon Valley. Everything about the place hooks you into the excitement: funny sayings on the walls like *'Move fast and break things,'* Hack-a-thons, eat-anytime kitchens, and even playrooms. They don't want to control anyone . . . it's clear they want to create an environment that does just the opposite. They want to unleash everybody's talent."

"Did you also notice how some of the women leaders talked about making the transition from an insistence on complete control to an attitude that was more supportive? It isn't always easy to let go and empower people," I observed.

"Yeah," replied Darcy, "I was surprised that Secretary Rice was so blunt about her own mistakes in learning to delegate. I mean, there we were in her office at Stanford, surrounded by her accolades and pictures of her with the world's major dignitaries, and she told us flat out that when she started as the university Provost she wasn't good at it. Her epiphany was that *'You'll drive yourself crazy trying to do everything . . . and you'll drive talented people away if you try to control them too much.'* I remember that because it made me feel better; I struggle with delegating important tasks when I lead a group, too. Rishika was really good at that. I learned a lot from her example."

"Sharon Allen had a turning point on the difference between leading and managing, too. Her big 'aha' came when a staffer told her she was a better leader in Portland than she was in Boise."

"I wondered about that," Darcy said, tilting her head inquisitively. "She was the same person in both cities, right? Why would things be different?"

"Since Sharon's career started in Boise," I reminded her. "She knew so much about the people and systems there it was easy for her to micro-manage. In Portland there wasn't that history, so she had to rely on the knowledge and abilities of others more."

"I get it!" Darcy's lightbulb glowed. "So, knowing less of the minutiae actually made her a better leader! That seems almost crazy."

"But it's important," I followed. "Women have a tendency to get too involved. Amy Pascal, the head of Columbia Pictures, said she has to re-sist the urge to apologize for other people's mistakes. And it took Marin Alsop ten years as a conductor to learn to 'desensitize' herself a little to her orchestra members' personal problems and stay focused on the music. She wanted to nurture them, but sometimes you have to back off and let people deal with their own issues. Because women's brains are wired to experience emotions intensely and to see and remember de-tails, we have the advantages and disadvantages those wires bring. Our great women leaders learned when to turn it off and when to turn it on."

"What *are* the advantages of the female brain?" Darcy mused, almost to herself. "Mema talked about her attention to detail as one of the keys to her success as chairman at the dairy. Eileen Fisher, too, seems like a good example. The company she built from the ground up is so unique."

I agreed strongly. I've heard repeatedly that women's brains have more connective tissue than men's brains, which makes us more adept at link-ing disparate thoughts and ideas to one another. Among scientists, there seems to be quite a bit of controversy over whether this is really true; but in the real world, it seems obvious. We women can't buy a car without talking about our kids, the insurance, the finances, the grocery shopping, our mother-in-law's astigmatism, a movie we saw in 1997 that had a car in it, and so forth. It's all connected. While men buy a car based on horse-power and gadgets, women buy a life facilitation device with wheels.

"When we were at Eileen's house in Irvington," I said to Darcy, "and all her senior team leaders explained what they do, it suddenly hit me that her company structure was more like the female brain—everything interconnected. Traditional organizational charts have a pyramid structure with hierarchies that determine whose turf belongs to whom. At the Eileen Fisher Company, though, half of the leadership titles included 'liaison' between departments or functions. Everything was linked."

"Yeah," Darcy concurred. "She was the ultimate collaborative leader. A big listener—she hardly ever talked. And the whole meeting was about connectivity between everyone and everything! They talked about their personal lives, their business news, and anything else they wanted to. They started with a gong and silent meditation. I thought it would have driven a man nuts, but the two guys in the room seemed to fit right in. I guess women have had to adapt themselves into a male-dominated model, but it looks funny to see men fitting into a more female model of how to do business." Darcy laughed.

"It seemed so strange to me," I agreed, "after a lifetime of more typical corporate meetings. But by the end I understood the crazy genius of it. Everyone left with a Gestalt understanding that could save explanation time later, create higher levels of cooperation and respect for one another's needs, and avoid problems. As Eileen pointed out afterward, they identified and solved several problems which would have gone unnoticed with a more structured agenda."

The complicated exit from the New Jersey Turnpike to Route 1 was looming on the horizon. While I focused on steering the car, Darcy steered the conversation in a new direction. "What did *you* learn from our trip, Mom?"

"One of my biggest takeaways was how much it matters that women help other women," I said slowly. "I know that seems obvious. But when you see it up close, it really hits home. Like the way Nicole Malachowski was surprised how much confidence her role as the first female Thunderbird pilot could give to thousands of little girls."

Darcy took the torch and ran with it. "Hillary Clinton brought together women leaders from across the globe to mentor the next generation at that luncheon we attended. Amy Pascal, too, prides herself on green-lighting movies that would have made her feel better about herself as a young girl. We didn't pick women leaders because they were impacting other women, but they just were. Everywhere we went."

"Without women in high places," I added, "all these things would be different. Somewhere along the road, I started seeing the world like that scene in *It's a Wonderful Life*, where the angel shows Jimmy Stewart what things would be like without him: and it all looks pretty bleak. Can you imagine a world with no woman Thunderbird pilots and no Hillary Clinton on the international stage? What if Geena Davis wasn't around to prove to big Hollywood studios that they put three male figures for every one female in kids' movies and television shows?"

"What if Noemi Ocana wasn't inspiring other women in Nicaragua to succeed in their own businesses?" Darcy joined my imagination game with enthusiasm. "What if Ellen Johnson Sirleaf wasn't standing up for the Liberian women who pressured the government to free her from prison and then elected her president?"

"If you could see our society in your mind's eye without the contribution of women leaders," I posed, "the world would look like a much harsher place. Not only would we miss out on what these leaders do, but our universe would suffer from the lack of help they provide for other women. Thoughts like that make me feel even more urgent about the next generation of women leaders. Like Secretary Clinton said, *'We don't want to lose the contributions that the next wave of gifted, caring women can make.'*"

"And Geena said," Darcy jumped in, "add women leaders, change everything! It's really true, isn't it, Mom?"

"That's what I saw. Women helping women makes a big difference to the whole world. But we need the support of men, too. That's another message I heard loud and clear."

"You mean their husbands?" Darcy asked, smiling. "So many women we met said that marrying the right man was the secret of their success." She began ticking them off on her fingers. "The head of the EPA, the UN Ambassador, the founder of Teach For America, the first woman

Thunderbird pilot, and the activist professor in Mexico . . . they all said it spontaneously in very similar words: a partner who is really an equal partner—one who accepts, embraces, and encourages what you do—is crucial."

"There were others, too." I couldn't help but correct her finger math. "Sheryl Sandberg felt strongly about it—she wants her daughter to have every career opportunity, and she wants her son to be a full partner as a parent. Geena Davis talked about how she and her husband are raising their sons to care about supporting women's leadership as much as her daughter does. Amy Pascal is co-chairman of the movie studio with a man. If men and women leading together makes the world a better place, men and women should be working together to make it happen."

"But the stay-at-home-mom choice still deserves respect," Darcy said, putting her hand on my arm. I reached over and held her hand for a moment.

"I am so glad you came around to that point of view. Did you know your auntie Susan Rice even took some time off from her high-level political work to stay at home with her kids for a while?"

"I know, I know," Darcy admitted ruefully. "I can admit now that I didn't feel much respect for homemakers until we sat down and really got to know Cathy Sarubbi. She's the support behind her heroic firefighter husband, her daughter the blind ski racer, the rest of her family, and everyone else in town—but she doesn't get the glory or the medals. It's not just because she can't do anything else, either. She had a big management job and gave it up to be the 'Momager' of her brood."

"Women like Cathy are the glue that makes everybody else's lives work." I told my daughter emphatically, "As a mom who works and travels a lot, I appreciate the moms who volunteer in our schools, run sports programs, and scoop up everybody's kids during a crisis like 9-11. If everyone acted like me, where would we be then?"

"It's almost like everything I thought I knew about leadership was wrong," Darcy admitted with a remnant of sadness. "Unconsciously, I thought stay-at-home moms were boring and lacked talent. I thought choosing the life of a senior leader meant an excruciatingly dull existence in straitjackets masquerading as business suits. The reality of getting to know these amazing women made all the difference. Each personality shined through. Each woman was both a leader and exactly herself. It actually shocked me. One woman's strength, perhaps, was another's weakness, but all of them excelled at what they do. It profoundly changed me to meet them, see how they lived, and hear what formed their core values—whether it was the death of a parent like Denise Dresser, or training to be a chemical engineer like Lisa Jackson. Each person's personal experience shaped them and made them a great leader in a different way."

"I know what you mean. Each woman we met was so much herself, and that's exactly what made her great."

"I thought at the beginning that 'leadership training' would make me into someone else, someone I didn't want to be. Now I see, especially after talking to both Secretary Rice and Ambassador Rice," she quipped, "that my desire to be a linguistic anthropologist is a good foundation for being a world leader. It isn't just an academic discipline, like I feared; it's about cross-cultural global understanding. My passion can make me a great leader in my own unique way. As a matter of fact, my role as a leader will rise out of who I am, not strangle my personality. I can lead *and* be myself."

Recent research reports that the ambitious, confident, and highly educated young women of Gen Y, like Darcy, are better prepared than any women in history to close the gender gap and walk through the corridors of power where their mothers and grandmothers fought to open the doors. Many of them don't want the top jobs because they fear a loss of personal autonomy, authenticity, and quality of life. Darcy's epiphany is crucial to the momentum of progress. Our journey had broken through her stereotypes about women leaders and revealed that she could carve her own path and create her own style. Setting high aspirations and leadership goals doesn't mean a life sentenced to conformity.

I reached up, pressed the button on our magic genie, and watched the white garage door roll up into the ceiling. "I'm so glad you changed your perspective," I responded as I slipped our blue pal into her parking space.

"One of the most profound realizations I've come to is that people—this applies to men as well, but it's particularly acute in women—will always gravitate toward the familiar."

"What do you mean?"

The drive completed, I could now give Darcy my full attention. "Think about it," I said. "Achievement in sports, for example, isn't easy, but when you grow up in an athletic family you see the fun of it and you just assume that you can do it, too. The hard work seems irrelevant. In families with musical talent, like Marin Alsop's, you grow up surrounded by harmonious melodies and the discipline to practice is something natural.

"Conversely, to do something unfamiliar to you is like approaching a big black box with no idea what's inside. The difficulties loom much larger than the joys when spheres of activity feel alien."

Darcy had that thoughtful, yet puzzled look that has come to replace her more childish "huh?" reflex. But I knew how to bring it home.

"Remember how you declared that you wanted to get a Ph.D. in linguistics when you were seven years old?" I continued.

It was as if her head exploded. She got it. "Right! I always knew Mema was 'Dr. Deane' and Grandma was Dr. Cremaschi. Plus my father has a Ph.D. and you have an honorary doctorate, too! I barely knew what a Ph.D. was, but I figured I oughta have one, you know. Why not?"

"That's it. Kids without that experience wouldn't even know what a Ph.D. was at age seven. If they did hear about it, they would think it sounded really hard and unreachable. But all *you* were thinking about was: since these people you love did it, you could, too. You'd worry about how hard it would be later."

We sat together on the long, burgundy sofa in the living room where we'd hatched all these plans so long ago.

"Did the adventure change you, Mom?"

"You know, it did. Sometimes I regret I didn't take the conventional path through business school and move up to be a major corporate executive. I used to compare myself to peers who won a seat in Congress or rose to the top of the Gates Foundation and think, I'm not really a leader. Now, after our extended conversation about leadership with these twenty extraordinary women, I am able to embrace my own power from where I sit, even though it isn't the corner office of a global conglomerate. In the last two years, I have stepped up to make a difference for the employment of people with disabilities as a board member for the National Organization on Disability. I am taking more of a thought leadership role in the corporate world. I convene researchers, practitioners, and ordinary folk to create tools and techniques that can help everyone to be more resilient in this stressful, fast-changing world."

"So you have embraced more deeply the leader in yourself and that changes what you do day to day?" Darcy asked, back in the role of interviewer.

"It really does. Even at my advanced age," I said, poking her in the ribs. "You have to continue to rekindle your faith in yourself over and over during your lifetime. You should never stop reaching inside to find your strengths—no matter how old you are. Think about it. Hardly any of the women we featured could have, at your age, had any reasonable expectation to achieve what they did. A woman fighter pilot was illegal when Nicole was little. The idea of a woman chairman at Deloitte, Sony, or even Northern Wairoa Dairy was absurd just twenty or thirty years ago. Let's not even consider secretary of state or president of a country!"

"Yet they all believed in themselves," Darcy said reflectively, leaning back on the soft, familiar cushions. "They followed their passions, skills, and beliefs to carve out new territory for women. They went beyond their own wildest dreams."

There was one more thing I needed to say as I snuggled closer to her on the couch.

"I am very glad we did this together. I could have spent all these hours away from you coaching clients, doing more keynotes, or writing a different book. I am really happy I invested a significant chunk of my time on an adventure with you—before you go off to college. It's been one of the greatest experiences of my life."

"Thanks, Mom," Darcy said softly. I think she blushed.

"At the same time, it wasn't a cakewalk, was it? From the outside, traveling together looks so perfect. But we struggled with rejections, late nights in airports, keeping your grades up, long hours writing to meet deadlines, plus peri-menopausal symptoms and teen hormones. And we still did it. Together."

Our hands spontaneously smacked together in a congratulatory high five.

Acknowledgments

When we began this crazy journey, Darcy and I knew we were taking on more than we could possibly manage on our own. So, as we said in Chapter One, we stepped out on faith. Fortunately, many others were inspired by our desire to seek out role models for the next generation of women leaders. Their belief, support, and assistance were critical in turning this quest that spanned four continents, twenty women leaders, and nearly two years of schlepping into a success.

First of all, we want to express our deepest and most sincere thanks to each of the women featured in this book. You opened up your lives, your hearts, and your unique wisdom in ways beyond anything we ever imagined. In almost every case, there also was a team of staffers who bent their schedules to coordinate with us, help us with research, and share with us their own behind-the-scenes perspectives. You know who you are. Please accept our undying gratitude.

Another crucial acknowledgment at this point, is that the "us" of which we speak includes Allen Haines who accompanied Darcy and me on many of the trips, made introductions to women leaders, and spent long hours slaving over a hot manuscript to convert our adventure into an entertaining narrative—while he humbly stayed out of the limelight. This isn't his first book with us, and we certainly hope it is not his last. Allen Haines, we love your writing, we love having you on our crew, but most of all, we just love you for you. Will you marry us?

Other key members of our inner circle include our beloved editor, Adrienne Ingrum, who, like an Olympic coach, continually pushes us to better our best. Adrienne, we could never do what we do without you. Our agent, Richard Pine, is always there with brilliant advice, support and encouragement every step of the way. Rolf Zettersten, Harry Helm, and the rest of the Hachette family have worked side by side with us for three books now, again supporting us to do better each time. I know that these relationships are rare and special. You all make it possible for us to do our best work.

My incredibly talented brother, Wayne St. John, took time out from his vacation to organize a busman's holiday photo shoot that captured the picture used on the back cover. We also commandeered my multilingual sister, April St. John-Keenoy, on her vacation to help with the translations for our background research. Many, many thanks to you both.

> I'd like to especially thank the principal at my school, Mr. Michael Zapicchi, and all of my teachers. Without your patience and understanding, I never could have managed to travel, keep up with my advanced workload, and stay on track for college. You made all this possible for me.

We are blessed to have run into so many wonderful people whose contributions made this book possible. Special thanks to: Connie Lindsey, Jennifer Mitrenga, Ruth-Anne Renaud, Melinda Wolf, Diana Taylor, Mark Settles, Robert Sirleaf, Lissa Muscatine, Dana Muldrow, Kerci Marcello-Stroud, Emily Bloomfield, Keri Devaney, Eric Kapenga, Alex McPhillips, Kathleen McGlynn, Julie Mikuta, Cherisse Young, Charles Garcia, Phil Witt, Josh Goldstine, Jim Kennedy, Christine Farrell, Harry Rhoads, Bernie Swain, Liz Morrison, Karla Alvarez, Elisa Lurkis, Barry Salzberg, Rick Frenkel, Stephanie Kretschmer, Elliot Schrage, Camille Hart, Lindsay Scola, Marilyn Banwell Stanley, Minyon Moore, and Sunny Bain for all your help in connecting us to the wonderful women in this book.

And finally, for a continual source of strength, courage, and perseverance beyond our own capacities, we give thanks to God.

Index

About the Authors

Bonnie St. John

Despite having her right leg amputated at age five, Bonnie St. John became the first African American ever to win Olympic or Paralympic medals in ski racing, taking home a silver and two bronze medals in downhill events at the 1984 Paralympics in Innsbruck, Austria. In recognition of this historic achievement, Bonnie was quoted on millions of Starbucks coffee cups and was honored at the White House by President George W. Bush as part of the 2007 celebration of Black History Month.

Bonnie has achieved the highest levels of success in a variety of endeavors throughout her life. In addition to her success as a Paralympic athlete, she is the author of six books, a highly sought after keynote speaker, a television and radio personality, a business owner, and the single mother of a teenage daughter. She graduated Magna Cum Laude from Harvard University in 1986, and won a Rhodes Scholarship to Oxford University, taking an M.Litt. in Economics. Upon her return to the United States, Bonnie was appointed by President Bill Clinton as a Director for Human Capital Issues on the White House National Economic Council.

Today, Bonnie travels the globe speaking, leading seminars, and researching her various writing projects. She frequently donates personal appearances to schools, homeless shelters, community groups, and other organizations in hundreds of locations while traveling for corporate clients. During the winter, she coaches disabled ski racers for the

Adaptive Sports Foundation in Windham, New York. Prior to the 2008 Beijing Olympics, Bonnie served as one of a handful of Paralympic ambassadors who helped train our athletes going to China to be positive representatives of the United States. In 2010, Bonnie once again represented the USA as a member of President Obama's official delegation to the Paralympic Winter Games in Vancouver.

NBC Nightly News called Bonnie, "One of the five most inspiring women in America." She has been featured extensively in both national and international media including: *The Today Show,* CNN, *CBS Morning News, NBC News,* and the *New York Times,* as well as *People, O,* and *Essence* magazines, to name just a few.

Darcy Deane

Darcy Deane is the seventeen-year-old daughter of Bonnie St. John and Dr. Grant Deane.

Homeschooled until sixth grade, Darcy has traveled extensively throughout all fifty of the United States and many countries abroad. She particularly enjoys spending summers, when she can, with her family in New Zealand.

Darcy attended middle school at the Dalton School in New York City and currently attends the Education Program for Gifted Youth Online High School through Stanford University.

In addition to continuing as an author and world traveler, Darcy is interested in pursuing a career as a linguistic anthropologist and is currently studying Chinese, Spanish, and Ancient Greek languages.